Seeing Chekhov

SEEING CHEKHOV

Life and Art

Michael C. Finke

CORNELL UNIVERSITY PRESS

ITHACA AND LONDON

First published 2005 by Cornell University Press

Printed in the United States of America

Library of Congress Cataloging-in-Publication Data

Finke, Michael.
    Seeing Chekhov : life and art / Michael C. Finke.
       p. cm.
    Includes bibliographical references and index.
    ISBN 0-8014-4315-6 (cloth : alk. paper)
    1. Chekhov, Anton Pavlovich, 1860–1904—Criticism and interpretation. 2. Self in literature. 3. Evolution (Biology) in literature. 4. Darwin, Charles, 1809–1882—Influence.
5. Dreams in literature. 6. Identity (Philosophical concept) in literature. I. Title.
    PG3458.Z8F56 2005
    891.72'3—dc22

                            2004030464

Cornell University Press strives to use environmentally responsible suppliers and materials to the fullest extent possible in the publishing of its books. Such materials include vegetable-based, low-VOC inks and acid-free papers that are recycled, totally chlorine-free, or partly composed of nonwood fibers. For further information, visit our website at www.cornellpress.cornell.edu.

Cloth printing   10 9 8 7 6 5 4 3 2 1

To my daughter, Rachael

Contents

Acknowledgments

Earlier versions of parts of some chapters have appeared in article form: the section in chapter 1 on "At Sea" in *Reading Chekhov's Text,* ed. Robert Louis Jackson (Evanston: Northwestern University Press, 1993), 49–60; rpt. in *Anton Chekhov: Modern Critical Views,* ed. Harold Bloom (Philadelphia: Chelsea House, 1998), 185–96; other sections in chapter 1 (parts of "Chekhov in the Theater" and "Chekhov in His Prose") in *Inchiesta letteratura* 30, no. 130 (October– December 2000), 49–55; the section in chapter 3 on "Ward 6" in *Indiana Slavic Studies* 8 (1996), 115–30; the section in chapter 3 on "Black Monk" in *Anton Čechov: Philosophische und religiöse Dimensionen im Leben und im Werk,* ed. V. B. Kataev, R.-D. Kluge, and Regina Nohejl (Munich: Otto Sagner, 1997); and the section "Seeing Hell" in chapter 4, in *Russian Review* 53, no. 1 (January, 1994).

The Slavic reference librarians at the University of Illinois, Urbana-Champaign, helped me past frustrating dead ends in my research. I had considerable assistance with illustrations from Lilla Vekerdy of the Becker Library at the Washington University School of Medicine; the staff at MedPIC at Washington University School of Medicine; Elena D. Mikhailova of the State Literary Museum, Moscow; the photographer Dmitrii Sherman, Moscow; and the Chekhov Museum in Yalta. Special thanks to Bernhard Kendler of Cornell University Press for seeing this project through, and to Ange Romeo-Hall and Amanda Heller for their editorial labors.

The late Marena Senderovich got me started on Chekhov and continues to influence and inspire my work. The impact of Savely Senderovich's Chekhov scholarship will be evident; he has also been a sharp and helpful critic. I feel a very deep gratitude toward three fellow Chekhov scholars in the United States who read much or all of the manuscript and offered invaluable insights and suggestions for improvement: Radislav Lapushin (University of Chicago), Cathy Popkin (Columbia University), and Julie de Sherbinin (Colby College). Others who were kind enough to read and comment on sections of the manuscript at various stages include Sara Dickinson, Robert L. Jackson, Donata Meneghelli, Yekaterina Vernikov, Robert K. Weninger, and Christl Weninger. No one caught more slips or helped me solve more organizational problems than my patient Japanologist colleague and wife, Elizabeth Oyler.

I have also been the recipient of much assistance and personal hospitality from wonderfully congenial Russian colleagues with encyclopedic knowledge of Chekhov. Above all I thank Alevtina P. Kuzicheva for generosity on many fronts, and Gennadii Shaliugin, director of the Chekhov Museum in Yalta, for his hospitality there and subsequent response to many queries. I wish to acknowledge, too, my indebtedness to numerous others, including Margarita Goriacheva, Vladimir Kataev, Margarita Odesskaia, Iurii Skobelev, and Anatolii Sobennikov. Colloquy with these scholars, visits to the Chekhov Museum in Yalta, and participation in Chekhov symposia at Melikhovo and on the shore of Baikal have made the study of Chekhov a special delight.

Not all of these scholars have always agreed with how I see Chekhov; I value their collegiality all the more.

Note on Citations and Transliteration

All references to Chekhov's writings are keyed to the fullest scholarly edition, A. P. Chekhov, *Polnoe sobranie sochineii i pisem,* ed. N. F. Bel'chikov et al., 30 vols. (Moscow: Nauka: 1974–1983). References to this edition are indicated by *S* for the eighteen volumes of Chekhov's writings and *P* for the twelve volumes of letters, followed by volume and page numbers; as a rule, however, letters are cited by date only so as to facilitate searching them out in translated sources. Ellipses not enclosed in square brackets appeared in the original.

Transliteration of Russian names and citations quoted in the original follows the pattern of System II as laid out in J. Thomas Shaw, *The Transliteration of Modern Russian for English-Language Publications* (Madison: University of Wisconsin Press, 1967): in essence, the Library of Congress method, but without diacritics. Nonetheless, certain familiar personal and place-names are rendered in their common American English spellings, for example, Tolstoy rather than Tolstoi, Yalta rather than Ialta, Meyerhold rather than Meierkhol'd, Gogol rather than Gogol'. All translations are mine unless otherwise indicated. Bibliographic information regarding translations reflects the spelling choices made at the time of publication, so there will be occasional variations (such as Nemirovich-Danchenko versus Nemirovitch-Dantchenko).

Seeing Chekhov

Introduction

In his remarkable objectivity, standing above personal sorrows and pleasures,
he saw and understood everything.

> —Aleksandr Kuprin, "Pamiati Chekhova"

We can still say, echoing the 1929 remark of one of Russia's most important early Chekhov scholars, that of all the major nineteenth-century Russian writers we know Chekhov least of all.[1] A wealth of biographical materials has been published since Chekhov's death in 1904 by his siblings, colleagues, and friends, as well as by scholars and archivists; recently, much that had been withheld until the era of *glasnost'* has also seen print. Nevertheless, Chekhov's personality remains to us, as it did to many of his contemporaries, quite closed.[2]

This is as Chekhov wanted it. No other major nineteenth-century Russian literary figure made greater efforts to keep his personal self apart from his literary products and inaccessible to his readers; indeed, most key figures of the tradition tended to insert themselves into their works in one way or another. Gogol offered interpretations of his major works as projections of his own psychological processes and the purging of his soul, and he eventually constructed for himself a prophetic persona from which his late works emanated.[3] Romantic poets such as Pushkin and Lermontov operated according to an expressivist literary code: their writings made them celebrities. Dostoevskii's reputation in the second half of his career was inextricably connected to his personal experiences as a convict in Siberia, about which he wrote.[4] (It is unthinkable that a publication with a title such as that of his journal *Diary of a Writer* [*Dnevnik pisatelia*] could have issued from Chekhov's pen.[5]) Turgenev, the author whose influence on Chekhov has probably been most remarked, averred that he always portrayed

I

himself in the failed lovers of his fiction: "First Love" ("Pervaia liubov'," 1860) was directly autobiographical,[6] and the hunter-narrator of his *Hunter's Sketches* (*Zapiski okhotnika,* 1852) cannot be disentangled from the author's self. Tolstoy's first published narratives were highly autobiographical, and his most ambitious novels are laced with personal and family history. Later in his life a veritable religious, philosophical, and ethical movement—popularly understood as echoing Tolstoy's personal convictions and practices—grew in response to his essayistic writings. If, to clinch the case, we consider Chekhov's contemporaries—let us take Gorkii, Korolenko, and even Bunin, all figures who were close to Chekhov and acquired great weight in their own right—then we have a set of authors whose works of greatest lasting importance, arguably, were memoiristic and autobiographical.[7]

Chekhov stands out for insisting that his verbal art speak for itself; about himself, Chekhov, the less said the better. "I have autobiographophobia," he wrote his medical school colleague and friend, the eminent neuropathologist G. I. Rossolimo (11 October 1899), when the latter was assembling the biographies of classmates, and he was hardly joking. That same year his publisher Adol'f Marks objected to Chekhov's wish that no photograph or biography of the author appear in the first volume of his collected works.[8] It is rather doubtful that Chekhov would have been bitten by the autobiographical bug even had he lived to an appropriately graybeard age, for he always attacked authorial self-exposure or "subjectivity" (*sub"ektivnost'*) in direct statements regarding poetics, particularly to his elder brother Aleksandr, in whose works he often found this failing. Even in Chekhov's journals, according to the Russian scholar who has studied them most closely, "'I' sounds almost like the third person. He writes 'I did this and that' in such an even, calm, businesslike tone that he seems estranged from his very self."[9]

Chekhov has had his way. However contentious many of the psychobiographical readings of the lives and works of the other nineteenth-century greats might appear, it is remarkable that there have been virtually no such attempts in Chekhov's case.[10] There is something quite special about the way we see Chekhov: on the one hand, we frankly acknowledge considerable blindness in regard to his inner life; on the other, he has in effect become the ego-ideal of Russian literature, the unquestionable model of an *intelligentnost'* still relevant to all educated Russians.[11] Thus the samizdat and emigrant author Sergei Dovlatov wrote, "You can delight in Tolstoy's mind, Pushkin's refinement, and Dostoevsky's deep psychological penetration, but the only one you can wish to be *like* is Chekhov."[12] So too the American novelist and essayist James McConkey, in an autobiographical work that simultaneously retells the story of Chekhov's journey to Sakhalin Island, admits, "Perhaps my love of T. [Chekhov] is narcissistic; perhaps he is but a mirror of my ideal self."[13]

If the critical tradition has viewed Chekhov as the most emotionally balanced and objective of all its authors, this is in large part due to our understanding of how Chekhov himself saw the world. And this understanding most often derives from a rather naïve appreciation of Chekhov's medical training and world-view. For it is clearly the case that Chekhov's professional identity as a physician depended on a certain kind of seeing. Chekhov's keen powers of observation—his *nabliudatel'nost'*—have been remarked by both memoirists who knew him well and scholars who approach him only through the written record and across the distance of many decades. The epigraph above, cited from Aleksandr Kuprin's memoir of Chekhov, is entirely characteristic in this regard; and Kuprin elaborates: "His eyelids hung somewhat heavily above his eyes, as one so often observes in artists, hunters, sailors—in a word, in people with a focused gaze."[14] To apprehend Chekhov means seeing how Chekhov sees, and the author's remarkable vision is understood as deriving from his occupational or professional training and identity.

This is the rhetoric from which legends are made. Chekhov himself participated in creating the legend, but he also spoke about his seeing in ways that complicate the facile causal attributions of critics and biographers. While he often credited his medical training for endowing his vision with a range and comprehension other authors lacked, in his fictional treatments of physicians he was apt to foreground the limits and troubling ethical ramifications of their professional gaze. And he certainly understood that medical seeing could not be translated directly into literary showing or telling; indeed, at times he suggested that the two modes of apprehending the world might well contradict each other. Ivan Leont'ev-Shcheglov recalls a conversation in which Chekhov criticized him for the strain of subjectivity in his writings. He ought to write about material other than himself, Chekhov told him: "A writer absolutely must develop himself into a sharp-eyed, indefatigable observer." When Leont'ev-Shcheglov suggested that Chekhov's training as a doctor made this easy for him, whereas altering his own artistic perspective at the age of thirty would be a far greater challenge, Chekhov answered that medicine "more likely interferes in giving way to free art, it interferes, you understand, in the sense of the immediacy of impressions [. . .] For example, a simple person looks at the moon and is moved: before him is something terribly mysterious and inaccessible. Well, an astronomer looks at it with completely different eyes . . . he has no, can have no treasured illusions! And I too, as a medical man, have few illusions . . . and that's of course a pity—it tends to make life dry."[15]

In the well-known autobiographical statement that followed Chekhov's profession of "autobiographophobia," Chekhov credited his medical training with helping him "avoid many mistakes" as an author. But while conferring benefits on his art, Chekhov's dual professional identity at times posed irresolvable contradictions as well. Where it was impossible to "take scientific data into account," he claims to have "preferred not writing at all." He continues: "Let me note in this connection that the principles of creative art do not always admit of full accord with scientific data; death by poison cannot be represented on stage as it actually happens. But some accord with scientific data should be felt even within the boundaries of artistic convention, that is, the reader or spectator should be made to realize that convention is involved but that the author is also well versed in the reality of the situation. I am not one of those writers who negate the value of science and would not wish to be one of those who believe they can figure out everything for themselves" (11 October 1899).[16]

The actor and future director Vsevolod Meyerhold reports Chekhov's annoyance at the naturalistic sound effects Stanislavskii's theater was inflicting on his *Seagull,* and his amusement at one actor's naïve explanation for the croaking frogs and howling dogs: "'It's realistic,' said the actor. 'Realistic,' A. P. repeated with a laugh. And then after a brief pause, he remarked: 'The stage is art. In one of [I. N.] Kramskoy's genre paintings he has some magnificently drawn faces. What if we cut the painted nose from one of these faces and substituted a live one? The new nose would be "real," but the painting would be ruined.'"[17] Art has its conventions and demands a certain quota of mystification; in science and medicine, by contrast, the ruthlessly objective eye prevails, or so Chekhov appears to affirm in the autobiographical statement directed to fellow physicians. In any event, Chekhov characterized his own seeing as having been fundamentally conditioned by his medical training and practice.

And so too have Chekhov's readers long seen as distinctive the way Chekhov saw the world. But we have failed to register, let alone understand, just what a central concern for Chekhov himself, and how deeply problematic, were precisely the issues of seeing and being seen. In Chekhov's oeuvre the professional gazes of doctors, judges, and detectives are always subject to corruption by calculated self-interest or sudden and involuntary accesses of affect; and as becomes most apparent in connection with his handling of the theory of degeneration, the mystifying and ideological components of scientific seeing—the bread and butter of today's field of medical humanities—were far from lost on him.[18] In regard to Chekhov's person, too, both seeing and being seen could be highly problematic. To illustrate this in the most banal and literal sense: Chekhov's eyes caused him no little suffering, and complaints about them rank with those provoked by blood spitting and hemorrhoids. He once explained to Aleksei Suvorin: "In Moscow I went to the eye doctor. One of my eyes is farsighted, the other, nearsighted" (26 June 1896).[19] Far more fascinating, however, and much remarked in the memoirs of Chekhov's intimates and by scholars since, were the discomforts aroused by his own increasing visibility as an author and celebrity.

In 1888 Chekhov responded vigorously to a letter from Aleksandr Plesh-cheev—the venerable poet, *petrashevets,*[20] and, more important, editor of *The Northern Herald (Severnyi vestnik)*—who had criticized him for writing "The Name Day Party" ("Imeniny") as though he were afraid of being identified as a liberal. This was a story that had come off well, Chekhov felt, because of his medical insight into pregnancy and childbirth; women were praising him lav-ishly. "It's not bad being a doctor and understanding what you're writing about," he boasted in a letter to Aleksei Suvorin (15 November 1888). Against Pleshcheev's indictment he defended himself vigorously: "It seems to me that you might sooner accuse me of gluttony, of alcoholism, of flippancy, of coldness, of whatever you like, but not of wishing to appear or not appear . . . I have never hidden" (9 October 1888).[21] And yet, I will be arguing in this book, Chekhov's sensitivity on this point is symptomatic of powerful and contradictory impulses both to show oneself and, in spite of such spirited denials, to hide.

In guarding against "subjectivity," in removing himself from his writings, Chekhov was less interested in accommodating the desires of readers (as his re-marks to Aleksandr would have it) than in protecting his self from the intrusions of others. Chekhov had a powerful (and, some might argue, a rather un-Rus-sian) inclination for privacy. In his notebooks he even experimented with a bio-evolutionary explanation making deference to others' privacy a defining feature of what it means to be human: "In animals there is a constant striving to un-cover the secret (to find the [hiding] spot, and this is why people have respect for another's secret, as a battle against their animal instincts" (*S* 17:51). Although he was apt to make literary use of the private lives of his friends, his own life he tended to handle with great discretion, and he vigorously resisted attempts by his friends to read his writings as pertaining to his self. He grew extremely un-comfortable with the fame he earned as a mature author, and he showed no de-sire to exploit his personal history in creating a public persona. This striving for privacy while engaged in an activity that conventionally involved self-exposure reached a bizarre extreme in the notorious practical joke accompanying his marriage ceremony with Ol'ga Knipper: Chekhov asked a friend to arrange a dinner party for him, then married in secrecy, with the fewest possible witnesses, and departed Moscow with his bride while confused guests waited. This was no simple act of shielding one's intimate life, but an exhibitionistic and theatrical staging of self-concealment.

Even Chekhov's most intimate friends found him closed, hidden. "His eter-nal peacefulness, balance, a sort of outward coolness, surrounded his personality in a seemingly impenetrable armor. It seemed that this person painstakingly de-fended his soul from the eyes of others," wrote Ignatii Potapenko.[22] At the same time, Chekhov had the reputation of a somewhat vain man. Many who knew him well—such as Aleksei Suvorin and Isaak Levitan, by no means backbiting rivals (though there were those who fell into both categories)—commented on his *amour propre*. In moments of dizzying triumph as well as spectacular failure, Chekhov can be seen struggling to modulate his sense of self and regain his equilibrium. The evidence suggests that he came to view the temptations of grandiosity that issued from success—the power of the other's admiring gaze to inflate one's self—as a greater threat than the risks posed by any given work's collapse. He wrote in his notebooks, "A person has his eyes open only during times of failure" (S 17:93); it is always better to see than be seen. But of course these are two sides of the same coin, and as an author, Chekhov was preeminently concerned with his own visibility in the text.

Chekhov's resistance to the gaze of others plays out, too, in his long avoidance of the status of medical patient. The tuberculosis that attacked him for nearly half of his short life, and that carried off close relatives, including his elder brother Nikolai, was met with denial verging on the pathological. Through thirteen years of blood-spitting and other overt symptoms, Chekhov refused to allow himself to be examined by a physician; the very notion of seeking medical attention, he wrote Suvorin in 1891, disgusted him (18 November). I shall be arguing that Chekhov's medical knowledge placed him in a terrible double bind regarding his own consumptive body, which, in the scientific discourse of the day, was "degenerate." The self Chekhov aspired to be—in particular his professional identity as a physician—very much hinged on his being the one who sees rather than the patient of the medical gaze. But in 1897 a massive, nearly fatal hemorrhage removed all choice in the matter.

In addition to the tuberculosis plaguing the family, the Chekhovs were beset by alcoholism, bankruptcy, and an ancestral history of servitude. Chekhov was quite sensitive to his class heritage: he was separated from serfdom by only one generation, and he was wont to explain such maladies as seasonal sleep disturbances among his family members by reference to the phylogenetic memory of their serf heritage. In one of his brighter moments—he had just won the prestigious Pushkin literary prize, his brother Nikolai was still alive, and his own health was relatively good—he famously described the self he had become as the result of a lengthy and painful process of squeezing the tainted blood of his recent ancestry out of his own veins "drop by drop" until, one day, he awoke feeling "real human blood" coursing through his vessels.[23] I take this metaphor quite literally. For Chekhov, submitting to treatment, subjecting *himself* to the medical gaze, would have exposed the vulnerabilities of this hard-won selfhood. When that self collapses, it will be because of a biological inheritance that cannot be disavowed. Among the unused anecdotes and ideas for stories in Chekhov's notebooks is a sketch of just such an unwanted patrimony:

Doctor N., born illegitimate, never having lived with his father and knowing him
little, his friend from childhood Z. tells him in embarrassment: "The thing is, your
father has gotten melancholic, sick, asks permission to cast at least one eye on you."
The father owns [the restaurant] "Switzerland." Fried fish, which he handles with
his hands, and only afterwards with a fork. The vodka he serves is like fusel oil. N.
went, had a look, ate—no feeling other than irritation that this fat peasant [*muzhik*]
with graying hair trades in such garbage. But once, passing by at 12 o'clock at night,
he glanced through the window: his father sits hunched over a book. He recog-
nized himself, his mannerisms . . . (S 17:88)

This doctor's selfhood has been based on rejecting the bloodline of his father;
to see himself in that "fat peasant" (whose mannerisms can only have been trans-
mitted biologically, since the son was raised apart from him) poses the most troubling questions about who he actually is.

Chekhov—who, incidentally, had ample opportunity to observe his own father, of peasant birth, trading in foul goods and hunched over holy books—was
faced with a similar conundrum. I have come to the conclusion that confronting
how he ought to view himself led him to interrogate the very nature of medical knowledge and, in particular, the professional gaze with which the physician (as well as other professionals) regards his object. Chekhov the medical
student had been entirely capable of displaying considerable hubris. There is evidence, quite out of character for the humble Chekhov of biographic legend,[24]
that in the early years his self was vulnerable to an inflation in proportion to the
growing powers, as he understood them, of his professional seeing; all the more
so when regarding the "inferior" female gender, as in his plan to write a dissertation on the topic of sexual difference, discussed in chapter 3.[25] But Dr.
Chekhov swiftly matured into a ruthless deconstructor of all such megalomaniacal identities. In the chapters that follow, we shall see how this dismantling
of professional, gender, and class identities operates in sustained readings of several Chekhov texts; but we can also observe it here in a nutshell, in one of
Chekhov's concise unused journal entries: "Conversation during a congress of
physicians. First doctor: everything is cured by salt. Second doctor, a military
one: everything is cured by not using salt. And both are demonstrating this—
one on his wife, the other on his daughter" (S 17:143).

Chekhov ascribed the transformation in the way he, in his capacity as a physician, saw himself and others to his experience as a suffering patient—even as
he stubbornly refused to present himself as a patient to another physician. When
in the mid-1890s it briefly (and mistakenly) appeared that Chekhov's book on
Sakhalin could earn him a doctorate and a teaching position at the Moscow
University faculty of medicine, Chekhov articulated the distinctive contribu-

tion he might make to the training of physicians: "I, for instance, suffer from intestinal catarrh and well understand what such a patient feels, what sort of mental tortures he experiences, but this is rarely comprehensible to a doctor. If I were a teacher, then I would try to draw my audience as deeply as possible into the realm of the subjective feelings of the patient, and I think that this could really be of use to the students."[26] Chekhov's teaching plans thus show him focusing precisely on *how the physician sees the patient*. And Chekhov grounds the empathetic vision he will impart in his own experience of possessing an ill body. Nevertheless, his description of the ailment afflicting him conceals, or at least avoids naming, the tuberculosis that truly defines him as a patient. Chekhov by no means proposes to make a spectacle of himself as a patient who transformed affliction into capital and talks back to physicians (a genre of life writing quite familiar to us today); rather, he fantasizes about a position (that of teacher) which will unify his identities as doctor, patient, and verbal artist. And he means to employ his technical abilities as an author to condition how his "audience" sees a character, or in this case, a patient.

This last point illustrates just how short-sighted it would be to understand Chekhov's concern with seeing and being seen, hiding and showing, as issuing chiefly from his training and experience as a physician, his sufferings as a patient, or both. There is a distinctively literary side to this question as well. No other major figure in Russian letters devoted so much of his mature authorial life to *looking at himself.* At the beginning of 1899, Chekhov sold the rights to his fiction to the publisher Adol'f Marks. The contract required submitting fair copies of every work he had ever published, regardless of merit, under the threat of crushing penalties for omissions; and the "convict labor," as Chekhov put it, of finding and rereading this vast body of work, and very often rewriting those items selected to appear in his collected works, constituted a study of one's self perhaps equaled only by Freud's legendary autoanalysis. But this process also constituted a study of one's own poetics, and it only accentuated a long-standing metapoetic dimension to Chekhov's oeuvre: his very first publications were simple parodies, and when the time came to publish an ambitious and lengthy work in a highbrow venue and so declare himself a serious author, the story Chekhov produced— "Steppe"—was highly self-reflexive.[27] Many of the features of Chekhov's poetics that made him a founder of modern short fiction and drama derive from a new and very particular handling of the panoply of aesthetic issues involving what is seen, how it is seen, and by whom this seeing takes place.

We are accustomed to speaking of Chekhov's innovations in the poetics of drama and prose as issuing, chiefly, from two sources: a desire to move beyond the hackneyed conventions he mastered while publishing in the small press, and the particular worldview of a physician-author trained in the sciences in the last quarter of the nineteenth century. As a dramatist Chekhov staged the unseen private life. Thus Vladimir Nemirovich-Danchenko, co-founder of the Moscow Art Theater, speaks of the "sad everyday realities of Chekhov. Nothing extravagant in the costumes; no violent make-up; a complete absence of crowd scenes; no cascade of external tints—in a word, nothing with which the actor might protect himself against revealing his individuality to the point of nakedness." He goes on, "Life unfolded in such frank simplicity that the auditors seemed almost embarrassed to be present; it was as if they eavesdropped behind a door or peeped through a window."[28] The theater owner F. A. Korsh, after a reading of *The Seagull,* told Chekhov, "My dear, this is not suitable for the stage: you have a person shoot himself offstage, and you don't even allow him to say a few words before his death!"[29] The very idea of a "theater of mood," in Meyerhold's felicitous phrasing, involved staging the ineffable, the individual and internal.[30]

The Moscow Art Theater was roundly criticized for such radical departures from theatrical tradition as having major characters on stage at length with their backs turned to the audience.[31] This and other heresies, like speaking in the tones and rhythms of normal speech rather than declaiming, were very much called for by Chekhov's poetics. As a result, the audience's experience was shifted toward the voyeuristic: for the first time, actors behaved and spoke as though unaware of the gazes directed at them from beyond the footlights—more as we have come to think of acting in cinema as opposed to theater.[32] Perhaps no other feature of the mature Chekhov play makes this so clear as his elimination of the traditional theatrical device of the soliloquy. The soliloquizing actor reveals his or her character's inner thoughts unnaturally, with a fullness and coherence absolutely uncharacteristic of inner speech, and demonstrating an orientation toward the eyes and ears of an audience. Chekhov, by contrast, "wanted his audience to feel that they were in the position of eavesdroppers, and that the author had stepped down and was allowing his characters to talk among themselves."[33] Hence the elliptical quality of the dialogue in Chekhov's drama, remarked by so many.[34] As Iurii Sobolev put it, "The internal drama, which doesn't reveal itself through external movements and masks itself behind words, which don't seem to have any relation to what's being experienced— the drama of 'undercurrents'—is the core of Chekhov's dramaturgy." He cites Chekhov's instructions to the actors in *Uncle Vania:* "All the meaning and drama of a human being is inside, not in external manifestations."[35]

Many of Chekhov's most interesting remarks about poetics of prose and drama are found in his correspondence with his brother Aleksandr. In spring 1889 Aleksandr sent Chekhov the manuscript of a play (now lost) for criticism and suggestions. Chekhov recommended that Aleksandr present this, and any other plays he might write, under a pseudonym: "Khrushchov, Serebriakov, something of the sort." (Interestingly, these same names would soon be attached to the chief characters of the play Chekhov was then gestating, *Wood Demon* [*Leshii*].) Chekhov hoped to avoid confusion between himself and his brother among provincial readers and playgoers, and he wanted above all to forestall the inevitable "repulsive" comparisons critics would make: "You're on your own, I'm on my own, but people aren't up to that, they can't take it. If your play is good, I'll catch it; if it's bad, you'll catch it." Chekhov asks his brother to protect them both from the risk of becoming part of the scene, a principle that went beyond the use of pseudonyms, and which will be taken up further in chapter 1. "The main thing is to watch out for the personal element. The play won't do well anywhere if all the characters are like you [. . .] As though there weren't life outside of yourself! And who's interested in knowing my life and your life, my thoughts and your thoughts? Give the people people, not yourself" (8 May 1889). Observe others, Chekhov tells Aleksandr, and stage this for your audience, but do not make a spectacle of yourself.

These principles became central themes of Chekhov's metaliterary *Seagull*.[36] There the authorial career of the play's chief character, Konstantin Treplev, follows a trajectory in many respects inverting Chekhov's own. *Seagull* opens with the catastrophic staging of Treplev's play; by the end, Treplev is publishing prose fiction pseudonymously. Trigorin breaches these defenses, however, arranging a kind of meeting between Treplev as author and his readers during his visit in act 4: "Your admirers send you bows. . . . In Petersburg and in Moscow they're quite interested in you, and always asking me about you. They ask: what's he like, how old is he, a brunet or a blond. And nobody knows your real surname, since you publish under a pseudonym. You're mysterious, like the [man in the] iron mask" (*S* 13:52). But Trigorin has not even bothered to read his latest publication — the pages of the journal where it appears remain uncut (*S* 13:53) — and this blow is among those leading to Treplev's suicide at the play's end.

Treplev's novel poetics of playwriting involves staging the intimate and invisible: "We ought to portray life not as it is, and not as it should be, but as it appears in dreams" (*S* 13:11). The result is terribly abstract and obscurely symbolic, with a chief character who represents the "world soul" rather than an individual human being. Nevertheless, in staging this disembodied work, Treplev very much stages his most private self as well. As the character Medvedenko sees it, in the course of the play's performance by Treplev's sweetheart, Nina Zarechnaia, the two young lovers' souls "will merge in the striving to render one and the same artistic image" (*S* 13:5); and although this interpretation is colored by Medvedenko's own unhappy romantic obsessions, one might indeed view the staging of Treplev's play as meant to enact a coupling of sorts. This autobiographical and performative aspect of the play is enhanced by its unique set design. The stage in effect comprises little more than a frame, through which is seen the same landscape that the estate's inhabitants view every day: the lake and what lies beyond. Treplev has drawn a frame around the familiar horizon of their everyday lives, demarcating a space where, as Arkadina and Dorn recollect, the love life of this locality has always been conducted.

There is also an extreme lack of distance between Treplev and his play's audience and critics; not only is the author seated among his public during the play's premiere, but this public consists entirely of family and friends. Treplev is particularly sensitive to the reactions of his mother the actress, but he craves more than her professional opinion: before the play he tears petals from a flower, seeking from fate an answer to the question whether "she loves me, [or] she loves me not." Conflated with the anticipated aesthetic judgment of a theater professional, then, is the more fundamental question of maternal love. When Arkadina subsequently calls her son a "decadent" (S 13:39), literary politics are fused with a mother's immensely damaging negative affect. For Treplev, his mother's regard answers the entire question of his selfhood, not just his success or failure as a playwright. Her gaze proves existentially determining, and in this respect Treplev remains rather infantile, and terribly vulnerable.[37]

Situations and verbal motifs of seeing and being seen pervade the play. The *Hamlet* device of presenting a play within a play, with which *Seagull* opens, can be read as an attempt to stage seeing itself; Chekhov's audience *sees* seeing, and what follows is a dramatization of the dangers entailed for an author who cannot keep his self outside of the scene. Nina finds it quite hard to reconcile what she witnesses of the private lives of Trigorin and Arkadina with their public personae: the famous actress cries over horses, the famous writer thinks only of fishing (S 13:26–27). Before Treplev's play begins, he and Arkadina recite the scene from *Hamlet* in which Hamlet indicts his mother; declaims Arkadina/Queen, "Thou turn'st mine eyes into my very soul" (S 13:12). Some time later Treplev presents Nina with the seagull he has shot, and he tells her: "Your gaze is cold. [. . .] Women don't forgive failure" (S 13:27). When Nina embarks on her acting career, Treplev follows her for a while, viewing her from the audience, but she does not want to "see him" (S 13:50). When she visits him in act 4, he calls her "moia nenagliadnaia," best translated, perhaps, as "my darling," but literally that which cannot be gazed upon enough, to the point of either satisfaction or indifference.[38] Treplev's final act in *Seagull* is a determined departure from the scene; and there could be no more dramatic realization of a simultaneous exhibitionism and its suppression than his shooting himself offstage at the end, an unorthodox device that rendered the play's most dramatic event unseen. Finally,

Chekhov is himself visible in *Seagull* to a remarkable and uncharacteristic degree: he parodies his own practices as an author in the character Trigorin; he imports an episode from his own life in the handling of the engraved medallion that Nina presents to Trigorin;[39] and the travails of the family intimate Lidiia Mizinova, who had borne a child out of wedlock with Chekhov's friend Potapenko, become those of the character Nina Zarechnaia.[40] One of Chekhov's intimates suggested that the play's failure had so deep an impact on Chekhov precisely because "*Seagull* is one of the most subjective works of this uncommonly objective Russian writer."[41]

Certain widely acknowledged distinctive features of Chekhov's poetics of prose arguably serve functions homologous to those of his drama which I laid out earlier. Consider, for instance, the effect on the reader of the celebrated plotlessness of Chekhov's stories, their slice-of-life casting, or, in instances where highly dramatic possibilities are raised, their tendency to opt for an ending in which these possibilities remain unrealized (the "zero" ending). The result is to deny the reader a particular viewpoint on the narrative, an aesthetic position outside the narrative's action that conceives it as a finished whole. Perhaps the strongest case in point involves the evolution of narrative point of view and voice within Chekhov's fiction—those aspects of style that delimit the reader's seeing and modulate the author's visibility in the text. The Russian scholar A. P. Chudakov has demonstrated a marked developmental trajectory in Chekhov's narrative method toward the elision of authorial voice. In the early stories, fictional author-narrators often speak in their own distinctive voices (which, however, cannot be taken as Chekhov's own, for even in these early works, isolating Chekhov's position in his deeply ironic narratives is notoriously difficult). Characters, too, speak for themselves in letters, monologues, or transcribed dialogues, at times punctuated by a fictional authorial voice intervening with opinions or statements of truth. Chekhov's mature stories, by contrast, contain far less dialogue, and the narration is almost always handled in free indirect discourse tied to the point of view of a particular character in the story.[42] The trajectory of Chekhov's career in prose fiction is thus toward eliminating the authorial position while exposing to the reader more and more of his characters' inner world. The mature Chekhov's poetics of prose can in this sense too be called a staging of the interior and unseen, a poetics of voyeurism, which simultaneously strives to conceal the position of the observing eye. Above all, the author's self is kept apart from the scene.[43]

Mikhail Gromov characterizes such tactics as a "special form of relationship to the reader," who is invited to "fill in" the blanks, thereby adding his or her own "personal ('subjective') vision and understanding of colors, images, allegories, and symbols."[44] In other words, suppressing the subjectivity of the author as a principle of poetics corresponds to increased potential for readers to inject their own subjectivity in the process of reception. This is presumably what Chekhov had in mind when he told Bunin, "You need to sit down to write [only] when you feel cold as ice": cold author, hot reader.[45] Without disputing such reader-response understandings of Chekhov's distinctive narrative manner, however, I mean to propose another frame of reference for making sense of it. For Chekhov's practices as an author do not belong exclusively to the abstract and extrapersonal domain of poetics. Habits, preferences, and such customs as publishing under pseudonyms (taken up in chapter 1) arguably respond to profound inner needs.

For instance, Chekhov—not surprisingly—required a certain measure of isolation while writing. Although he often wrote in close quarters with family and friends, his creative process remained deliberately opaque. This was perhaps less true in the early years, when, according to Vladimir Korolenko, "Anton Pavlovich's sister told me that her brother, whose room was separated from hers by a thin partition, would often knock on her wall at night in order to share a theme, or at times an already finished story, which had suddenly popped into his head." But things changed as Chekhov's works became more serious, no longer "playthings" to share with the family but "great valuables." One of Chekhov's most famous remarks on his writing practice was a boast to Korolenko of how easily he wrote his comic trifles: "He looked over the desk, grabbed the first thing that his eyes settled on—it turned out to be an ashtray—put it in front of me, and said: 'If you want, tomorrow you'll have a story . . . Its title: *The Ashtray.*'"[46] But this is an explanation that mystifies at least in proportion to what it reveals. Chekhov generally destroyed the drafts of his works, rendering apprehension of what the Russians call his "creative laboratory" (*tvorcheskaia laboratoriia*) a greater challenge than is the case with many other authors. According to Potapenko, "Chekhov's creative work could not withstand another's gaze, and since he was always creating, and even when in immediate contiguity with life and with people he would operate in a somehow special way, in his own distinct way—creatively—he had to hide that work, and that's why the closest people [to him] always felt a certain distance between him and themselves."[47] When Chekhov had the means and the space to do so, he created working environments that protected him from the eyes of others without removing himself entirely from their field of vision; hence the detached studio he had built at Melikhovo and the dacha he purchased some distance from Yalta at Gurzuf.

I will be tracing a wide and varied pattern of such habits and behaviors in Chekhov's personal life that might best be understood as responding to deep-seated anxieties and desires connected to issues of seeing and being seen, hiding and showing. Chekhov loved to peep and eavesdrop, and his delight in observing was so intense that it could in turn render him something of a spectacle, as in this instance late in his life:

> Once he [Ol'ga Knipper's Uncle Sasha] was among Olga and Chekhov's guests at a small gathering in Moscow. Since Olga refused to offer him any wine, he soon slipped off to the kitchen, where the cook and maid were happy to keep filling up his glass while he settled himself in comfortably and regaled them with stories from his military campaigns. Realizing that Uncle Sasha had disappeared, Chekhov quietly made his way towards the kitchen, opened the door very slightly and began to observe the scene, doubling up every so often with soundless laughter. Aware of Chekhov's absence, Olga and her sister-in-law left the room as well and amused themselves in turn watching Chekhov watching Uncle Sasha.[48]

If Chekhov loved observing, and at times even flaunted this predilection, there were circumstances under which being seen was an entirely different matter. His discomfort at participating actively in official celebrations or other large social gatherings that would make him a center of attention often aroused such "terror" that he fled; quite well known in this regard was his hasty departure from Moscow to avoid the role expected of him in the jubilee celebration of Dmitrii Grigorovich, the elderly author credited with "discovering" Chekhov's talent.[49]

Chekhov's passion for travel, a hankering to transform the self through seeing new things, far exceeded his financial means and stressed his physical limits as well. His sister Mariia remarked: "I have to say that in general, Anton Pavlovich had a passion for constant movement, for journeys to new places. He always wanted to set out for someplace far away, see and observe something new, not yet known to him. These yearnings for new impressions were obviously the instinctive demand of a litterateur, the demand of his creative sense of self."[50] Bunin reports Chekhov as saying: "A writer should be fabulously rich, so rich that at any minute he could set out on a voyage around the world on his own yacht, outfit an expedition to the sources of the Nile, the South Pole, Tibet, and Arabia, buy himself the whole Caucasus or Himalayas . . . Tolstoy says that a person needs only three *arshins* [seven feet] of land. Nonsense—it's a dead person that needs three *arshins,* a live one needs the whole globe. And especially a writer."[51] But what Chekhov has in mind here is not so much space for living as broad new expanses for *seeing.*

The high level of *amour propre,* or sheer vanity, remarked by Chekhov's intimates (and by Chekhov himself), points at bottom to concerns about how the self is seen by others. It was a character trait that lent itself to Chekhov's outstanding principledness, but it was also a vice, a weakness that had to be hidden or else overcome through self-discipline. As Potapenko wrote: "In reality, in his

soul alongside generosity of spirit and humility lived also pride and vanity; next
to fairness, bias. But like a true wise man he was able to manage his weaknesses,
with the result that in him they acquired the characteristics of virtues." Potapenko witnessed in Chekhov a "torturous internal struggle" to achieve the even-
ness and sobriety that struck everyone.[52] There is also the discretion with which
Chekhov handled his affairs of the heart, and again, the extent to which he hid
his illness from others and in some respects himself. Even after the critical year
of 1897, when his life became increasingly organized around his poor health,
"he never resembled a sick person, and no matter how badly he felt, he never
complained, never showed it. None of his family or friends ever really knew
when Anton Pavlovich felt sick. That was characteristic of Anton Pavlovich until the end of his life."[53]

It should be no surprise, then, that seeing and being seen, showing and hiding, prove absolutely central to Chekhov's life and works. They are ubiquitous
themes in his narratives, becoming especially prominent at times when Chekhov
himself is climbing a new rung on the ladder of his literary career, and therefore becoming more visible. They point to a fundamental coherence between
the comic trifles of the early Chekhov and his mature productions; they are implicated in a persistent and profound self-reflexive or metapoetic dimension to
Chekhov's writings; they are key to his identities as a physician, as an author, and
as an ailing patient; and they provide a way to talk about some of the most remarkable episodes of his life and some of his oddest personal behaviors. In short,
seeing and being seen, hiding and showing, are obsessive concerns of Anton
Chekhov. These terms nominate a thematic complex that knots together Chekhov's writings and his life, and exploring their appearance in these mutually
implicated planes lets us see Chekhov and his writings anew.[54]

In what follows I lay out many well-known but often curious biographical
and textual facts that make new sense in connection with this theme, in effect
providing a very partial outline of Chekhov's life skewed to illustrate the centrality of the theme of seeing and being seen, showing and hiding, in his life and
art. Although my approach is biographical, I have eschewed a comprehensive
chronological account and instead proceed thematically. Good biographies of
Chekhov are readily available, and new ones have been appearing with striking
frequency.[55] Therefore, rather than relating new facts about Chekhov's life, I
make new sense of the material that has been gathered on Chekhov in the century since his death. Among the benefits of this approach is a new grasp of the
fundamental coherence of Chekhov's oeuvre. Instead of depicting the two
Chekhovs of critical tradition—the expansive comic improvisational genius
with a satiric edge who gave way, in maturity and illness, to the gloomy iro-
nist—I follow those scholars who, while sensitive to Chekhov's development

and transformations as an author, are even more struck by the unity of his vision throughout his career.[56]

I also confound the boundaries literary scholars tend—to a greater or lesser extent, depending on the fashion of the day—to erect between the historical personage of the author and his texts. Chekhov's self-declared "autobiographophobia" is at once a biographical fact and a feature of Chekhov's poetics. If both the organization of Chekhov's personal life and the development of his literary practice manifest an urge to hide his self from the public, then even a critic of formalist bent must concede the possibility of considering Chekhov's person while addressing his texts. The very absence of an overtly autobiographical dimension to Chekhov's work, when considered together with the resistances and compulsions Chekhov himself invoked by alluding to a "phobia," simultaneously wards off and invites psychobiographical reading. The challenge, as always, is to develop an interpretive framework that allows space for its subject to continue breathing.

The first chapter takes up the question of Chekhov's "autobiographophobia" in two areas where the person and the literary practice are unavoidably entangled. Writing for the theater meant making one's person accessible to a variety of audiences in ways that publishing fiction did not, and Chekhov's own characterizations of this distinction and management of the problems it represented for him constitute a fascinating aspect of his biography. Chekhov's prose, by contrast, could be published under pseudonyms, which in fact was the case for the first several years of his career. For Chekhov, it proves fair to say, writing prose was to writing for the theater as publishing under a pseudonym was to signing one's proper name: the common term underwriting each comparison is the author's relative visibility. These facts of Chekhov's biography are at once facts of his poetics, and both are best understood as motivated by and reinforcing the psychological dynamics pertaining to the vectors of seeing. This thematic complex becomes increasingly apparent in Chekhov's writings as it grows central to his life, a parallel process that emerges quite clearly in the short story to which Chekhov first deliberately attached his proper name, "At Sea," a story, tellingly, about peeping.

In chapter 2 I read a series of Chekhov's works, spanning his career, that associate the thematic complex of seeing and being seen, hiding and showing, with professional identity in the broadest sense. Since Foucault, it is perhaps all too obvious how such disciplinary identity might be constituted in relation to, as he calls it, the gaze. As we shall see, Chekhov by no means handles this theme exclusively in connection with the medical profession; it conditions his portrayal of legal professionals, government inspectors, theatrical professionals, schoolteachers, a spy, butlers and other house servants, medical patients, and even prostitutes. What is more, in Chekhov's texts all of these social, occupational, or, as I loosely call them, professional identities are defined in relation to the individual psychological dynamics of seeing and being seen, hiding and showing. The chapter culminates in sustained readings of two brief stories, centrally concerned with this theme, with demonstrable origins in Chekhov's own medical practice.

The third chapter focuses more narrowly on Chekhov's critical engagement with certain ideological components of medical seeing in his day. This has to do with the theory of evolution, and the subsequent twists Darwin acquired in late-nineteenth-century sociological applications, which today appear to us as peculiar distortions in the optics mediating the medical gaze. While still a medical student, Chekhov outlined a doctoral research project on the topic of the evolutionary inequalities between males and females of the human species. He operated with, and very clearly felt personally empowered by, theories of social Darwinism and degeneration. But Chekhov can be said to have worked himself into a position of deconstructing these components of the medical gaze, revealing falsities in its claims to objectivity and always embedding scientific discourse in an individual psychological context. The trope of seeing is key to his treatment of social Darwinism and degeneration, which tends to foreground the individual psychological and ethical problems issuing from situations in which certain humans (most often physicians, males) *view* others (most often patients, females). For Chekhov, possessor of the degenerate consumptive body of a serf's descendent, these became issues of deep personal significance.

Chapter 4 is the most speculative and intrusive in regard to Chekhov's person. I discuss the mechanics of desire in Chekhov, based on documentary evidence left by Chekhov himself and by intimates, and complemented by interpretations of Chekhov's oddest, most dreamlike, and most overtly erotic stories, as well as his last, unrealized idea for a play. This exploration of the erotics of seeing in Chekhov is followed by a treatment of certain archetypal and oneiric implications of the thematic complex in Chekhov: the masterplot of the journey to hell (katabasis) pervades Chekhov's fiction and drama, and it operates also as a fantasy motivating how he plotted his voyage to Sakhalin and the book he wrote about it.

In the conclusion I consider Chekhov's visibility in the things he arrayed around him, most notably the home he designed and had built in Yalta toward the end of his life, known as the "White Dacha," which today houses the most important Chekhov museum. I end with a discussion of Chekhov's illness, and how he conditioned the seeing of his own "thingness," his bodily self, in life and after his death.

CHAPTER I

To Be Seen or Not to Be Seen

In general, exhaustion and a feeling of annoyance. It's disgusting, although the play was a great success [. . .] Korsh had never had an author summoned to the stage after the second act.
—Chekhov to his brother Aleksandr 20 November 1887,
after the premiere of *Ivanov.*

Many aspects of Chekhov's literary practice were also personal life choices that might tell us much about Chekhov the individual. The story of his involvement with the theater, for instance, turns on the question of how he managed the visibility of his person to his audience; the same issue was a factor in his notorious reliance on pseudonyms in publishing (chiefly, but not exclusively) his early fiction, including works that today are considered short masterpieces. In both situations Chekhov's initial tactics appear quite conventional for the literary scenes in which he is operating, and therefore of questionable significance regarding the author's individual psychology. And yet, the overall course of Chekhov's career (or better, careers), as well as his own remarks on the matter— recorded in his letters and journals, and in the memoirs of his associates—suggest an intensely personal dimension to the question; so too does his treatment of the theme in his fiction and drama.

Chekhov in the Theater

In the theater. A gentleman asks a lady to remove her hat, which is impeding his vision. Murmurs, annoyance, requests. Finally a confession: Madam, I am

the author! The answer: What difference is it to me? (The author is in the
theater incognito.)

—from Chekhov's notebooks, ca. 1898

Let us begin, rather than at the beginning, with a famous episode from the author's maturity. In the first week of December 1895, Anton Chekhov traveled
to Moscow from his estate at Melikhovo with a newly finished play, *The Seagull*. Chekhov arranged for the manuscript to be typed up and sent to his close
friend and publisher Aleksei Suvorin in St. Petersburg, and he made two attempts at presenting the play for evaluation in Moscow—first to a literary-the-
atrical salon gathered at the actress Lidiia Iavorskaia's hotel, and then to fellow
author and playwright Vladimir Nemirovich-Danchenko (future co-founder,
with Konstantin Stanislavskii, of the Moscow Art Theater). The first reading of
the play went poorly: neither Iavorskaia nor the theater owner F. A. Korsh cared
for its novelties, and even Chekhov's ardent supporter and literary disciple
Tat'iana Shchepkina-Kupernik was unsettled by the play's allusions to the private lives of their mutual friends. All could see that the experience was far from
pleasant for the author. Shchepkina-Kupernik later recalled "the expression,
whether of confusion or indignation, on Chekhov's face."[1]

When it came time to hear Nemirovich-Danchenko's opinion of the play,
however, Chekhov made sure there could be no future recollections of his
pained face.

> I sat before the manuscript at my writing-table, while he stood at the window, his
> back toward me, his hands as always in his pockets, never turning toward me once
> during at least half an hour, and not missing a single word. There was not the least
> doubt that he listened to me with extraordinary attention, at the same time giv-
> ing the impression that with equal attention he followed something which was
> happening in the tiny garden outside the windows of my apartment; at times he
> even peered closer to the window and slightly turned his head. Did this arise from
> a desire to lighten my task of expressing myself freely, to avoid embarrassing me
> with eyes meeting mine? Or was it, on the contrary, an effort to preserve his own
> *amour propre*?[2]

What we know of Chekhov's demeanor while his work was being evaluated
comes from memoirists writing long after he had died; they inevitably recall
their first encounters with the play through the prism of both its subsequent
traumatic failure when first staged in Petersburg and its eventual triumph with
the Moscow Art Theater. Nevertheless, these accounts are in accord with the
signs of vulnerability Chekhov would famously demonstrate in response to the

play's unsuccessful premiere: Chekhov fled from his seat in the Aleksandrinskii Theater long before the play ended; he literally hid under his blanket and refused to talk afterwards at the Suvorin house, where he was staying;[3] and he immediately departed Petersburg without taking leave of his hosts and friends. Some measure of how shaken the episode left him may be indicated by the fact that at the end of his journey home by rail, the usually precise Chekhov managed to forget one of his bags on the train. Above all, Chekhov swore many oaths to "*never* write or put on plays" again.[4] The play's failure he interpreted "as the failure of his own personality,"[5] and he was unable to take pleasure in the genuine success it achieved in performances after the shaky first night. To be sure, Chekhov soon recovered his sense of balance, and he did renege on his oaths; but he also took care to protect himself from similar circumstances in the future.

Why was involvement with theater so perilous to Chekhov? And how did writing for the theater differ in this respect from writing fiction? Chekhov's most ambitious literary aspirations, starting with the massive play he attempted while still an adolescent, had been oriented toward the theater from the very beginning of his career. But writing for the theater also involved exposing the self in a way that appears to have been, at least at times, terrifying for him. Virtually all who tell the story of *Seagull*'s stagings—whether the fatal premiere, in October 1896 in St. Petersburg, or the revival in Moscow two years later (December 1898)—emphasize how mortally dangerous the theater had become for Chekhov. Both Chekhov's sister Mariia and his youngest brother, Mikhail, assert that Chekhov's medical condition worsened "from the moment" of the Petersburg failure of *Seagull,* as evidenced by the grave lung hemorrhage he suffered a few months later.[6] The acute sensitivity of an ailing playwright, and the notion that another such failure could perhaps kill him, have long been central motifs of the Chekhov legend.

Nemirovich-Danchenko attributes Chekhov's vulnerability to the author's excessive vanity. In his memoirs and in direct correspondence with Chekhov he speaks of his friend's "self-love" and "reserve" (*samoliubie* and *skrytnost'*—literally, "hiddenness"), a characterization of Chekhov that one also finds elsewhere among the author's closest friends—including in letters to Chekhov—and, indeed, in remarks Chekhov made about himself.[7] And Nemirovich-Danchenko's memoir illustrates, too, certain behaviors by which Chekhov apparently defends himself in the face of threat: turning his back to Nemirovich's critical gaze, hiding his own reaction to the other's judgment, feigning indifference to it while attending to some activity on the street, or perhaps splitting his attention. In short, writing for the theater involved exposing the self in a way that must have been appealing, indeed, irresistible—otherwise why do it?—yet terrifying. In

Nemirovich-Danchenko's account, the mechanisms Chekhov appears to have employed for coping with that terror were: (1) hiding, which defends the self from the gaze of others; and (2) compensating for injuries to the self that issue from being seen while vulnerable by, in turn, actively gazing at others, that is, moving from a "passive" to an "active" position.[8]

With Chekhov still smarting from the Aleksandrinskii Theater debacle, it took a great deal of epistolary persuasiveness, in April and May 1896, for Nemirovich-Danchenko to obtain permision from Chekhov for the Moscow Art Theater to attempt staging *Seagull*. "As I recall now," Nemirovich-Danchenko later wrote, "Chekhov rejected my proposal because of his confessed sensitiveness and self-consciousness: he wrote that he had no desire and had not sufficient strength to experience again the theatrical perturbations which had in the past caused him so much pain."[9] Even after Chekhov had relented, his sister came to Pushkino, where the theater was rehearsing *Seagull,* and "asks who are these bold people, deciding to play *Seagull* after it had caused so much suffering for Chekhov— she asks, worrying for her brother." This anxiety was keenly felt by all connected with the new production.[10]

So goes the Chekhov legend. If one examines the facts more closely, however, it appears that the most notable feature of Chekhov's anxieties regarding further production of his play is that they chiefly concerned *the place where he was.* Nemirovich-Danchenko could not understand why Chekhov wished to block the performance of *Seagull* by his new theater when the play was being put on in Petersburg and the provinces, and after superb reviews had appeared in Odessa and Kharkov newspapers.[11] Just a few weeks after the Aleksandrinskii catastrophe, Chekhov gave Elena Shavrova permission for the Society of Drama Writers to put on an amateur performance of *Seagull,* on condition that this occur "as far away as possible from Serpukhov! In this city [the chief one in the district where Chekhov's estate was located] I wish to be a juror, a member of the *zemstvo* [rural district council], a normal citizen, but not a dramatist. If they put *Seagull* on in Serpukhov, I'll lose all prestige in my district" (7 November 1896). Chekhov here is only half joking: all evidence suggests that he feared not so much the staging of his play and the possibility of its failure but the staging of the play where he was—as though he feared *becoming part of the spectacle himself.*

This is precisely what had happened in his first theatrical success. Years earlier, in November 1887, Chekhov had prepared for the opening of his *Ivanov* at the Korsh Theater in Moscow "as though for a wedding."[12] When a revised version of the play later opened at the Aleksandrinskii in St. Petersburg, the sensational public response provoked a giddy Chekhov to flee to Moscow with almost as great a haste as he would after the *Seagull* fiasco seven and a half years later. Having returned to Moscow, he apologized for not having visited the author K. S. Barantsevich; he had been "overcome by fumes," he wrote, and "fled Peter[sburg]," where "I was exhausted, and I felt ashamed the whole time. I'm braver when I'm unlucky than I am when lucky. In times of success I cower and feel a powerful impulse to hide under a table" (8 February 1889).[13] Nine days later Chekhov wrote Mariia Kiseleva:"There are now two heroes in Petersburg: [the painter-academician] Semiradskii's naked Phryne and the clothed Chekhov. Both are a sensation. Despite all this I am bored and would gladly flee to dear Babkino . . . [the Kiselev estate, where the Chekhovs had summered 1885–87]" (17 February 1889). The allusion is quite telling. Phryne was the fourth-century B.C. courtesan and model for Praxiteles and Apelles. She served as the model for Praxiteles'Aphrodite of Knidos, from which the whole Western tradition of female nudes in the plastic arts issues; and, according to Quintilian, she also won acquittal on capital charges by means of the "the sight of her exquisite body, which she further revealed by drawing aside her tunic."[14] In short, Chekhov's reference to "naked Phryne" invokes the very paradigm of scandalous representation of female nudity, not just its exposure but its exhibition, indeed, exhibitionism itself.

As a successful young playwright, then, Chekhov was a sight to see. Here, as so often in Chekhov, metonymy suggests a metaphoric association as well: the comparison with Phryne suggests that Chekhov felt himself feminized, unmanned, as the object of others' gazes. And according to those who saw him, he was none too comfortable in his moment of triumph: summoned to the stage by the audience after the performance, Lidiia Avilova reports, he "stood erect, awkward, as if tied up."[15] Chekhov's sister recalled: "All his life my brother was afraid of publicity, speeches, presentations, and so on. It was, in a sense, simply physically painful for him to take the stage during applause, or to bow; and he took to running away from the theater toward the end of his plays, or else hiding in the actors' dressing rooms."[16]

In a letter to Suvorin following the Petersburg staging of Ivanov, Chekhov wrote: "Tell Anna Ivanovna [Suvorin's wife] that I only pretended to be indifferent, but was horribly agitated. The attention with which she listened to the play had an effect on me like kalium bromatum [bromide potash]. I saw only two people during the play: her and [the painter] Repin. Why? I don't know" (4 February 1889). At the premiere of his play, in public and part of the spectacle to be observed by others, Chekhov found his own powers of observation strangely impaired. And his remark to Suvorin notwithstanding, he must have had ideas about the "why" of this phenomenon; indeed, he had written about it in "The Kiss" ("Potselui"), a story he was working on during the first staging of Ivanov in Moscow and finished only after that premiere. There the artillery officer Riabovich is dazzled by the family and social life of the retired general who is receiving him and his fellow officers: "Like a reciter, first appearing before the public, he saw everything that was before his eyes, but what he saw was somehow poorly understood by him (physiologists call this condition, where the subject sees but doesn't understand, 'psychic blindness')" (S 6:409). The plot of "Kiss" may be described in large measure by Riabovich's translocation, in his view of himself, from position of observer (and reader) to actor in the scene—with dismal consequences.

In the case of Chekhov, it is quite clear that both glory and humiliation made him anxious; it was a question not so much of failure as of being in the public eye at such critical, self-defining moments. After the *Seagull* fiasco, Chekhov wrote Suvorin's wife that he had planned to leave St. Petersburg the day after the premiere even in the event of success: "The noise of glory stuns me, after *Ivanov*, too, I left the following day" (19 October 1896). What mattered was not the fact of success or failure but the vulnerability of his person to the gazes of others; all his anxieties seem to have revolved around the issue of seeing and being seen. Thus the only acquaintance to speak with Chekhov before he left St. Petersburg after the *Seagull* fiasco, the author Ignatii Potapenko, recalled that Chekhov was willing to see him because, in Chekhov's words, "you aren't one of the eyewitnesses to my triumph of yesterday. Today I don't wish to see any of the eyewitnesses." He wanted to leave Petersburg immediately, he told Potapenko, so as to avoid seeing the others, who would "come and try to comfort me, with faces like those seeing off close relatives who have been sentenced to hard labor."[17] Chekhov could not bear to see in their faces signs of the way others were seeing him. In later years he never read his plays aloud and was embarrassed if present at readings; according to Stanislavskii, during rehearsals he positioned himself "somewhere in the back rows" rather than at the producer's table, to which he was routinely beckoned. But if he could be simply an observer, and not part of the action, then, Stanislavskii recalls, Chekhov's unselfconscious delight at watching a good production of a play he liked—by some other author—was remarkable.[18]

Nevertheless, from the time of his first failed effort at writing for the theater, which he himself carried to the actress Mariia Ermolova, Chekhov's person was very much in play in his playwriting. This was particularly true when he was in residence in the place where his work was being staged, which generally meant participating in the preparation, being summoned to the stage if a premiere was successful, and finding himself made into a public figure caricatured in the popular press in any event. There were, to be sure, certain advantages to this situation, particularly if Donald Rayfield's account of Chekhov's many affairs with actresses can be credited.[19] But the signs of Chekhov's irritation are more numerous and more overt. During the period of *Ivanov*'s production, Chekhov wrote Suvorin that "the stage is a scaffold upon which dramatists are executed," and he called theater "a form of sport. Where you have success and failure, you have sport and gambling."[20] Chekhov often spoke of "a particular authorial psychosis that afflicts a person putting on a play," and claimed that he suffered from this illness during the production of *Ivanov*: "A person loses himself, ceases to be himself, and his psychological health depends on trifles of a sort that he wouldn't even notice at other times: the facial expression of the director's assistant, the way an actor exiting the stage walks."[21] Chekhov persistently attempted to dissuade certain colleagues from writing for the stage; hence his words of advice to I. L. Leont'ev-Shcheglov (reported by Potapenko): "Give up the theater and its wings. In essence it's an infirmary of vanities. With the exception, perhaps, of a dozen real talents, they're all suffering from *mania grandiosa*."[22]

After *Seagull*'s Aleksandrinskii fiasco, Chekhov protected himself by avoiding the premieres of all his subsequent plays. He was at his new home in Yalta when *Uncle Vania* (*Diadia Vania*) made it to the stage. Rehearsal of *Three Sisters* began while Chekhov was in Moscow, but he left for Nice before the premiere. And then, a few days before opening night was to take place, he departed Nice for Italy, "flitting rapidly from city to city [. . .] justifying the suspicion that he was running away from news of the results of the premiere. Or he would again put on his armor of indifference. After all, after *Seagull* this was his first new play, his return to the theatre. Not only a letter, but even a telegram failed to find him."[23]

Although Chekhov did attend part of the first performance of *The Cherry Orchard,* the conditions of his presence underlined his defensive tactics. On January 17, 1904—Chekhov's forty-fourth birthday—*Cherry Orchard* premiered at the Moscow Art Theater. Unaware that the evening had been dedicated to the celebration of his jubilee he had remained at home, continuing his policy of avoiding the premieres of his plays. But after the second act Nemirovich-Danchenko sent him a note asking him to come to the theater: the play was going well, the audience had called for the author after the second act, and the cast would very much like to have him in the theater for the last intermission. And he told Chekhov that the audience, now knowing that Chekhov was not among them, would not summon him to the stage again. Caught by surprise when they did, Chekhov found himself compelled to take the stage and remain standing—visibly uncomfortable, weak and coughing—for a lengthy ceremony that must have been at least as damaging to his health as *Seagull*'s failure. This was the moment Chekhov had feared all his professional life.

Whether critical or loving, conveying trauma to the self or provoking its aggrandizement, the gazes that an author inevitably encounters in the theatrical sphere were felt to be perilous in the extreme: they upset one's sense and control of self. Under these conditions, modulating that self meant maintaining "distance," keeping oneself out of the spectacle, which in turn required *physically* hiding. That, from the time of *The Seagull's* failure, is precisely what Chekhov did. And of course he also wrote prose fiction, which as a rule involves a far less immediate encounter with the audience than writing for the stage.

Chekhov in His Prose

> Once you've finished writing, sign it. If you're not chasing after fame and are afraid of getting beaten, use a pseudonym.
> —Chekhov, "Rules for Beginning Authors"
> ("Pravila dlia nachinaiushchikhavtorov," 1885)

In an 1895 letter Chekhov told Suvorin that he was "probably not destined to be a dramaturge." He went on: "But I don't despair, for I haven't ceased writing stories—and in that domain I feel at home, whereas when I'm writing a play I experience discomfort, as though someone were pushing on my neck" (13 December). Elsewhere in his letters, as well as in his metaliterary fictions and plays, seeing and being seen become tropes expressing the difference between writing prose fiction and writing for the theater. After the sensation of *Ivanov's* staging, for instance, a shaken Chekhov reproached Aleksei Pleshcheev for having helped the play arrive at production so quickly, and added (adapting an analogy he frequently applied to his dual identity as a physician and author): "Belle-lettres is a restful and sacred thing. The narrative form is one's lawful wife, while the dramatic form is a showy, noisy, impertinent, and tiresome mistress" (15 January 1889).[24] Writing for the theater draws attention to and makes a spectacle of the author; fiction writing, by contrast, is domestic and unseen, and it places Chekhov *outside* the spectacle, as an observer. This is in keeping with how he describes his practice as the author of short tales in a 13 May 1883 letter to his eldest brother, Aleksandr: "I'm a newspaper hack, because I write a lot, but that's temporary . . . I won't die one. If I'm going to write, then it has to be from afar, from a crack in the wall . . . " If writing for the theater is depicted as an exhibitionistic activity, here Chekhov figures writing prose as a kind of voyeurism.[25] Much later, in an 1898 letter to Maksim Gorkii (in which, incidentally, Chekhov avers, "I have no desire to write for the theater anymore"), Chekhov still makes use of his old tropes in discussing Gorkii's shortcomings as a prose author: "You are like a spectator in the theater who expresses his delight so unrestrainedly that he interferes with himself and others listening" (3 December 1898). The proper position of a prose author is in the audience, observing; Gorkii's flaw is his tendency to make himself part of the spectacle.

Most interestingly, peeping became a frequent motif in Chekhov's early pseudonymous, and often metapoetic, stories, as Marena Senderovich has revealed.[26] Although this and closely related themes—such as hiding, showing oneself, shame from sudden exposure, and anxieties regarding one's name—animated Chekhov's writing from the start of his career to his death, the richest groupings of such stories arguably occur in two periods when Chekhov's own profile was acquiring a sharply increased visibility to the reading public: during 1883 and 1885–86. And a significant aspect of this visibility derived from the author's use, finally, of his proper name.

The 1883 remark about writing "from a crack in the wall" appeared at a time when Chekhov had acceded to a new and more profitable venue, the St. Petersburg humor magazine *Oskolki*, which began publishing him in late November 1882. In a series of immensely self-assured letters to Aleksandr, Chekhov demonstrates pride at having surpassed his eldest brother, also a writer; whereas once Aleksandr had instructed Anton in poetics and helped him get published, now it is Anton who condescends to Aleksandr. Chekhov appears also to have begun to sense the possibility of success in the literary field, but this possibility aroused quite ambivalent feelings: after all, he was entering his last year of study at the medical faculty of Moscow University, and in one of these letters (17–18 April 1883), which will be discussed in depth in chapter 3, he elaborates plans for doctoral research. That same year Chekhov for the first time deliberately signed one of his publications with his own name rather than a pseudonym; this was "At Sea" ("V more"), a story that depicts a pair of sailors aboard the steamer *Prince Hamlet,* father and son, spying on a pair of newlyweds in the ship's bridal cabin.

Because it appeared under his name, "At Sea" occasioned a kind of self-exposure that Chekhov had been avoiding to date, and the story's central themes of voyeurism and prostitution prove uncannily appropriate and self-reflexive, as we shall see. But this was no less the case with the many other stories depicting peeping, hiding, and embarrassing exposure that Chekhov published during this period. Two cases in point are the very brief "The Proud Man (A Story)" ("Gordyi chelovek [rasskaz]," 1884), and "A Lady-Hero" ("Geroi-Barynia," 1883), both pieces that Chekhov later judged unworthy of inclusion in the Marks edition of his collected works. In "Proud Man," a guest is thrown out of a wedding party by the best man because he refuses to give his name or show his invitation. "I'm not so stupid as to explain my title to any person I happen to meet," says the guest. "I'm not paying any attention to you" (S 2:377). After he is tossed down the stairs, however, he has his footman explain who he is, where he works, and how much money he makes; now he is cordially invited to rejoin the party. "Without pride you can't get by in this world," he explained. 'I'll never give way to anyone! No one! I know my value. On the contrary you

ignoramuses can't understand that!'" (S 2:379). The motifs of pride and anonymity in this story were provocatively reduplicated at the level of authorship,
in that Chekhov was in effect compelled to reveal his identity to gain access to
print: in contravention of Chekhov's wishes, *Moskovskii listok* published the story
under his real name (A. Chekhov). But this appearance of Chekhov's name was
calculated to further mystify the readership rather than reveal something true:
the unscrupulous editor N. I. Pastukhov had been publishing the stories of
Chekhov's brother Aleksandr under exactly the same signature, A. Chekhov,
hoping to deceive readers into thinking that Anton—the brother with the
greater reputation—was a regular contributor. (Chekhov had told Leikin the
previous December that he used his real name only under very particular circumstances, and that he was in principle ready to begin signing all his works
with his proper name—which was not quite true—but that he would never
do so for Pastukhov.)[27]

In "A Lady-Hero," the chief character, Lidiia Egorovna, has just received a letter from her husband informing her that the uncle to whom he appealed in financial desperation refused to help them; he has therefore sold her estate and is
proceeding to Odessa for a couple of months on "important business." Lidiia
Egorovna suspects, however, that the real purpose of her husband's side trip to
Odessa is to rendezvous with his mistress (S 2:149). The story thus opens with
Lidiia learning that she is bankrupt and a deceived wife. The setting and characterization of Lidiia Egorovna constitute an ambivalent combination of self-
exposure and hiding: while reading the letter she is taking her morning coffee
on the terrace of her dacha, that is, in an exposed, visible position; but in spite
of the summer heat, she wears a black silk dress "buttoned up to her chin." Her
self-presentation deliberately combines bold, attention-getting features (her
golden curls) with self-containment and abnegation (buttoned-up black): "She
knew that this black color went well with her golden curls and stern profile, and
parted with it only at night" (S 2:149). This flattering fashion choice reflects,
too, an emotional need; and for the rest of the story Lidiia entertains guests while
struggling to hide her anger and humiliation.

Lidiia's cousin and neighbor, a retired general, arrives with an acquaintance
the general jokingly calls a "liberal" and "red." Here begins a humorous riff on
the attention-drawing color red that highlights the dangers of attracting attention to oneself—or, in other words, exhibitionism. The general tells how the
red lining of his uniform coat once startled a Georgian bull, which charged him
(S 2:150). And he tells of one colonel in his battalion who so craved promotion
to general that he continued to serve into his seventies. He had become gouty,
could no longer sit astride a horse, and, if he drew his saber on maneuvers, could
not return it to its sheath; in other words, the man was a wreck. While waiting

for the rank of general—public recognition of a powerful status—he had become manifestly, visibly impotent, and precisely when his promotion finally came through, he was struck by partial paralysis (presumably from a stroke). The newly retired general then made a practice of showing the red lining of his coat everywhere he went: the man whose decrepitude was on display for all proudly displayed himself, because he saw only the red color that indicated his status as general. Eventually he lost his vision, and his housekeeper stole the fabric to sew an adornment for herself, replacing the lining with grayish calico; but the general, unaware, continued his buffoonish practice of proudly opening his coat to display the absent red lining indicating a general's rank.

This embedded tale of absurd pride and the dangers of exhibitionism serves as a counterpoint to the frame situation, in which Lidiia Egorovna buttons up her feelings of anger and injured self-esteem. As her cousin tells his story, she thinks, "He's gone to Odessa for two months . . . to that . . ." and "He's in Odessa now . . . the débauché!" (S 2:150). This inner train of thought eventually becomes public, bursting out as though stays or buttons on her dress have popped. During dinner a guest asks where she procured such delicious radishes; here, as in the cousin's tale, the motif of red becomes associated with self-exposure, for Lidiia responds inappropriately: "He's in Odessa now . . . with that woman" (S 2:152). At night, alone, "maintaining etiquette was no longer necessary, and she could sob!" (S 2:152).

"Lady-Hero" is thus an exemplary story entirely structured around motifs of showing and hiding, pride and shame, and incorporating these motifs in both comic and mundanely tragic modalities at one and the same time.[28] But what is its connection to the moment in Chekhov's literary career? The motif of bright red cloth on a blind man's garment points toward another frame of reference for reading the story. In his 1885 sketch "In the Train Car" ("V vagone [razgovornaia perestrelka]"), a journalist complaining of the difficulties of the authorial calling remarks, "Glory, as one of my colleagues put it, is a bright patch on the filthy tatters of a blind man" (S 4:69–70). This hack writer's "colleague" is none other than Aleksandr Pushkin, from whose "Conversation of a Bookseller with a Poet" ("Razgovor knigoprodavtsa s poetom") the image has been borrowed.[29] The banality of success, the hazardous temptations of pride, the drive to suppress both feelings of grandiosity and shame—these overt themes in the story are tied by a few red threads to the literary sphere, and to Chekhov's own situation in it. And then there is the theme of the adulterous husband: Chekhov repeatedly characterized his own dual professional identity in terms of adultery—medicine, he would write, was his lawfully wedded wife, literature, his mistress[30]—and the theme of a disloyal husband in Chekhov's narratives is very often freighted with metapoetic significance.

The next significant advance in Chekhov's literary career occurred in the spring of 1885, when *Petersburgskaia gazeta,* a St. Petersburg daily for which Chekhov had been doing some court reporting, offered him weekly publication of his stories (on Mondays). This new venue was not particularly profitable for Chekhov, but it was willing to publish pieces that were longer and more serious than those acceptable to the small humorous press.[31] As "A. Chekhonte" he was attracting ever greater attention. Therefore it is not surprising, and very likely self-reflexive, that the theme of how one handles one's proper name was central to the very first story Chekhov sent the newspaper. In "The Last Mohicanness" ("Posledniaia mogikansha"), a shrewish wife berates her husband, who, lacking self-esteem, "forgets his title [*zvanie*]" and "embarrasses our family name [*nashu familiiu konfuzit'*]" by such undignified activities as going hunting with a certain Gusev, who is a lowly clerk (or scribe, *pisar'*, from the verb *pisat'*, "to write"). "How dare you even give a peep in the presence of a scribe, let alone talk with him," she remonstrates. With this publication in *Peterburgskaia gazeta* Chekhov shames his wife (medicine) and forgets his title (Dr.) by taking a deeper step into the writerly professsion. ("Gusev," incidentally, was Chekhov's nickname for his brother Aleksandr. As we saw in the case of "Proud Man," Chekhov's pairing with Aleksandr could indeed be problematic for the prestige of his name.)

At the end of 1885 Chekhov visited St. Petersburg for the first time. It came as a shock to learn that he was being read by the literary elite, and that he was considered a major emerging talent. After returning to Moscow, he wrote Aleksandr that he was "stunned by the reception given me by Petersburgers," that he "became terrified." "Had I known they were reading me, I wouldn't have written like that, to order" (4 January 1886). Similar remarks can be found in other letters following Chekhov's return. Now such well-known literary figures as Dmitrii Grigorovich, the onetime roommate of Dostoevskii, were urging Chekhov to take himself seriously as an author. This would mean addressing serious issues of the day in longer narratives, and it would mean, too, signing his works with his proper name. On 25 March 1886, Grigorovich famously wrote Chekhov that for the past year he had been reading "everything signed 'Chekhonte,' though he was inwardly made angry by a man who valued himself so little that he considers it necessary to have recourse to a pseudonym"; he ended his letter by urging Chekhov to sign his forthcoming collection of stories with his real name.[32] Soon thereafter, in a letter referring to Grigorovich's view on the matter, Chekhov instructed the publisher of his second pseudonymous collection of stories, *Motley Tales* (*Pestrye rasskazy,* May 1886), to add "A. P. Chekhov" in brackets to the book's second title page.[33] Meanwhile, in February 1886, with his debut in Suvorin's important Petersburg daily *Novoe vremia,*

Chekhov had finally begun to publish on a regular basis under his own name. Although he continued to use pseudonyms for stories appearing elsewhere, he could no longer avoid feeling the eyes of the public upon him, and his career had taken another significant step forward. To his brother Aleksandr he boasted that he had taken the place of his once powerful literary patron: "Leikin has gone out of fashion. His place has been taken by me" (6 April 1886). After another visit to Petersburg he wrote his uncle Mitrofan Egorovich, "I have to tell you that I am now the most fashionable writer in Petersburg" (18 January 1887).

Not surprisingly, stories involving peeping, exhibitionism, shameful exposure, and hiding are quite characteristic of this period.[34] Among them are two whose timing and content suggest roots in their author's life. While Chekhov was in Petersburg, his story "The Truth Will Out" ("Shilo v meshke")[35] appeared in *Oskolki*. In it, a government inspector traveling incognito to investigate abuses by officials in a provincial town fantasizes about the commotion he will create when he arrives. He asks his driver if he has ever heard of Posudin, that is, himself. It turns out that the driver knows not only who Posudin is but also all the intimate details of Posudin's life—that he drinks heavily when alone, that his housekeeper bosses him around. He knows, too, that the inspector is expected in the town to which he is secretly traveling, that misdoings have been well covered up, and that delicacies have been ordered to wine and dine him. In short, the fantasy of power Posudin has been savoring—the anticipation of a scenario resulting from operating clandestinely, then exposing his true identity in a lightning strike reminiscent of the ending of Gogol's *Government Inspector (Revizor)*—evaporates in a flash. He who imagined himself the observer was in fact the observed and, in consequence, impotent. Posudin abandons the mission and returns home. This story was apparently written while Chekhov was planning his trip to Petersburg, where over two hundred of his pieces had been published pseudonymously, and where his name was known in editorial offices, but his person had never before been seen. Now Chekhov, who had been "writing from a crack in the wall" (i.e., been the observer), would make his self available for inspection.

The second story, published in August 1886, very likely reflects Chekhov's ambivalence regarding the laurels that had begun to come his way. In "The First-Class Passenger" ("Passazhir 1-go klassa"), which appeared under Chekhov's name in *Novoe vremia,* a civil engineer who has completed many important projects complains of remaining unknown: he never sees his name in the newspapers, while far less distinguished individuals receive great recognition. He relates, for example, how his mistress, a third-rate actress in the provincial city where he was building a great bridge, upstaged the bridge's opening ceremony merely by strolling past the site along the opposite bank of the river; the next day it was she, rather than he, who appeared in the newspaper (indeed, he was known in town not as the builder of the bridge but as "some sort of engineer" with whom the actress was living). The engineer's monologue is delivered in a first-class waiting room to a man who turns out to be an equally unknown but important and much-published scholar, and the story ends with their complicitous laughter. At a time when Chekhov's own name was beginning to appear in newspapers of both capital cities, Chekhov repudiates celebrity, as though there were an inverse relationship between the value of one's work and the size of one's public profile. In his letter to Mariia Kiseleva of 13 December 1886, Chekhov negates the value of his own fame, while associating himself with perhaps the most famous female exhibitionist of the late nineteenth century, Zola's fictional actress and prostitute Nana: "Alas and alack! In Piter [St. Petersburg] I'm becoming as fashionable as Nana. At the same time that editors hardly know the serious Korolenko, all of Piter reads my drivel [. . .] It's flattering for me, but my literary sensibility is offended . . . I'm embarrassed for the public, which chases after literary toy poodles for the simple reason that it's unable to notice the elephants, and I deeply believe that there won't be a single dog that recognizes me once I start working seriously . . . " Chekhov's visibility is an index of the public's blindness.

What had it meant for Chekhov to write under pseudonyms, and what did it mean to give them up? Pseudonyms had served as that fissure in the wall Chekhov wrote of to his brother: they rendered the author's person invisible, transforming a process that might naturally be conceived as reciprocal—one observes others and in turn subjects oneself to the gazes of others—into a kind of voyeurism. That is, to the extent that publishing put Chekhov's person before the public, then Chekhov protected himself by writing under pseudonyms.

Now, there are certainly factors that mitigate the individual psychological significance of Chekhov's recourse to pseudonyms. Publishing pseudonymously was, rather than a matter of personal choice, common practice in the so-called small press where Chekhov got his start. Thus an 1886 letter to his brother Aleksandr rebukes the latter for attaching his real name (Al. Chekhov) to a cartoon for which he had supplied the theme: "Don't allow them to sign your full name to trifles [. . .] Do you want to thoroughly shame yourself?" (27–30 December). Some years later Chekhov altered the signature on a story he was placing for one of his protégés, Elena Shavrova: she might feel her appearance in the "small press" under her own name to be *mauvais ton,* he explained (24 March 1892). The variety of Chekhov's pseudonyms also had a quite practical function: it was a way of appeasing the inclinations to exclusivity of Chekhov's various publishers. Thus, when Leikin, the publisher of *Oskolki,* berated Chekhov for giving a piece, "The Dance Pianist" ("Taper"), to the rival *Budil'nik* during a period of intense competition for subscriptions, Chekhov could answer, "I *promise* not to give anything to humorous journals in December, January, and the end of November, anything with the signature A. Chekhonte, or any signature known to the readers of *Oskolki*" (23 November 1885). Ernest Simmons has argued that there was nothing expressive about Chekhov's early tales, no risk to the self that would bestow meaning on publishing pseudonymously: "So lightly and impersonally did he regard these early contributions that on one occasion, at least, he allowed a fellow writer the use of his pseudonym, Antosha Chekhonte, to help him place his pieces, and agreed to turn over the payments to him."[36] But in this matter the generally reliable Simmons was shortsighted. It is precisely in the early tales, as should be becoming clear, that the self-reflexive aspect of Chekhov's art is most palpable. Moreover, the sheer quantity of different pseudonyms Chekhov used—more than fifty if one counts all variations[37]—far exceeds explanation by reference to normal practice in the small press. Chekhov's own remarks on the topic, too, point toward an internal psychological motivation for his use of pseudonyms, and these same demands would be met by other means once he began to sign his works with his proper name.

Chekhov once told the minor author Ieronim Iasinskii that writing under a pen name "was just like walking naked with a large mask on and showing oneself like that to the public."[38] This analogy makes hiding a facilitator of exhibitionism, with the pseudonym functioning as a theatrical suppression of the compulsion to expose oneself. The same could be said for the rather transparent pen name that became Chekhov's favorite (especially for stories in *Oskolki* and *Petersburgskaia gazeta*), Antosha (A. or An.) Chekhonte. Marena Senderovich, who has published by far the most interesting and penetrating treatment of Chekhov's use of pseudonyms—I rely very heavily on her work—argues that truly hiding behind such a pseudonym was impossible:

> Its use is more likely a final theatrical gesture of playful defense in the spirit of Chekhov's humorous texts. Thus Chekhov's relation to his texts is twofold: on the one hand, the pseudonym provides a means for concealment when it is unsuitable for Chekhov's authorship to be made manifest; on the other hand, the Russian author was playing hide-and-seek with himself, as children do when they close their eyes and say, "Come and find me." He does not try to avoid being found, but he avoids calling out his own name and at the same time hints at it. If one gives some thought to the question of this game, its meaning becomes clear: it establishes aesthetic distance between the writer and what he has written. Chekhov hides from himself just as he hides from his reader under a pseudonym—a typically Chekhov-

ian correspondence (there are insufficient social and cultural motives otherwise to explain the use of the pseudonym); behind it one finds both shame for an action and fear of ridicule, which magically disappear under the enchanted hood of pseudonymity.[39]

Rather than aesthetic, however, I might speak of a *psychological* distancing of the author from his public; for it is not his relationship to the literary work as an aesthetic object that troubles Chekhov, but the extent to which he is himself visible in that work to those who are reading it. As in the notorious case of Stendhal, which comes to mind thanks to its elegant treatment by Jean Starobinski,[40] the use of pseudonyms alters the author's situation in respect to the gaze of others; but unlike in Stendhal's case, for Chekhov the pseudonym functions to protect the one genuine self. Thus Chekhov justified employing pseudonyms by asserting that he was saving his name for the medical research he hoped to publish someday (*P* 1:195–97). Chekhov's masks never became his real life: he never disavowed his family, his origins, his professional identity as a physician, or his friends. One could in no sense speak of a kind of deliberate multiple personality disorder as with Stendhal, for whom, according to Starobinski, "the mask and the pseudonym generate a dynamic of pure irresponsibility."[41]

In November 1885 Chekhov wrote a letter to his publisher Leikin that opens with a lament about the misery and expense of being a "family man" (Chekhov was of course still single, but had assumed responsibility for his parents and siblings). "I've got trouble!" he declares. And he ends the letter (in which he asks for Leikin's help with arranging regular payment from *Peterburgskaia gazeta*) with a footnote asterisked to his signature: "My signature begins to acquire a definite and consistent character, which I explain by the enormous quantity of prescriptions I have to write—most often, of course, *gratis*" (17 November 1885). Chekhov's family and medical practice leave him economically poor, but solid in identity; he, like his signature, has acquired definition. His literary practice under a variety of pseudonyms—this letter precedes by a week the one promising to use "Chekhonte" only in Leikin's journal—remains chiefly a financial matter.

After 1886, when Chekhov's professional identity as a writer had crystallized, the situation became far more complex. When Chekhov prints his proper name along with his pseudonym on the title page of *Motley Tales* (*Pestrye rasskazy*), he as much as declares he will hide no longer. Nevertheless, he inscribes a copy of that collection to himself—"To the esteemed Anton Pavlovich Chekhov from the author. 86.V.24"[42]—as if to separate his true self (the reader or observer) from the authorial persona, or at least to joke about such a possibility. And he continues to use the pseudonym for stories, some of them among his short masterpieces, published in the least prestigious and least profitable of his vehicles (*Oskolki, Petersburgskaia gazeta, Budil'nik*). *Novoe vremia* pays enough to merit Chekhov's genuine signature, and the stories he publishes there are his best; now the pseudonyms "A. Chekhonte" and "Man without a Spleen" (Chelovek bez selezenki) are used, apparently, to maintain conventions that have been established between Chekhov and his readers in the small press, while also signaling a certain detachment from these trifles.

This would appear a stable arrangement. For Chekhov, however, visibility as such remains problematic; once he has been seduced into exposing his name and his self, new strategies of concealment are required. Marena Senderovich has argued that the bifurcation between Chekhov stories and pseudonymous stories soon gives way to a further bifurcation, this one between what has already been published and what remains secreted in the author's mind. She cites a letter to Suvorin of 27 October 1888, in which Chekhov claims, "I have not yet begun my literary activity, even though I won the [Pushkin] prize"; "I don't like it that I've been successful; those plots sitting in my head are annoyingly jealous of what's already written"; "I don't like and am bored with everything that gets written now, whereas all that is still sitting in my head interests, touches, and agitates me." The logic is that of Chekhov's story "First-Class Passenger": what is known to the public, by definition, loses value. But Chekhov's own exposure is irreversible, and his task now is to establish a private self and a private life apart from his famous name. This motif of what Senderovich calls "name alienation" appears in both Chekhov's letters and his fiction of this period, culminating in "A Boring Story" ("Skuchnaia istoriia") of 1889, whose hero, a celebrated professor of medicine, despairs, unloved and misunderstood, in a life apart from his famous name.[43] And there were still problems that arose from sharing this name with brothers who also appeared in print. Thus Grigorovich's fall 1888 letter informing Chekhov that the latter would receive the Pushkin Prize (and praising the new story "Steppe") also expressed annoyance at Chekhov's brothers, who dared to publish under the name Chekhov: "It confuses readers, and works get attributed to you that shouldn't be."[44]

The mature author who signed his own name to substantial prose works found new strategies of self-protection. Chekhov tended to get quite upset and defended himself vigorously when critics made inferences about the author's self from his writings: thus in a letter to Suvorin he railed against readings of "Boring Story" that attributed the hero–narrator's weltschmerz to Chekhov (17 October 1889). And yet scholars and biographers have never ceased to associate this story with the difficult personal moment in Chekhov's life surrounding the death of his brother Nikolai (in June 1889, from the same consumption that afflicted Chekhov), and with many documentary indications of spiritual malaise. During the period when he was conceiving "Boring Story," Chekhov wrote a critical response to the manuscript of a play (now lost) sent him by his brother Aleksandr: "The main thing, watch out for the personal element. This play won't be of use anywhere if all the characters are similar to you [. . .] What good are Natasha, Kolia, Tosia? As if there weren't any life outside of yourself! And who's interested in knowing my life or yours, my thoughts or yours? Give people people, and not your own self" (8 May 1889). This letter provides a key to understanding the provocative title of "Boring Story": this confessional tale rarely bores its readers, but it does contain a great deal of the "personal element" against which Chekhov cautions Aleksandr. The title of the story appears to be a kind of private joke regarding the story's subjective side and its expressive function. The emphasis here is on "private," however; Chekhov ridiculed the pretensions of those who would see his soul in this or other works.[45]

Interestingly enough, although Chekhov now signs his fiction, he obscures the authorship of essays such as his obituary for the explorer Przheval'skii (1888) and his denunciation of practices at the so-called research station of the Moscow Zoo ("Fokusniki," 1891). That is to say, Chekhov attaches his proper name to works of fiction while maintaining vehemently (and disingenuously) that they have no connection to his person, but withholds his signature from essays and editorials that directly express their author's opinions. (One exception was his signed obituary in December 1891 for his friend and medical colleague Zinaida Lintvareva.)

Celebrity status, which of course increased the frequency and boldness of remarks about him, made self-defense more difficult for Chekhov. In one Moscow newspaper alone Chekhov was mentioned almost six hundred times in the last twenty years of his life.[46] The author's response to this situation: "When I see my last name in that nice newspaper, I get a feeling as if I had swallowed a wood louse. Ugh!"[47] Toward the end of 1901 he wrote in his notebook, "It's better to perish because of fools than to receive praise from them" (S 17:85). As a rule Chekhov attempted to ignore publicity, adopting the posture of a living target who is confident of the poor aim of those stalking him. One incident did, however, provoke an uncharacteristic, angry outburst. A review article that appeared in *Russkaia mysl'* shortly before Chekhov's departure for Sakhalin had listed Chekhov among the "priests of unprincipled writing," and this could not go unanswered. Most interestingly, Chekhov's letter of 10 April 1890 to Vukol Lavrov, the journal's editor and publisher, deploys the rhetorical tactic of redefining the self that has been attacked such that it no longer legitimately falls under the purview of literary criticism. Because he is about to leave Russia, perhaps never to return, Chekhov writes, he cannot restrain himself from answering a slander. He attaches no great value to most of what he has published, but he refuses to be ashamed of his writings. Moreover, he is above all a doctor and primarily known as such to his acquaintances. This identification of himself as first and foremost a physician is a doubly effective shield against the article's invective: the *zemstvo* physician—employed by the rural district council and devoted to public health—was the living icon of "principledness" in Russia at the end of the nineteenth century; as a doctor whose literary dabblings are insignificant, Chekhov should be not be held to standards that might be appropriate for a socially significant author.

Chekhov also took to leaving Moscow for long voyages. Perhaps the expedition to the prison island of Sakhalin in far eastern Siberia best exemplifies wanderlust as a way of both hiding oneself and indulging what might be called, in a loosely Freudian idiom, the drive to see. This heroic journey, which has often been interpreted as a therapeutic measure to combat depression over his brother Nikolai's death, feelings of alienation and ambivalence, and intimations of mortality, was a kind of escape, a means of hiding temporarily from family, friends, critics, and his illness—the same illness that had cut down his brother. Thus Senderovich argues that Chekhov "made that journey so he could escape from an inauthentic existence into which his famous name had plunged him. The trip constituted a flight from the name, paradoxical as it may seem, that Chekhov no longer felt was his own and that deprived his life of authenticity."[48] But the trip was also a triumph of the gaze: "Really, I have seen such riches and have had so much pleasure that even dying now does not frighten me" (to Suvorin, 27 June 1890); "I can say: I've lived! I've had my share. I've been in the hell of Sakhalin, and in heaven, on the island of Ceylon" (to Leont'ev-Shcheglov, 10 December 1890). Traveling facilitated an inner translocation to a more active and positive self during a time of crisis. In other words, the journey to Sakhalin served the same psychological demands that had once been met by writing under a pseudonym, "through a crack in the wall." By now, Chekhov, a celebrity about whose voyage much was written in the popular press, could protect his true self only by removing his very person from view. Traveling to Sakhalin carried out, on an epic scale, a maneuver analogous to the one described by Nemirovich-Danchenko when the latter was reading Chekhov's manuscript: by turning his back on Moscow, Chekhov made himself unseeable; and from the position of the observed, he moved into that of an observer—sociologist, ethnographer, and writer of travel sketches.

Chekhov asserted that he was going to Sakhalin not for literary purposes but to pay his debt to medicine.[49] Traveling east, he became a different person, not the one readers and critics of his fiction presumed to see. In fact, Chekhov made remarkably spare literary use of this and other voyages; the author of *Sakhalin Island* (*Ostrov Sakhalin*) was a man of science rather than a man of letters.

Soon after returning to Moscow (December 1890), he again removed himself from view by traveling to western Europe (March and April 1891) and eventually buying a small estate and moving to the country (February 1892). On that estate he built himself a refuge, a small outbuilding to which he could retreat to write;[50] later, after he had moved to the Crimea, the dacha at Gurzuf would offer a similar level of privacy and detachment from the family home. Nevertheless, over the next decade, literary fame would make Chekhov ever more visible to his public. Memoirists who knew him in his last years never fail to remark the impudence of admirers who, on any number of pretexts (or with none at all), would show up at the door of Chekhov's home in Yalta. Chekhov seems to have been utterly incapable of resisting such assaults on his privacy, though he could find subtle means of defending himself. The most striking of his practices at such moments was to occupy himself with a pair of binoculars: when others took him as an object to be viewed, he defended himself *psychologically;* rather than turn away his visitors, he adopted the stance of the one who looks, assuming the active position of viewer.[51] But there were pleasures to be had as well. The artist Aleksandra Khotiaintseva tells of Chekhov's delight in listening, ear to the wall of his pensione room in Nice, as a young couple from Kiev read his stories aloud next door.[52]

Chekhov's sister, Mariia, tells two tremendously revealing anecdotes along similar lines that relate to the last years of Chekhov's life. In the first instance, Chekhov walked out of a concert that he, his sister, and Ol'ga Knipper had traveled some distance to hear when other patrons took note of his presence. This occurred in the Crimea, at the Vorontsov Palace at Alupka. The trio was drinking tea before the concert's start when a stranger from a neighboring table stood to pronounce a "bombastic speech about the writer Chekhov, now among us"; and when everybody turned toward Chekhov, he rose and made for the exit. His sister and Knipper found him pacing the palace grounds, extremely upset and adamantly refusing to return to the concert. In the second instance, Chekhov was traveling with his sister on a train when a naïve fellow passenger started a conversation about literature, and in particular Anton Chekhov, "one of the best contemporary authors." Traveling incognito, like the hero of "The Truth Will Out," Chekhov pretended to know nothing about the literary scene or this outstanding author, and he resisted to the end his sister's prodding to disclose his identity.[53] According to Mariia, he thoroughly enjoyed hearing himself praised while hiding, as it were, behind a mask of anonymity. Meanwhile, his concealed genuine identity remained utterly anchored and secure; after all, his sister was seated beside him. This episode, like the one related by Khotiaint-seva, realizes the metaphor of "writing through a crack in the wall," and may be taken as emblematic of the conditions Chekhov considered comfortable for an encounter with his readers.

A Case in Point: A Psychoanalytic Reading of Chekhov's "At Sea"

> It's worth being just a bit more honest: throw yourself overboard entirely, don't stick yourself into the heroes of your novel, renounce yourself for at least ½ hour.
> —Chekhov to his brother Aleksandr (20 February 1883)

With the publication of "The Requiem" ("Panikhida") in February 1886, Anton Chekhov made his first appearance in *Novoe vremia*, Aleksei Suvorin's Petersburg daily. He had submitted the story under the pseudonym A. Chekhonte, but was persuaded by the paper's editors to attach his real name.[54] That this moment receives special mention in biographies of Chekhov is natural, given the significance Suvorin was to have in the development of Chekhov's career and the meaning Chekhov clearly attached to signing his proper name. It is in equal measure odd, however, that so little attention has been afforded the first story published under the name of A. Chekhov at the author's own initiative. This was "At Sea," a very short tale published in *Mirskoi tolk* in 1883.[55] Two more stories signed by Chekhov, "He Understood!" ("On ponial!") and "The Swedish Match" ("Shvedskaia spichka. [Ugolovnyi rasskaz]") soon also appeared in different journals.

Once written, the story clearly troubled Chekhov. Soon after posting it, he grew nervous enough about the provocative subject matter to write a letter to the editors asking that they return the story; he was told it was too late, although the editors would be happy in the future to receive "less spicy" tales. A short time later, in a letter to Nikolai Leikin (25 December 1883), Chekhov complained of the tactics of unscrupulous publishers regarding his name.[56] He explained, "I sign with my full family name only in *Priroda i okhota* [where 'He Understood' appeared], and once I put it under a large story in *Strekoza* [this was 'The Swedish Match']." Less than two months after "At Sea" appeared in *Mirskoi tolk*, Chekhov neglected to mention it when listing the few stories he had published to date under his own name—a disavowal that, arguably, indicates some ambivalence toward the story.

Almost two decades later Ivan Bunin asked Chekhov to contribute something to a projected almanac by the publishing house Skorpion. Chekhov, who had been revising his early pieces for the Marks edition of his collected works, offered a slightly reworked "At Sea" under a new title, "At Night." But he was then appalled by the decadent company in which he found himself printed. He was also irritated by the sloppy proofs Skorpion sent him to correct, and angry that the proofs arrived with postage due. What seems to have especially provoked Chekhov, however, was the overly prominent use of his name to advertise the almanac in the newspaper *Russkie vedomosti*. As happens to the narrator of "A Boring Story," Chekhov saw his name detached from his self and circulated as a coin of exchange. His letter of complaint to Bunin (14 March 1901) ended with a pun: "Having read this announcement in *Russkie vedomosti,* I swore never again to become involved with scorpions, crocodiles, or snakes."

If the first publication of a story under Chekhov's own name involved a great deal of anxiety, then republication of the same story many years later became an occasion for manifestly hostile feelings; in both instances the issue of Chekhov's name was central. When revising the story, Chekhov did not disturb its spicy plot, nor did he remove some astonishingly suggestive erotic imagery. Indeed, Skorpion's edtor, Valerii Briusov, complained in his diary that Chekhov had intentionally sent a story that would be unlikely to get past the censors.[57] What Chekhov suppressed—or what, perhaps, he wished he had suppressed before he sent the story in eighteen years before—were overt signals of intertextual connection with Victor Hugo's *Toilers of the Sea* and Shakespeare's *Hamlet* and certain lurid details concerning the story's sailor-narrator, his father, and his late mother. Chekhov normally cut material when making revisions. But most often such cuts were of the stylistic variety, intensifying Chekhov's trademark laconicity. In the case of "At Sea," the anxiety and ill will that accompanied each publication of the story, together with the singular fact of Chekhov's signature, lead one to suspect an uncomfortable (for Chekhov) degree of personal involvement in the tale; and, as we shall see, Chekhov's revisions appear oriented toward eliding precisely the author's visibility in the text. The motif of peeping in "At Sea" suggests reading it as another in the series of tales from this period thematizing the position of an author who writes "from a crack in the wall," a metaliterary interpretation that is supported by a remarkable series of literary allusions. But the story is also saturated with what can only be called Oedipal motifs, and these are implicated in the self-reflexive aspect of "At Sea." There is a deep nexus between the story's provocative erotic plot and imagery and the author's revisions, anxieties, and signature.

The plot tension of "At Sea" is explicitly based on the dynamics of erotic desire. The sailors aboard a steamer have drawn lots to determine which two of them will spy on a newlywed English pastor and his young wife in the bridal suite. The winners are father and son; and since the son is also the first-person narrator, the reader's position is no less voyeuristic than the narrator's: both anticipate the payoff of observing the newlyweds' coupling. The familial relationship between the two peeping Toms creates additional expectations, however; scenes of mastery and initiation will occur on both sides of the wall.

The two sailors take their places at the peepholes, but there is a hitch in the bridal suite, where the bride appears reluctant. When she does finally assent, we peeping Toms, who were unable to hear the husband's words, assume that he has been pleading for himself and that the marriage's consummation will follow. In the surprise denouement, a banker with whom the couple had been socializing earlier enters, gives the pastor some money, and is left alone with the bride. The stunned sailors leave the peephole without witnessing the sexual act, thereby also depriving the reader of the promised voyeuristic titillation.

The denouement provokes a moral reevaluation of the sailors, earlier self-described by the narrator as "more disgusting than anything on earth." For had the peepers' desires been strictly pornographic, the exchange of privileges for money should have been no cause for them to give up their stations. At the same time, a man of the cloth is the last husband we would expect to be pimping his own bride. Last, the roles of father and son are reversed: the son, whom his father addresses as "laddie" or "little boy" (mal'chishka), becomes father to his own father as he helps him up the stairs.

Every detail in this miniature relates to the denouement, either as anticipated by the sailors or as it actually takes place. The setting at sea and at night—Chekhov underlined both aspects in the various versions he published by alternately using them as titles—suggests a space cut off from the normal world where anything might happen, tailor-made for liminal states. Each of the first three short paragraphs ends in an image that, if interpreted with the story's anticipated denouement in mind, evokes erotic culmination—the heavy clouds wishing to let go of their rain in a burst; the joking sailor who, as lots are drawn to determine who will spy on the newlyweds, crows like a rooster; and this bold image suggestive of a male orgasm: "A little shudder ran from the back of my head to my very heels, as if there were a hole in the back of my head from which little cold shot poured down my naked body. I was shivering not from the cold, but from other reasons."

Next follows a digression that sets up an opposition between the debauched seaman's world and the virginal world of the newlywed pastor, his bride, and idealized love. This opposition is most explicit in the passage juxtaposing the space where the peepers stand with the space of the bridal suite, and it will be reversed in the denouement. For the moment, however, the narrator focuses on the sailor's world. His view of his own and his comrades' moral state is summed up by the special kind of space they inhabit. Both literally and figuratively, it is the vertical space necessary for a fall: "To me it seems that the sailor has more reasons to hate and curse himself than any other. A person who might every moment fall from a mast and be immersed forever under the waves, who knows God only when he is drowning or plunging headfirst, needs nothing and feels pity for nothing in existence." Here the sailor embodies man in his fallen state, man who falls all the time, compulsively. In the denouement the narrator jumps back from his peephole "as if stung" or bitten, as by a serpent (the Russian word here, *uzhalennyi,* would be used for a snakebite). The father's face is described as "similar to a baked apple"; this motif has special resonance in the context of a story about falls, carnal knowledge, and egregious sin. The inhabitants of this anti-Eden are compelled to repeat forever the moment of the Fall.

The digression ends, "We drink a lot of vodka, we are debauched, because we don't know who needs virtue at sea, and for what." Yet the anticipated coupling between pastor and bride is special precisely because of its aura of idealized love and virtue, while the sailors' reactions in the denouement demonstrate that virtue is necessary to them, even if they do not expect to take part in it. Here we might compare the way negotiations are carried out between the banker and the pastor with the sailors' method of deciding who among them will receive voyeuristic satisfaction of their erotic desires. The latter cast lots; they rely on luck, God's will, to decide the matter. For the pastor, God's representative on earth, he who can pay gets what he wants. The woman whom the sailor idealizes as a love object becomes a commodity for the pastor and the banker.

"At Sea" begins as a story about the depravity of the sailor's world but ends as a tale depicting the depravity of the "aristocratic bedroom"—a reversal perhaps banally moralistic, but not untypical of the early Chekhov. The last image is one of the father and son moving upward in space.

Chekhov's revisions of "At Sea" can be divided into three chief areas: his handling of references to Hugo, his handling of references to Shakespeare, and his decision to drop certain details regarding the familial relationship of the two peepers.

The characters and setting are quite exotic for Chekhov, and one suspects from the start that they have been imported. The Russian scholar R. G. Nazirov has revealed the story to be a parody of Victor Hugo's *Toilers of the Sea (Les travailleurs de la mer,* 1866).[58] "At Sea" picks up where *Toilers* leaves off: the English pastor, Ebenezer, is departing on a steamer with his bride, Deruchette. Left behind in despair is the extraordinary seaman, Gilliatt, who once saved Ebenezer's life and to whom Deruchette was promised. Chekhov's story echoes the opposition between the coarse laborer of the sea and the refined representative of

God, and it repeats certain central motifs, such as that of peeping: the lovesick Gilliatt spies on Deruchette for four years before he takes action to win her; he is spying on her when the pastor declares his love and kisses her for the first time; and even at the novel's melodramatic end, as Gilliatt commits suicide by allowing the rising tide to cover him where he sits, he is watching Deruchette and Ebenezer hold hands on the deck of a departing steamer. To Nazirov's findings can be added Chekhov's handling of the plot device of reversal: men whose exemplary virtue is remarked on by Hugo's narrator repeatedly turn out to be utter scoundrels. Chekhov's revisions distanced "At Sea" from Hugo's novel. In particular, notes Nazirov, "Chekhov cut a direct 'bibliographic key,' a line making rather explicit allusion to the original object of parody: 'the loud, drunken laughter of *toilers of the sea.*'" To be sure, the customary strategy of improving the rhythm of his prose, shortening dialogues, and pruning some of the melodramatic imagery eliminated the excesses so characteristic of Hugo's style and thereby weakened the links between this parody and its target text; but Chekhov's motivation was by no means exclusively stylistic.

The second subtext obscured in the revisions was *Hamlet.* Chekhov had a career-long involvement with Shakespeare, and especially with *Hamlet.* As one Russian critic has put it, "Shakespeare is mentioned so often in the stories and plays of Chekhov that one could call him one of Chekhov's heroes."[59] Just as Chekhov actually incorporates the title of the Hugo subtext into his narrative, in the 1883 version of "At Sea" the steamer's name, *Prince Hamlet,* is mentioned five times—this in a work of under five pages. Not surprisingly, this "bibliographic key" opens a number of subtler allusions to Shakespeare's tragedy.

The cock's crow and the narrator's shudder, discussed earlier, recall the appearance of the ghost of Hamlet's father:

BARNARDO: It was about to speak when the cock crew.
HORATIO: And then it started like a guilty thing
    Upon a fearful summons.[60]

For the sailor imitating the sound and those who are amused by it, the cock's crow is an erotic allusion; for the narrator, however, who has been contemplating his fallen state and is full of self-reproach, it is also a "fearful summons" heard by a "guilty thing." In the Gospel tale of Peter's denial, retold in Chekhov's short masterpiece of 1894, "The Student," the rooster's call has a similar meaning.

In *Hamlet* this shudder at the recollection of one's guilt is repeated when Claudius sees his crime portrayed in Hamlet's "mousetrap," his play within the play.[61] The moment is paralleled in "At Sea" in the narrator's reaction during the dumb show of the wedding night: if the crime of treating the bride as an object to be bought and sold stuns him, this is perhaps because it echoes what he and his shipmates did when they created and raffled the use of the peep-holes—or so the logic of *Hamlet* would suggest. In both cases, the anticipated pleasures of observation—the mousetrap's lure—vanish with the moral shock of recognition.

In the original version of the story, the narrator goes on deck and previews in fantasy the scene to be staged in the bridal suite:

> I lit a pipe and began looking at the sea. It was dark, but there must have been blood boiling in my eyes. Against the night's black backdrop I made out the hazy image of that which had been the object of our drawing lots.
>
> "I love you!" I gasped, stretching my hands toward the darkness.
>
> This expression "I love" I knew from books lying around in the canteen on the upper shelf.

As he utters "I love you" and stretches his hands toward the phantasm he has conjured, the narrator imagines himself in the place of the bridegroom. In a sense, this fantasy places the narrator on the other side of the wall at which he will soon be standing. The motifs of dreaming and reading also associate the narrator with Hamlet; in particular, they recall act 2, scene 2, where Hamlet enters reading, in which he utters the line "Words, words, words," and which ends with a torrent of self-reproaches, including his calling himself "John-a-dreams." As we have seen, the narrator of "At Sea" is no less liberal with criticism of himself. It is also in act 2, scene 2, that Hamlet calls Polonius "Jephthah, judge of Israel," thereby accusing the father of sacrificing Ophelia to gain favor with Claudius. There is a clear thematic connection with "At Sea," in which the bridegroom sacrifices his wife for financial gain.

Chekhov's recourse to *Hamlet* in this story differs from such references in his other early narrative works. There allusions to Shakespeare are usually comically distorted citations that sharpen a character's speech characteristics, reveal a farcically pretentious character's lack of culture, or lampoon Russian pseudo-Hamlets and latter-day superfluous men.[62] Something more substantial is taking place in "At Sea." And yet Chekhov chose to obscure the story's connection with *Hamlet* when revising it.

The third area of Chekhov's revision of "At Sea" involves suppressing all mention of the narrator's late mother and toning down the hostility between the narrator and his father. In the 1883 version, the elder sailor addresses his son after they win the lottery:

"Today, laddie, you and I have gotten lucky," he said, twisting his sinewy, tooth-less mouth with a smile.

"You know what, son? It occurs to me that when we were drawing lots your mother—that is, my wife—was praying for us. Ha-ha!"

"You can leave my mother in peace!" I said.

The "that is" (in Russian, the contrastive conjunction *a*) separating the two des-ignations "your mother" and "my wife" underlines the different functions this one woman had for the two men. (The erotic connotations that can be associ-ated with "getting lucky" work in Russian as well as in English translation.) In the 1901 version this exchange is replaced by the father's words: "Today, laddie, you and I have gotten lucky [. . .] Do you hear, laddie? Happiness has befallen you and me at the same time. And that means something." What this odd coin-cidence "means," perhaps, is what it has displaced from the story's earlier ver-sion: the mother.

In addition to leaving the mother in peace, Chekhov cut out explicit motifs of antagonism between father and son. In the original version, when the father asks the son to switch peepholes so that he, with his weaker eyes, might see bet-ter, the son strikes his father. "My father respected my fist," he says.

"At Sea" is so laden and ready to burst with motifs of Oedipal strivings that, had the story not been written some sixteen years prior to Freud's first public discussion of Oedipus and Prince Hamlet in *The Interpretation of Dreams*,[63] one would be sorely tempted to conjecture about Freud's influence on Chekhov. To the extent that Chekhov departed from the situations and configurations of the characters given him by Hugo's *Toilers* and, at a deeper level, *Hamlet,* his alter-ations of these subtexts in the original version of "At Sea" directly parallel Freud's interpretation of Shakespeare's play: they superimpose direct conflict with the father onto an impossible erotic desire. And both the ship metaphor and the motif of games of chance figure prominently in the *Oedipus Rex* of Sophocles. "We are all afraid, like passengers on a ship who see their pilot crazed with fear," laments Jocasta; and "Oedipus has drawn it for his lot" to kill his fa-ther and succeed him in the marriage bed.[64]

The story's English characters and Shakespearean ship led the censors to take its original version as a translation from English; the 1901 version, "At Night," was received as an imitation of Maupassant.[65] Perhaps this helps explain why, in spite of Briusov's concerns, the story was passed by the censors: giving works non-Russian settings and characters and presenting an original work as a trans-lation or an imitation of a foreign author were long-standing techniques for evading prohibition. But if elements of foreignness acted as a screen from gov-ernment censors, might this not be true of Chekhov's internal censor as well?

Recourse to the exotic Hugo subtext and to *Hamlet* may have facilitated the emergence of very sensitive material. Years later, when Chekhov revised the story for Skorpion, he attenuated the agonistic relationship with the father and the Hugo and *Hamlet* connections in equal measure.

Behind the incident of voyeurism we can see many features of the "primal scene," that archetypal peeping situation.[66] In "At Sea" the scene is portrayed with idiosyncrasies and distortions characteristic of the work of the defense mechanism of repression. These include splitting the father into two figures, the old sailor at the peephole and the pastor (or reverend father), whose conjugal place the narrator has already taken in his fantasies (when he is on deck with outstretched arms in the story's first version). They also make it possible for father and son to share the object of desire even as they contest for her; that is, there is a transformation in which the "either me or you" or "not me but you" as rightful agents of erotic desire for the mother figure become "both me and you."[67] This helps explain the uncanny stroke of luck — "that means something" — by which both father and son have won the right to stand at the peepholes.

The narrator's positioning at his peephole actually begins as a dreamlike image of penetration into a low and dark place: "I felt out my aperture and extracted the rectangular piece of wood I had whittled for so long. And I saw a thin, transparent muslin, through which a soft, pink light penetrated to me. And together with the light there touched my burning face a suffocating, most pleasant odor; this had to be the odor of an aristocratic bedroom. In order to see the bedroom, it was necessary to spread the muslin apart with two fingers, which I hurried to do." The Russian here for orifice, *otverstie*, can refer to an orifice in the anatomical sense as well. The aristocratic bedroom, with its ambivalently perceived scent, is revealed only after a parting of the hymeneal "muslin"; the notion of the hymen is, after all, what makes the anticipated coupling of newlyweds special and, presumably, piqued the banker's interest and opened his wallet.

The dialogue between father and son as they are waiting in anticipation at their stations vocalizes, after a process of displacement, thoughts belonging to the situation of the primal scene: "Let me take your place" and "Be quiet, they might hear us." In theory it is the child who can be traumatized by his lack of potency in the Oedipal stage; here the old man complains of his weak eyes. We can interpret the "stung" reaction of the narrator at the denouement — once again, on a different plane of meaning — as just such a castrating trauma, with potency redefined in pounds sterling and the idealized pastor-father exposed in his lack of it. The shock is all the more effective when juxtaposed with the images of excessive and impatient potency at the story's start. At the same time, the exchange represents the uncanny event of a wish fulfilled: the narrator's investment in this scene is predicated on a fantasy of taking the pastor-father's place, and now, before his eyes, just such a substitution is made. Once again, on the model of Hamlet's mousetrap, the sailor's conscience has been captured—with the difference that his most serious crime was no more than a transgressive wish. The narrator's sudden solicitous attitude toward his father—he helps him up the stairs—may be interpreted as an attempt to undo this fantasy.

A full-scale psychoanalytic interpretation of the story would only be beginning at this point. One might depart from Freud's sketch of the vicissitudes of the peeping compulsion, where scopophilia and exhibitionism are treated as inextricably linked opposites "which appear in ambivalent forms."[68] This is certainly the case in "At Sea," where Chekhov can be said to expose himself—this time, without wearing a mask—in a story depicting scopophilia. The narrator's fantasies and voyeurism are fundamentally autoerotic acts, while the contradictory situation of father and son peeping together, which then culminates with the father's order to desist, could at once dramatize a wish for union with the father and the father's injunction against autoerotic activity, both features of ambivalent Oedipal dynamics.[69] The narrator portrays his father as laying down the moral law and so impinging on his natural process of maturation: "Let's get out of here! You shouldn't see this! You are still a boy." By now, however, this gesture of paternal authority appears ludicrous.

Chekhov wrote "At Sea" as a twenty-two-year-old medical student, who at the time, incidentally, was following a patient in a clinic for nervous disorders.[70] The past few years had seen a "tangling up of the family sequence" in which Chekhov had become in a sense the father of his own brothers, sister, and parents.[71] This was chiefly a result of his ability to bring money—that same signifier of authority that displaces the Bible in "At Sea"—into the household after his father's disastrous bankruptcy. In Chekhov's own family, moreover, the Bible can be associated with Chekhov's pedantically religious father, who was fond of reading scriptural texts aloud. Just what Chekhov's new status meant to him is hinted at in Tat'iana Shchepkina-Kupernik's retelling of a favorite story of Chekhov's mother: when still a student, Chekhov came to her and announced, "Well, Mama, from this day on I myself will pay for Masha's schooling!"[72]

The psychological issues glimpsed in "At Sea" resonate throughout Chekhov's life and art. Chekhov's coy, ironic, at times nearly sadistic bearing toward women with whom he skirted serious involvement (see chapter 4) recalls Hamlet's treatment of Ophelia and his mother, the women he claims to love. It happens that the measure by which Hamlet quantifies his love for the dead Ophelia—more than the love of "forty thousand brothers" (5.5.269)—was a favorite citation of the early Chekhov; in humorous paraphrasings it became a ready synonym for "a lot."[73] More to the point, some of Chekhov's later, full-length stories that are notable for their representation of psychopathological states very carefully situate certain characters' psychological problems in respect to their relations with their fathers; this topic, which is addressed in chapter 3, can perhaps best be seen in the lengthy stories "Ward 6" (1892), "Three Years" (1895), and "My Life" (1896).

Psychoanalytic theory has it that the son's identification with the father, his accession to the father's name, closes the Oedipal stage.[74] This comes about after acquiescence to what is perceived as the father's threat of castration and the renunciation of erotic desire for the mother. Fully one third of "At Sea" involves the narrator's self-reproaches, all of which are based on his sailor's calling, that is, the professional identity shared with and given him by his father. It is clearly an uneasy identity. For Chekhov, too, any identification with his real father would have been terribly problematic; but the Oedipal victory of far surpassing the father raises its own set of complications.

Chekhov's very first ambitious literary attempt, the play he wrote while still in Taganrog and subsequently destroyed, was titled *Fatherlessness* (*Bezottsovshchina*); just before collapsing at the end of the last act in that play, the chief character, Platonov, declares, "Now I understand Tsar Oedipus, who gouged out his own eyes" (*S* 11:177). The first story Chekhov signed with the name of his father, "At Sea," depicts a son overtaking the father; in subsequent years Chekhov was to sign his own name only after he had already become a prominent literary figure and his ascendancy over the family of his father (and his first literary patron, Nikolai Leikin) was beyond dispute. Later in life, just after his father died—when he must have been meditating on his relationship with his father—Chekhov made an oblique association between his own family and that of Oedipus. On receiving a telegram of condolence from V. I. Nemirovich-Danchenko on behalf of Konstantin Stanislavskii and others at the Moscow Art Theater, Chekhov replied in a letter of 21 October 1898: "I am waiting for *Antigone*. I'm waiting, for you promised to send it. I really need it. I'm waiting for my sister, who, as she has telegraphed, is coming to me in Yalta. Together we'll decide how to arrange things now. After the death of our father, our mother will hardly want to live alone in the country. We've got to think up something new." Chekhov sets up a parallelism ("I am waiting for *Antigone* [. . .] I'm waiting for my sister") that casts the shadow of Oedipus' family onto his own, with the upshot: now that my father is dead, my mother will want to live with me.

The peeping situation of "At Sea"—and its overtones of the primal scene and complex Oedipal dynamics—found reflection, too, in certain of Chekhov's written remarks about his own marriage a few years before his death. It was at the time of the story's revision and republication in 1901 that Chekhov finally decided to take this step. In fact, Chekhov informs Knipper that the story has come out right in the middle of the three letters in which he proposes a wedding and honeymoon (22, 24, and 26 April 1901). What is more, Chekhov suggests two alternative cruises for the honeymoon (south along the Volga, or north to Solovki), and then immediately proceeds to inform Knipper of the publication of "At Sea," a story about two peepers observing newlyweds on a shipboard honeymoon. As is so often the case in Chekhov, a textual contiguity that appears accidental and perhaps even disjunctive masks a striking similarity: he has proposed a honeymoon like that of the spied-upon couple in "At Sea."

Chekhov's first letter to his brother Aleksandr after the wedding—written from the koumiss therapy sanatorium in Aksenovo where the couple had traveled on account of Chekhov's deteriorating health—plays with Oedipal motifs. Chekhov adopts the persona of a wayward son who, erotically precocious, has violated the father's rule and expects punishment: he addresses his brother as "pater" (*otche*) and asks, "Are you angry?" He explains: "I'm guilty before you: I didn't ask your permission and blessing. You see, I have, in a kind of a way, gotten married!" (21 June 1901). This joke on the theme of the father's authority and a son's Oedipal anxieties continues a long-standing epistolary tradition: in the early years the two brothers had honed their considerable skills of verbal mimicry by parodying the peculiar authoritarian discourse of their pedantic and once fear-inspiring father. Here, mocking the father gives way to a bawdy exhibitionistic allusion to another of Chekhov's early stories: his postscript— "N.B. This is not your England!"—echoes the punch line of his early tale "The Daughter of Albion" ("Doch' Albiona"), where it is spoken as the male character exposes himself to an indifferent English governess in his employ.[75] Embedded in each of these little jokes are fantasies about how others see his marriage and allusions to scenes he has staged previously in his fiction.

In his letters to both Knipper and Aleksandr, then, Chekhov deliberately entangles his life with his art. He all but invites us to read his own marriage through "At Sea"—an operation that, indeed, proves quite revelatory. The oddest feature of Chekhov's wedding (and one of the most famous facts of his biography) was Chekhov's insistence on a secret ceremony, though it pained Knipper.[76] He excluded all of his family, even his brother Ivan, who alone knew of Chekhov's plans. "I am somehow horribly afraid of the wedding ceremony and congratulations, and the champagne, which one has to hold in one's hand and accompany with a certain indeterminate smile," he excused himself to Knipper (26 April 1901). The usual explanation of this fear—Chekhov's aversion to convention, and to the banality or *poshlost'* of the wedding situation—fails to consider deeper psychological motivations for Chekhov's peculiar handling of this event. I see here a deliberate inversion and cancellation of the peeping scene of "At Sea." Chekhov does not wish to be observed; he is positively scopophobic about it (which may suggest that he is himself in the grip of a powerful scopophilic drive, with all the attendant implications). With dread he fantasizes himself as, rather than a participant in a meaningful social ritual, the object of peepers: the "indeterminate smile" ("neopredelenno ulybat'sia") that he imagines being compelled to display would be the visible and readable sign of his intimate life. To put it otherwise, he cannot project his own wedding as other than a spied-upon primal scene. But he does get married, and his clandestine fulfillment of the groom's role could surely be likened to writing pseudonymously, or, to recall yet again that vivid metaphor, walking about naked with a mask on. After all, Chekhov did not merely elope: he called tremendous attention to his wedding by arranging a dinner party that took place while he was getting married, and from which he and Knipper remained absent. He did not organize a private event; he staged a theatrically private event.

From a psychoanalytic perspective there is little difference between exhibitionism and such theatrical suppression of the compulsion to expose. The same logic applies to what can be called, in the loose sense of the term, the very contradictory Oedipal features of this scene of hiding, showing, and peeping. The marked exclusion of family from Chekhov's wedding makes it all the more a family affair. Knipper, like several previous romantic interests, had become a close friend of his sister. Might not suppressing the idea of a family romance have involved suppressing, literally, his family from the wedding? In prohibiting his family from the event, and in separating his wife from her close friend Mariia Pavlovna, Chekhov wards off any hint of incestuous ramifications while simultaneously preserving his strikingly close nuclear familial arrangement with his mother and his sister. "Dear Mother, bless me, I'm marrying. All will remain as before," he informs his mother by telegram (25 May 1901). Mariia perhaps understood better when she wrote Ol'ga that she herself would get married now that her brother had done so (P 10:316); after all, during his lifetime Chekhov had more than once given his sister to know that she ought to reject suitors for her hand.[77]

Does it make sense to speak of the Oedipal, too, in Chekhov the author? The allusions in "At Sea" to Hugo and Shakespeare—and their elimination in the story's revision—invite consideration of Chekhov's relations with his literary fathers.[78] "At Sea" juxtaposes two subtexts of vastly different literary value. In parodying Hugo's melodramatic situations and stylistic excesses (as he had done in the 1880 spoof "One Thousand and One Horrors," dedicated to Victor Hugo), Chekhov treats this predecessor as the sailor-narrator treats his own father. Hugo may be openly and easily displaced; Shakespeare, however, is another matter. Whether imitated by would-be authors, misquoted by pretentious buffoons, or performed by untalented actors, Shakespeare in Chekhov's works is a benchmark against which pretension stands revealed, very often to comic effect.

And this notion of pretension might apply equally to the ill-equipped young-ster who boldly advances an erotic claim on his parent and to the young author who declares his identity as an author for the first time by signing his proper name.

When Chekhov wrote "At Sea," the figure of Prince Hamlet had served Rus-sian literature for decades as a paradigm for the inability to translate desires and talents into action. The allusion to *Hamlet* in "At Sea" is a kind of joke about that paradigm, but one that perhaps nevertheless indicates anxiety about failure and a wish to forestall it. In a letter to Suvorin of 25 November 1892, Chekhov contrasted his own generation of authors with its more impressive predecessors, stating of the former, "If you lift up the skirts of our muse, all you see is a flat area," while of the more virile elders he wrote, "They have a certain goal, like the ghost of Hamlet's father." The author of that generation with whom Chekhov was most often associated, and whom he was at times accused of im-itating, was Ivan Turgenev.[79] In 1887 Chekhov himself joked about being mis-taken by local inhabitants for Turgenev—presumably the Turgenev of *A Hunter's Sketches* (*Zapiski okhotnika*)—when he wrote his family of his wanderings afoot during his tour of the southern steppes (11 May 1887). And it was Turgenev who, sometime around Chekhov's first blood-spitting in 1884, appeared to Chekhov in a nightmare to warn him that his life would be short; or so Chekhov told Suvorin in 1894: "Some ten or so years ago I took up spiritualism, and Tur-genev, who had been summoned by me, answered: 'Your life is drawing close to its sunset'" (11 July 1894). By the time Chekhov revised "At Sea" in 1901, his place as an author was secure, but death was without doubt nearer and more real. There is considerable evidence, too, that he had become a conscious theo-rist of Oedipal anxieties and their implication in the problems of authorship. In *The Seagull* the young writer Treplev, who laces his speech with citations from *Hamlet,* must contest an established author of the preceding generation for both the affection of his mother and recognition as an author.[80]

In any case, the early Chekhov repeatedly associated with *Hamlet* the fateful moment of asserting one's identity in spite of feelings of inadequacy and prob-able failure. In "Baron" (1882), the seedy prompter, a failed actor who had shown great talent but lacked courage, is carried away during a performance of *Ham-let* and begins declaiming the lines he should have been whispering to the red-haired youth playing the prince. It is his end. He is kicked out of the theater altogether, but at least for once in his life he has shown boldness: he has de-claimed. For once he has ceased to be invisible, unheard by the audience. How appropriate that the story in which Chekhov decides to be Chekhov, to sign his own name, should be engaged with *Hamlet.*[81]

CHAPTER 2

Looking the Part

Medicine gets in his way; if he weren't a doctor, he'd write even better.
— Tolstoy to Maksim Gorkii, regarding Chekhov

If Chekhov had not been such a remarkable writer, he would have been an excellent doctor [. . .] And there would be nothing surprising if his diagnosis proved more complete and penetrating than a diagnosis established by some sort of fashionable star. He saw and heard in a person—in his face, voice, movement—that which was hidden from others, which didn't give itself away, which eluded the eyes of the average observer.
— Aleksandr Kuprin, "Pamiati Chekhova" (1986)

What distinctions arise between referring to the visual thematics in Chekhov's life and art as "seeing, being seen, hiding, showing" or, alternatively, "scopophilia, scopophobia, and exhibitionism"? Neither formulation is particularly graceful. The first series of relatively neutral terms describes behaviors without invoking a larger interpretive context; the second, by contrast, belongs to a discourse in which they are associated with "partial instincts" or "drives" and Freud's notions of perversion. They are key terms in the psychoanalytic paradigm of the Oedipal complex, and in the fantasy of the "primal scene" at the center of that complex.[1] In works such as "At Sea" and *The Seagull,* this interpretive valence is activated, as it were, by overt material; while this is not necessarily a fact about Chekhov's psychological makeup, it is most certainly so about these texts, in which peeping and exhibitionism appear in plots involving triangular familial conflict and allusions to *Oedipus Rex.* But this is by no means always the case in Chekhov's handling of the thematic complex in his works.

The works read in this chapter raise additional, and often quite different, psychological issues, both as literary themes and in regard to Chekhov's person.

Seeing and being seen are central to a variety of psychoanalytic models that describe how the self is formed and buttressed, and how it can be threatened or damaged as well. Seeing and being seen, hiding and showing, are construed in these theoretical contexts as fundamental to the dynamic psychological processes, narcissistic (and pre-Oedipal) in nature, that shape and maintain the self; and this extends to professional identity as well. Chekhov's handling of the thematic complex in connection with professional identity foregrounds precisely this psychological dynamic. His writings very often represent characters for whom a certain kind of seeing or being seen, or both, also constitute the *distinctive* activities on which a social, occupational, or professional identity is based.

This grounding of identity in the vicissitudes of seeing is exceptionally clear in the case of physicians, who see what remains hidden from others, be this the body itself or organs and processes internal to it, and whose visual penetration would be either impossible or transgressive were it not carried out by a professional. In Chekhov the defining function of vision is by no means limited to the medical profession, however; rather, it appears connected with the very notion of professional or occupational identity in the widest possible sense, and primarily as a fact of individual psychology.[2]

What does it mean in Chekhov's poetic world to see professionally? It means to view with a gaze that differs from everyday seeing, a gaze that operates according to the conventions of one's discipline and is therefore ostensibly objective, affect-free, and detached from libidinal drives. What does it mean to be seen as a professional? One either looks the part or one does not; one measures up to expectations in the eyes of others or one does not; one is either a success or a failure. In terms Chekhov habitually applied to the playwright's métier, as we saw in the last chapter, the component of exhibitionism inevitably involved in maintaining one's professional identity places selfhood at perennial risk of catastrophic collapse in a high-stakes "form of sport."

How this theme in Chekhov's writings might relate to the author's psyche can be approached only speculatively, and with nuance. We are not dealing with a topic that is peculiar to Chekhov, or one that is always best understood in terms of individual psychology. In medicine we know that seeing and being seen, hiding and showing, surely reflect the pragmatics of professional identity—the training, habits, discipline, and typical situations of practice; they are also key tropes of cultural discourses (whether broad or narrowly disciplinary) that endow that practice with meaning. What appears emphasized in Chekhov's writings, however, is the individual psychological component in such complex inter- and extrapersonal dynamics. Just why this is so remains open to a tantalizing variety of explanations, none of which are mutually exclusive. Did Chekhov's medical training attune him to problems of observing and being observed? Did it aggravate a psychological disposition peculiar to him? Or might his early, formative practice as an author of brief comic tales have led him to focus on the inherently comic plot devices of pretense and exposure?

In this chapter I gauge the medical disciplinary dimensions of seeing and being seen by means of a digression into the memoiristic and autobiographical narratives of two other Russian author-physicians, Chekhov's successors Vikentii Veresaev (1867–1945) and Mikhail Bulgakov (1891–1940). These authors treat aspects of the experience of becoming and practicing as a physician that are never directly addressed in Chekhov's writings—there is relatively little in the written record about Chekhov's own medical education—and provide something of a control on the inferences we might make from examining the case of Chekhov alone. We are indeed dealing with a phenomenon far from unique to Chekhov.

That caveat notwithstanding, witnessing the range and depth in Chekhov of the thematic complex involving seeing and being seen, hiding and showing, does build a persuasive case for understanding it as revealing something distinctive about the person of Chekhov. After treating a brief exemplary selection of works in which the complex plays out in connection with medicine and other occupational identities, I proceed to readings of two short tales, "The Mirror" ("Zerkalo") and "A Work of Art" ("Proizvedenie iskusstva"), that are wholly structured around the themes with which we are concerned. These stories emerged from a traumatic event in Chekhov's own medical practice, and this connection underwrites a psychobiographical understanding of the thematic complex in Chekhov.

Vicissitudes of Seeing and Professional Identity in Veresaev and Bulgakov

Unlike Chekhov, both Vikentii Veresaev and Mikhail Bulgakov left fictionalized memoirs of their practice as physicians. Veresaev's *Memoirs of a Physician* (*Zapiski vracha,* 1901) melds the narrative of a young doctor's education and introduction to practice and research with an essayistic and, on balance, appreciative critique of the profession; Bulgakov's *Notes of a Young Physician* (*Zapiski iunogo vracha,* 1926–27) is a cycle of highly polished short stories, each with the same fictional doctor-narrator, who relates tales of his initiatory practice in a very challenging place and time. In both, seeing and being seen, hiding and showing, prove central.

Veresaev's semi-fictional memoir at times makes use of colleagues' experiences as the memoirist's own and openly declares that certain representative episodes are invented.[3] It begins with a summary of the author's training in the faculty of medicine at the university in Dorpat. The first two years involved theoretical study, and in particular the study of anatomy, during which Veresaev's new knowledge translates into a power of seeing: "I personally got used to corpses very soon and would for hours on end, fascinated, sit through their dissection, which revealed before me all the secrets of the human body; over the course of seven or eight months, I was passionately occupied with anatomy, having given myself over to it entirely—and for that period my view of the human being became somehow amazingly more simple."[4] While observing a passerby in the street he sees "an animated corpse"; an attractive girl might make his heart beat fast for a moment, "but at the same time all she's made of is well known to me, and there is really nothing special about her: her brain has the same convolutions that I have seen on hundreds of brains, her muscles are just as permeated through and through with fat, which makes the dissection of female corpses such an unpleasant task; in general, there is really nothing in her attractive or poetic."[5] The budding professional's gaze is powerful, penetrating, and de-eroticized.

Then Veresaev enters the clinical phase of his education, and his seeing changes: "Instead of abstract science, living man came to the fore; the theories of inflammation, microscopic preparations of tumors and bacteria gave way to genuine sores and wounds. Sick, mutilated, and suffering people stretched before my eyes in an endless line [. . .] I was struck by the sheer mass of suffering, by the variety of the most subtle, unbelievable tortures that nature prepared for us. A fleeting glance at these sufferings sufficed to terrify the soul."[6] Veresaev's empathic response in the clinic, his loss of detachment from what he sees there, undermines his professional gaze and, temporarily at least, his very identity as a physician. He identifies with his patients to such an extent that he becomes one: following a dream in which he is hit by a carriage and suffers lung damage, he twice presents himself to his professors, first for an irritated mole under the arm that he takes for a sarcoma, and then after incorrectly diagnosing himself with diabetes.[7] The professional gaze, when turned inward, nearly undoes him altogether.

The first chapter of Veresaev's memoir and exposé thus sets up two extremes of seeing as defining the boundaries, so to speak, of the professional identity to which he is acceding. Much of what follows involves charting a tenable path between these extremes. Chapter 2 opens: "The subject of our study now became the live, suffering human being. It was difficult to watch these sufferings, but even more difficult in the beginning was the fact that we also had to study precisely these sufferings [. . .] One had to try to persuade oneself that, after all, it's not hurting *me*, after all, I'm completely healthy, it's that *other person* who's in pain."[8]

But there are other kinks in seeing for a budding physician to negotiate. Veresaev has "to blush for himself" when he tells of the first time he witnessed a young female patient disrobe. "I sat there all red, trying not to look at the patient," he recalls. "Was there any voluptuous feeling in me when the patient stripped before our eyes? There was, but very little; the *fear* of such a feeling predominated. But afterwards, at home, the recollection of that experience acquired a delicately voluptuous tint, and I reflected, with a secret pleasure, that in the future many similar scenes awaited me."[9] In addition to negotiating a path between the extremes of a cold, objectivizing, and pitiless eye and the gaze that feels the other's inner life so as to identify with the other, the physician must struggle against the erotics of seeing; he must suppress the libidinal potential of his key professional tool. (Later in the memoir Veresaev also devotes a lengthy section to the feelings of shame that inhibit females from seeking medical attention from male physicians.)[10]

And then there is the question of how the physician is seen. During the first autopsy Veresaev witnesses, a professor of pathology exposes the fatal error of one of his colleagues, a surgeon whose intervention resulted in the patient's death. Although the pathologist declares that "unfortunate accidents happen to the best surgeons" and the two professors shake hands at the end, Veresaev is stunned: "The reasons for the failure are stated with utter calm; the person responsible, even if he is upset, is upset only as a consequence of his vanity . . . Meanwhile, the matter has to do with nothing more and nothing less than the destruction of a human life, something immeasurably horrifying, which ought to have provoked the inevitable question: might such a surgeon dare to continue practicing medicine?"[11] Veresaev's own errors, which more than once result in a patient's death, make him "ashamed to look my patients in the face."[12] Being seen threatens exposure as a pretender.

An acute sense of medicine's limits now brings Veresaev to the point of "medical nihilism." Medicine, he decides, is *blind:* "It blundered in the dark, and only pretended to know something." "I shut my eyes to the means and limits of science, to what it accomplishes, and mocked it for not being able to do *everything.*" Faith returns, however, when Veresaev witnesses a professor's demonstration of differential diagnosis on a patient whose problems had confounded Veresaev in the clinic. The professor's progress is figured as a transition from blindness to a vision that penetrates the opaque body: "And at last the professor began his deductions. He approached them slowly and warily, like a *blind man* walking along a steep mountain trail." The diagnosis at which he arrives is indeed verified by autopsy after the patient dies one week later, and Veresaev is able to *see* the extracted tumor that the professor divined while it was still hidden in the body: "I was examining the soft bloody tumor, lying on a wooden plate, and I suddenly recalled our village elder, Vlas, a fiery hater of medicine and doctors. 'How can doctors know what's happening inside me? Can they really see through?' he asked with a contemptuous laugh. Yes, in this case they did indeed see through. My attitude toward medicine changed sharply."[13]

It is not only one's seeing that must be trained; self-presentation, controlling how one is seen, becomes no less important. With the incurable one must be able to "play the hypocrite and lie [. . .] It is necessary to be an actor everywhere and at each step." One must cultivate a certain shamelessness, not just to maintain one's self-esteem and professional identity, but because "disease is cured not only by prescriptions and medicines, but by the patient's own soul as well."[14] When Veresaev indulges in honest but critical reflection regarding the diagnostic and therapeutic powers of his discipline, soberly resisting grandiosity in his self-regard as a physician, the result is not simply to make him feel ashamed for disrespecting medicine; he may actually be degrading those therapeutic powers he does possess.

The book ends with discussions of the physician's social, legal, and economic situation, in many respects quite bleak. Here we learn that the physician's professional identity makes him visible to the public in unique ways. By law a physician cannot refuse a summons for assistance, on penalty of a fine up to 100 rubles and arrest lasting from seven days to three months. A physician has no legal right to hide. And when unfortunate results are trumpeted in the press without regard to norms of practice and reasonable expectations, the shame of exposure often leads to suicide.[15]

Mikhail Bulgakov's cycle of stories, *Notes of a Young Doctor,* was published with the help of Veresaev's influence. If Bulgakov ended his career with highly self-reflexive narratives on what it meant to be an artist in the era of high Stalinism, he began it with no less self-reflexive accounts of what it meant to be a physician during the cataclysmic years of World War I, the Russian Revolution, and the Civil War. The first and last stories from that cycle (in terms of the cycle's narrative chronology) turn on motifs of seeing and being seen.[16]

"The Embroidered Towel" ("Polotentse s petukhom") tells of the fictionalized Dr. Bulgakov's arrival at the remote hospital where he is to serve. The cold, jolting journey into this veritable heart of darkness all but strips him of his professional self. "My legs were ossified with cold, so much so that as I stood there bemused, I mentally leafed through the textbook pages in an inane attempt to remember whether there was such a complaint as ossification of the muscles or whether it was an illness I had dreamed up while asleep the night before [. . .] What the devil was it in Latin?"[17] Something nightmarish from the depths of his psyche has emerged to contaminate the knowledge that made him a physician. When the watchman takes him for a student, the doctor affects a more mature bearing and thinks, "I need to get glasses"—not so he can see better, since his vision is fine, but to alter the way he is seen.[18] He feels like "The False Dmitry—nothing but a sham."[19] Above all, he fears confronting an entrapped hernia. (Incidentally, the nonfictional Bulgakov had acquired quite a bit of surgical experience by the time he was sent to serve in the isolated clinic described here, and he went there not alone but with his wife.)

His baptism under fire is the case of a young woman whose legs have been mangled by threshing machinery. At first his seeing is curiously nonmedical: "On her white face, motionless as a plaster cast, a truly rare beauty was fading away before my eyes. Seldom in life does one see such a face [. . .] the mother must have been a beautiful woman."[20] The *feldsher* bares her injuries, and the doctor begins work on a patient who, he knows, will nevertheless die. Afterwards he reads surprise and respect in the eyes of his assistants, then examines his face in the mirror of a dark window: "No, I don't look like Dmitry the Pretender, and, do you know, I seem to have aged."[21] The face in the mirror belongs to a seasoned professional. In this moment in which the self is defined, what matters is not so much what he accomplishes but how he is seen—both by others and by himself. The outcome of the surgery is not even reported, for the patient's death has been inevitable from the start.

There follows a hiatus of two and a half months. The "young girl of enchanting beauty" did survive after all; she and her father have come to thank the physician. But this visit, while affirming the doctor's authenticity and prowess, in effect threatens to undermine them as well. "'Kiss his hand,' the father suddenly commanded her. I was so flustered that I kissed her on the nose instead of the lips." In the ending's twist, seeing and being seen again emerge as problematic. Now the narrator struggles to achieve the proper professional detachment while modulating his sense of pride and suppressing his attraction to the girl; the result is blushes and confusion. When the girl surprises him with a gift— a towel that she embroidered while in the hospital but kept hidden during his bedside visits—he affects an exaggeratedly severe, professional mien: "I can't accept it,' I said sternly, and even shook my head. But she put on such a face, such eyes, that I took it."[22]

"The Vanishing Eye" ("Propavshii glaz") opens with the narrator marking the anniversary of his arrival in the village before a mirror: "Yes, the difference is enormous. A year ago this mirror, just unpacked from my trunk, reflected a shaven face. [My] upper lip now wears a solid growth rather like a harsh yellow toothbrush; my cheeks feel like a cheese-grater, so that if my forearm happens to start itching while I am at work I get relief by rubbing it against my cheek. It always gets like that when I shave only once a week instead of three times."[23] Interruptions in his shaving are caused by emergency cases. His whiskers grow, his razor gets rusty—when he looks in the mirror, his half-shaven face reminds him of criminal types whose photographs he saw in a book about the prison island of Sakhalin[24]—but these are markers of the time required for him to become a grizzled, confident veteran physician. At the end of the year he sums up the numbers, reviews his achievements in the mirror of recollections, and is proud of what he sees: "My hand had acquired courage and did not shake. I spotted all tricky complications and had learned to make sense of the words of peasant women that nobody could understand. I interpreted them like Sherlock Holmes deciphering mysterious documents [. . .] I cannot . . . honestly imagine being brought a case that would stump me. . . . How I used to shudder whenever there was a knock at the door, how I winced with fear . . . Now, though . . ."[25]

The following morning, on the first day of the doctor's second year, just such a case arrives: a year-old baby who appears to have no left eye, only a swelling in its place. The child's "vanishing eye" is at once the doctor's vanishing eye: his powers of observation fail him utterly; he cannot conceive of what is going on behind the superficially visible. He tells the mother that her child *has* no eye, though the mother assures him the child had one only two days ago. The doctor urges surgery; the mother takes the child away but returns a week later, after the abscess that swelled to cover the eye has burst on its own and the child looks healthy. A story that, until the last page, has celebrated the acquisition of clinical prowess—a professional self-image and a powerful professional gaze—ends by undercutting both.[26]

In Veresaev and Bulgakov, then, motifs of seeing and being seen, hiding and showing, are portrayed as fundamental to the creation and maintenance of a physician's professional identity. This finding both validates and complicates our approach to the phenomenon in Chekhov. It affirms the soundness of the thematic focus on issues of seeing, being seen, hiding, and showing in connection with Chekhov's identity as a physician and his treatment of the medical sphere in his fiction and drama. Rather than the result of a peculiar critical focus, we seem to be on the track of something that is central to the experience and identity of physicians, or at least Russian physician-authors of the last decades of the nineteenth century and the first decades of the twentieth. At the same time, the memoirs of Veresaev and Bulgakov caution against interpreting behaviors that may be generated or conditioned by the medical profession as manifestations of an individual's fixations in the psychoanalytic sense.

Chekhov's Professionals

I'm always tormented when I have to inspect, and I let three quarters of the
baggage go by without being opened, but the time will come when I'll
really catch it for that. It's infinitely shameful to creep into another's suitcase
and see the color on a passenger's cheek when his dirty socks are uncovered,
or a crumpled shirt, covered with vomit . . . Examining a woman's
baggage—that's entirely different. It's fun. A certain lady very willingly and
politely displays her entire suitcase down to the smallest details, but tries to
hide one little corner. The customs official's eyes light up: in expectation of
reward, he puts his paw right in that sacred little corner and instead of some
silk material pulls out a chemise with signs of menstruation. . . . I myself
love to inspect women, because they always have some edible reserves in the
form of *pirozhki* and cookies, especially Frenchwomen [. . .] By the way: do
you know whom we suspect most of all? Pregnant women. It always seems
to us that their womb consists of lace. But even if your elbow is nearby, you
can't give a poke; and I'd happily inspect, but . . . Anna [his wife] won't
permit it."

—Chekhov's brother Aleksandr, while serving in customs
in Novorossiisk, in a letter to Chekhov (21 November 1885)

Chekhov's treatment of seeing and being seen, showing and hiding, is by no
means limited to representations of the medical context. The thematic complex
and a panoply of attending dangers are also predictably central in works having
to do with criminal investigations and trials, the sphere of the theater, the profession of writing, and prostitution. The thematic complex is implicated, too, in
defining a character in terms of social status rather than occupation. In the
broadest sense, I am talking about how the self is defined, for oneself and for
others, by the dynamics of seeing and being seen. What unites the subject of
professional or occupational identity and social status in Chekhov—and this is
as true of the early comic Chekhov as it is of his mature productions—is its
treatment in connection with the gaze.

It proves possible to generalize. Certain professionals, such as judges, criminal
investigators, physicians, and the spying revolutionary of "Story of an Anonymous Man," are apt to be defined by their active positions: they do the seeing.
Prostitutes, actors, criminals, and the ill, by contrast, are defined by their position as object of the observing eyes of others. The marker of high social status
is a cultivated blindness to one's inferiors, on the one hand, and utter invulner-
ability to their gaze, on the other. Very often the active and passive positions are
combined in the treatment of one and the same type, or the plot actually turns
on a character's movement from one position to the other.

Stories about medicine and the law that center on the professional's act of seeing thematize either the psychological and ethical consequences of taking others as objects of a detached professional gaze, or else the consequences of a de-sublimated gaze, a seeing in which the necessary detachment is corrupted by affect. Works that portray such professionals as objects of the gaze are typically comic and involve pretense and imposture, that is, showing a fake self. But included under this rubric would also be works such as "Ward 6" and "A Boring Story," in which the transformation of physician into patient—that is, the ironic shift from an active position to that of the passive object of the gaze of others or oneself—becomes tragic.

In tales involving actors, actresses, prostitutes, and patients, selfhood depends on how one is seen, and for whose pleasure. In effect, we are adopting the passive-versus-active distinction around which Freud's discussion of instincts and their vicissitudes was structured,[27] though as we shall see, the passive position does not always equal powerlessness, and the act of watching can be associated with passivity and weakness as well as with aggression and strength.

Let us begin establishing the range and significance of this theme in Chekhov with a representative set of stories involving medicine.

In "Late Blooming Flowers" ("Tsvety zapozadlye," October–November 1882), a fatherless gentry family on the skids summons the most prominent doctor in the area, a man who as an orphaned child had been the family's serf. The doctor is utterly professional and refuses to engage in small talk of any kind; nor does he acknowledge his previous relationship with the family, including their footman, who is his uncle and who raised him. His proud, businesslike bearing, self-confidence, and apparent wealth impress his former masters, and in particular the daughter, Marusa, who is of marrying age but without a dowry. "An amazing man, an omnipotent man!" she tells her brother. "How omnipotent his art! Judge for yourself, George, what a lofty exploit: to battle with nature and to overcome it!" (S 1:401). Even the mother would not be averse to this young man as a suitor for Marusa, if only he were not of "low birth" (S 1:402).

The doctor's surname, Toporkov, is derived from the Russian for "axe," a conventional symbol of the rude peasantry and its penchant for violent revolt. And Toporkov has rebelled, through his acquisition of an education and a deliberate and haughty self-presentation. Key to this posture is his insistence on seeing others with a relentlessly professional eye, which is to say, even his former masters can enter his field of vision only as submissive patients. In spite of his chilly bedside manner, his display of wealth and success keeps his reputation bright and the waiting room of his medical office filled. The love-struck Marusa often observes him driving to visit his patients, though her gazes are never returned by the upright, forward-looking doctor: "Nothing was visible from behind the fluffy collar of his bearskin overcoat, except for a white, smooth forehead and gold glasses, but for Marusa that was enough. It seemed to her that cold, proud, contemptuous rays proceeded from the eyes of this benefactor of humanity through those glasses. 'This man has the right to feel contempt!' she thinks [. . .] 'What a strong man one must be to be born a lackey but make oneself as un-approachable as he is!'" (*S* 1:410). The heroic self-overcoming Marusa sees in the doctor's pride cannot but remind us of how Chekhov, many years later, would express to Suvorin the triumph of the son of a serf "squeezing the slave's blood out of himself drop by drop." Toporkov appears entirely defined by this feat.

When a matchmaker arrives with an offer of marriage from this "plebeian," on condition that a dowry of sixty thousand rubles accompany the bride, the bankrupt gentry family is deeply offended. But the smitten Marusa does not re-alize that the matchmaker has been charged with finding a bride—any bride—who will provide the capital Toporkov seeks, and that Toporkov is unaware of the matchmaker's offer to her. Even after Toporkov marries a wealthy merchant's daughter, Marusa's affections remain bound to the doctor, who she imagines married the merchant's daughter out of injured pride. As her own situation de-clines—her mother has died, their home has been sold by creditors, and her dis-sipated brother has brought her to the most abject poverty—she scrapes together the large fee needed to see the doctor in his office. Illness is but a pre-text; she hopes to speak to him of what she alone has construed as their secret love for each other. Marusa is stunned by Toporkov's cruel professional distance when he orders her to disrobe and, impatient, unbuttons her chemise without ceremony (*S* 1:424). Twice she visits without summoning the courage to speak of her affections, but during the third visit she blurts out a declaration of love. Toporkov, having never before heard these words addressed to him, is shaken: "He stood before her, read pleading in her eyes, and felt that he was in the most horrible position. In his chest his heart was pounding, and in his head some-thing impossible and strange was going on . . . A thousand unsummoned rec-ollections piled up in his burning mind. Where had these recollections come from? Could they really have been called forth by these eyes, with their love and pleading?" (*S* 1:429). As happens most notably in Chekhov's later masterpiece "Rothschild's Fiddle" ("Skripka Rotshil'da," 1894), the reemergence of sup-pressed memories—a disavowed part of the self—occasions a dramatic alter-ation in a character's ethical stance and overall personality.[28]

Here it is first and foremost Toporkov's *seeing* that changes: "'What can I do?' he whispered one more time, looking at Marusa's eyes. He was shamed by those eyes" (*S* 1:430). The very next day he accompanies Marusa, who is in the last

stages of consumption, to the south of France. After she dies, "Toporkov, returning from France, began living as he had before. As before he took care of
the ladies and piled up five-ruble notes. However, there has been a noticeable
change in him. When speaking with women, he looks to the side, into space . . .
For some reason it becomes horrifying for him when he looks at a female face"
(S 1:431). In the ironic structure of this story—one of Chekhov's most ambitious to date—characters are either masters or slaves. By the end, Toporkov has
become a weak man and is taken advantage of by Marusa's brother, who now
lives at the doctor's expense, just as he had ruined his mother and his sister—all
the result of a change in Dr. Toporkov's seeing.

In March 1883 Chekhov deployed the theme of the perils of the professional
gaze in a series of cartoons, "In the World of Science" ("V uchennom mire," S
3:461–63). Western readers of Chekhov may not be aware of his collaborative
ventures into the visual arts (at times involving his brother Nikolai) during the
first period of his career. In this genre, too, Chekhov's humor was apt to turn
on questions of seeing and being seen. In four of the six cartoons of "In the
World of Science," characters misapply scientific seeing.

In "A Victim of Science" ("Zhertva nauki"), the professor's seeing is so thoroughly sublimated and professional that he abandons his wife as an erotic object; in "Specialists in the Steam Bath" ("Spetsialisty v bane"), similarly, the
pathologist and the artist view the bodies of fellow steam-bathers with a mis-
applied professional eye. In "The Anatomist Gruber Is Guilty" ("Anatom Gruber vinovat"), the "family problem" of the hysterical young wife is presumably
caused by the extension of her husband's failure in the anatomy course to a lack
of sexual competence in their conjugal life. Finally, the twist of "A Scholarly
Lovelace" ("Uchenyi Lovelas") is the utterly scientific and professional (phreno-
logical) purpose behind what first presented itself as a lecherous program of
seduction. (See figures 1–4.)

The theme broadens to include fraudulent self-presentation in the story "The
Night before My Trial" ("Noch' pered sudom," 1884/1886[29]). The narrator, a
landowner en route to the town where he is to be tried for bigamy, takes lodg-
ing for the night at a post station. Barefoot and undressed, he hops around a stove
to warm himself until he realizes that a highly amused woman has been watching him from behind the screen separating his space from the neighboring one.
Being seen in such an undignified pose unnerves him: "This means she saw me
hopping! That's bad. . . . " The narrator regains his equilibrium, or restores his
damaged self, by fantasizing in pictures, "each finer and more tempting than the
other," about this female—until, that is, bedbugs claim his attention. When he
overhears the woman complaining about the bugs, he seizes the moment and
calls out to offer her a powder to repel them. She suggests that he simply push

Figures 1–4 "In the World of Science"
("V uchenom mire", *Oskolki* (1883); theme by A. Chekhonte, drawings by V. I. Porfir'ev.

1. "A Victim of Science" ("Zhertva nauki")

"During the day you give your disgusting lectures, after dinner you sleep like the dead, at night you look at stars through the telescope . . . All night! And this has gone on since our wedding day! It's awful! Can it be, you barbarian, that you have no need for progeny?"

2. "Specialists in the Steam Bath" ("Spetsialisty v bane")

"When I look at those people, it seems like I'm back at work in the morgue."
"And to me it seems like they're all nude models posing for paintings."

3. "The Anatomist Gruber Is Guilty" ("Anatom Gruber vinovat")

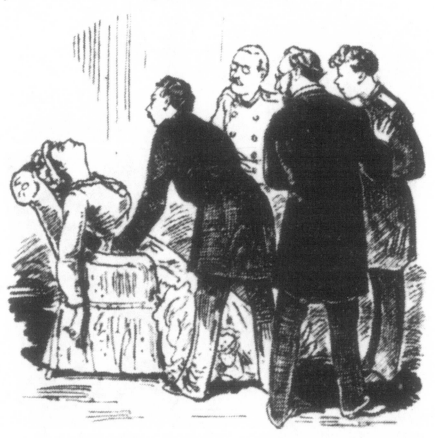

"Don't bother her, gentlemen! Let's leave the room . . . She's got a family problem, the poor thing! Her husband received a failing grade in anatomy!"

4. "A Scholarly Lovelace" ("Uchenyi Lovelas")

"Hee-hee-hee . . . I got her to come . . . plied her with dinner and champagne . . . I promised to buy her a bracelet . . . And when she was drunk and leaned her head on my chest, I went and measured her skull! A fine Gallic type! You know what the rear-to-front diameter of her skull comes to? You won't believe it!"

the powder through the screen; the narrator lies: "I'm a doctor, and doctors have the right to intrude into the personal lives of others." The woman instead sends her husband, previously unmentioned, who in turn asks the doctor to examine his wife for tightness in her chest. And so the impostor gains a pleasure of seeing disguised as professional examination. He writes a bogus prescription and the next morning receives payment of ten rubles. The following day, however, the narrator discovers that the husband is the prosecutor in his case (*S* 3:118–23).

The narrator's position in this story oscillates between that of the examined and that of the examiner: he is traveling to subject himself to the court's purview; he examines his lodgings and berates the station-keeper for their foul smell; he is watched by the woman; he gives her an examination while posing as a physician; and at the end, the stern eyes of the court are upon him. The fake prescription, in which is inscribed the Latin saying "Sic transit gloria mundi" (so passes worldly fame), contains the wisdom of the ancients on the meaning of being widely seen. In sum, this story deploys all the key motifs of the seeing and being seen complex as it intersects with the theme of medical professional identity, as well as the judicial sphere, in a thoroughly comic key.

"Fakers" ("Simulianty," June 1885) is a short Chekhonte piece with a different twist on imposture. Here both physician and patients are "fakers." A general's wife fancies herself a homeopathic doctor and treats all who come for help. Her patients have learned that she is particularly susceptible to flattery, especially if it is accompanied by the denigration of traditional allopathic medicine; what is more, with proper buttering up this wealthy woman will address financial problems as well as bodily ones. In effect, this impostor pays her patients—who, she fails to notice, are not really ailing—so that she can see herself as a successful healer (*S* 4:40–44). The plot of this story found an echo in Chekhov's own life many years latter. Aleksandr Kuprin recounts how a certain "Tambov landowner"—or so Chekhov called the man—demanded medical attention from Chekhov in Yalta, even though Chekhov averred that he had long since quit practicing medicine and was not up to date. The man insisted on hearing Chekhov's advice regarding his medical condition, after which he laid two gold coins on the table; when Chekhov was unable to persuade him to take the money back, he told the man that he would donate them to a Yalta charity and wrote out a receipt to this effect. The man left, delighted: it turned out that he had visited Chekhov with the sole aim of acquiring the famous physician-writer's autograph; he had been attempting to wangle a prescription out of him, but this receipt would do very nicely. Chekhov told Kuprin the story "half laughing, half angry."[30]

In "Aniuta" (February 1886) a medical student has his mistress strip and marks her up with charcoal pencil so that he can cram for his anatomy exam; when finished he lends her to his friend, a painter who needs a nude model for a painting of Psyche. Here, turning the professional gaze to the body that should be an object for libidinal seeing becomes an act of cruelty.[31] In "A Work of Art" ("Proizvedenie iskusstva," December 1886), which will be read in depth later in this chapter, the situation is inverted: a doctor gets rid of a sculpture of female nudes because it threatens to sexualize his seeing.

In "A Male Acquaintance" ("Znakomyi muzhchina," May 1886) the complex of seeing and being seen is inflected through the professional spheres of medicine and prostitution and in connection with the use of pseudonyms. The dance hall girl Wanda—her real name is Nastas'ia Kanavkina—has been in the hospital and unable to work. Having pawned the last of her valuables, she hopes to get some money from one of her customers, "the tooth doctor Finkel, a convert, who three months ago gave her a bracelet and on whose head she once poured a glass of beer at dinner in the German club" (S 5:116). Wanda goes to Finkel's office but loses confidence as she approaches the door. When in drunken company, dressed according to her trade, and operating under a pseudonym, she has always been bold, but now she will be seen in ordinary clothes, "like a beggar or some petty bourgeoise" (S 5:117). And, indeed, the doctor does not even recognize her: he "gazed at her importantly, coldly, like an official, and he was chewing something" (S 5:118). The libidinal seeing that formerly characterized their relations has been replaced by a medical professional's objective eye. Without her dancing clothes and her alcohol-induced high spirits, Wanda is no longer Wanda. Intimidated, she complains of a toothache, and the dentist proceeds to extract a perfectly good tooth. When Nastas'ia presents herself pseudonymously, as Wanda, dressed in fancy clothes, a vigorous and voluptuous object of desire for male admirers, she feels in control: Finkel only smiled and shook his finger at her after she poured beer over him. But as the patient Nastas'ia, fresh out of the hospital and dressed shabbily, she becomes a passive victim. And this duality is duplicated in the dentist. When drinking, Finkel the converted Jew behaves like a generous and expansive Russian, and his seeing is delightfully libidinal. In his office, however, Finkel's seeing is not merely cold and professional, it is incompetent, and, even worse, that of a stereotypical greedy yid. "Who will pay me for the work?" he demands as a stunned Wanda prepares to leave, and she gives him her last ruble.

The 1887 "Doctor" ("Doktor," S 6:309–14) lacks the explicit lexical motifs of seeing and being seen that are found in the other works, but it turns on the irruption of very disturbing and hateful affective emotions into the professional attitude of a family physician attending a nine-year-old boy dying of tuberculosis of the brain. Having quite bluntly told the mother that the prognosis is hopeless, and doing nothing that we can see to ease the child's sufferings, the doctor takes his leave. He puts on his coat and picks up his stick, but, obeying an inner compulsion, returns to interrogate the mother. At this critical moment there is one thing he wants to know: Was this child his? It turns out that he has been paying child support all these years, and only now confronts the mother with his knowledge that she has been receiving support payments from two other men as well.

In "A Boring Story" (1889), which was discussed in chapter 1, the professional eye turned inward—upon himself and his family—proves paralyzing and self-destructive to the mortally ill professor of medicine. Where once he shone when all eyes and ears were on him in the lecture hall, now he reads in the mirrors of these eyes not his professional potency but his physical and emotional decomposition. In "Ward 6" ("Palata No. 6," 1892), to which I will return in depth in the next chapter, the whole story's trajectory may be delineated by the translocation of the central character, Dr. Ragin, from the position of physician to that of patient. Dr. Ragin abdicates his professional duty to see: he hates examining patients, and he turns a blind eye to the corrupt and cruel behavior of the hospital staff under his supervision. He is forced out of his position as hospital chief, taken on a journey abroad—during which he refuses to sightsee—and in the end himself becomes the object of others' examination, at which point he understands that he is finished: "When they tell you that you have something like bad kidneys and an enlarged heart, and you start undergoing treatment [. . .] in a word, when people suddenly pay attention to you, then you might as well know that you've fallen into a vicious circle from which you'll never emerge" (*S* 8:118–19).

Now let us turn to some works treating professional, occupational, or socially hierarchical identities other than that of a physician.

In the comic masterpiece "A Daughter of Albion" ("Doch' Al'biona," 1883), a district marshal of the nobility, Ottsov, arrives at the estate of his friend Griabov to learn that the latter's wife and children are away, and that the master has been down at the river fishing with the governess. Ottsov hesitates—he presumably wonders what exactly is transpiring between Griabov and his employee during the mistress's absence—then sets out for the river. What he finds is quite the opposite of the reader's likely expectations: instead of interrupting a tryst, he comes upon the man and woman haughtily ignoring each other, except to exchange contemptuous glares. Since the English governess does not understand Russian and Griabov knows no English, the two cannot communicate verbally, and Griabov mocks her to her face: "She's no woman, she's an old maid." "I can't see her indifferently," he tells Ottsov, because of the contempt with which she looks at him and at everything around her (*S* 2:196).

Then Griabov's hook gets caught on a rock; he will have to strip and enter the water to retrieve it. He orders the Englishwoman to leave, but she ignores him, so Griabov strips in front of her: "Griabov took off his boots and trousers, removed his underwear, and stood there dressed as Adam. Ottsov grabbed his belly and turned red from both laughter and embarassment. The Englishwoman moved her eyebrows and her eyes twinkled . . . A haughty, scornful smile flashed across her face [. . .] 'If she would at least get embarrassed, the despicable creature!' said Griabov [. . .] Going into the water up to his knees and stretching to his full huge stature, he winked and said: 'This, brother, is not her England'" (S 2:198). There is a profound and complex interplay between seeing, being seen, eroticism, and power in this light comic tale. The Englishwoman refuses to register the insult to her sex in Griabov's self-exposure; nor does she respond to his manhood other than to laugh. Griabov's proud exhibitionism makes explicit his contempt for her as a woman, and it places her in the category of a servant before whom the master can, by definition, feel no shame. A situation that at the start appeared likely to involve the erotic is instead all about shame and pride; in a kind of stalemate, each maintains his or her dignity (while appearing utterly ridiculous to the reader) by refusing to feel shame.

The Englishwoman's unflappability also reflects a conventional national stereotype. The psychoanalyst Theodor Reik, for instance, relates an anecdote about an exhibitionist exposing himself to an Englishwoman in the Parisian Bois; she merely worries that he might catch cold.[32] In "A Daughter of Albion," contemptuous maligning of the other gender is superimposed onto nationalistic sentiment. When Griabov proclaims, "This, brother, is not her England" ("Eto, brat, ei ne Angliia!")," he manifests his connection with his Russian male friend (they are on intimate *ty* terms) and his denigrating perspective on both women and the English. It may be no accident that such sentiments emerge in a story about exhibitionism and staring: in Freud's treatment both scopophilia and exhibitionism hark back to fixations on the visible signs of sexual difference. What, after all, is Griabov referring to when he exclaims that "this" is not England?

An analogous play on seeing and being seen, in which, however, gender roles are reversed and the erotics of seeing are underscored, appears in the 1883 cartoon Chekhov conceived and published in collaboration with A. I. Lebedev, "A Classical Woman" ("Zhenshchina-Klassik"; see fig. 5). The reply of the severely décolletée "classical woman" asserts a social standing superior to that of the male admirers sharing her box, and it presumes that seeing across socially hierarchical divisions is somehow de-libidinized. But this rhetorical fig leaf for the woman's exhibitionism is belied by the theatrical setting, the attention given her by the surrounding gentlemen, and the opera glasses at rest on the ledge before her: she has come to the theater not to see but to be seen.

5. "A Classical Woman" ("Zhenshchina-klassik"), *Oskolki* (1883), drawing by A. I. Lebedev, theme by A. Chekhonte.

"You are terribly décolletée! Aren't you ashamed of such dress in our company?"
"Not in the least! Roman women were not ashamed to undress or even bathe before their slaves. I'm following the example of Roman matrons."

This theatergoer's proud and invulnerable display of herself in a sense doubles the self-exposure that defines an actress's profession. In "An Impresario under the Couch" ("Antrepener pod divanom," 1885) a young provincial actress is outraged when, while changing in her dressing room, she discovers the theater manager under her couch. No peeper, however, he is hiding from the husband of his mistress, a man to whom he also owes five thousand rubles. The actress allows him to stay after he promises financial rewards, including a benefit performance; exhilarated by this shift of power between them, and imagining that she has acquiesced "for her art," she begins to enjoy undressing in his view. The story establishes a parallel between her public performance, when crude local merchants shout propositions at the stage, and what happens in the dressing room. In other words, once she feels in control of the situation, this professionally catastrophic and offensive moment becomes an affirmation of one naïve actress's professional self; unfortunately, the manager will renege on his agreement.

The professional gaze corrupted by passion is both the overarching plot device and a prominent theme in Chekhov's only novel, a serialized potboiler, *The Shooting Party* (*Drama na okhote [Istinnoe proisshestvie]*, 1884–85). In the novel's initial frame situation, a journal editor recounts how the former court investigator (*sudebnyi sledovatel'*) Ivan Petrovich Kamyshev brought him a manuscript detailing a true story of love and murder from his professional career. In the concluding frame situation, the editor accuses the author of having carried out the murders described in the account and framed the man who was convicted of the crimes. Kamyshev finally admits that he killed the victim, Ol'ga, and attributes the murder to "affekt," or affect, passion: "Life is entirely composed of affect," he excuses himself (S 3:414). This perversion of the professional investigator's capacities is underlined in a series of footnotes attached by the editor, "A. Ch." (the novel was published under the "Antosha Chekhonte" pseudonym). For instance, during his interrogation of the witness Kuz'ma, the investigator becomes enraged and orders the subject taken away. The reproachful footnote begins: "A fine investigator! Instead of continuing the interrogation and forcing out a useful piece of evidence, he *got angry*—an occupation outside the duties of this official" (S 3:398). And shortly thereafter, when Kamyshev is relieved of his office and in his account writes, "I began to figure in as a witness," the editor glosses his remark as follows: "A role, of course, more appropriate for Mr. Kamyshev than that of investigator; in the Urbinin case he could not be an investigator" (S 3:402).

Kamyshev could not be an investigator because, as both reader and editor know at this point in the narrative, he is involved in the case as the secret lover of the victim, Ol'ga, who was in turn the wife of the accused. Under these circumstances it was highly unprofessional for Kamyshev to take jurisdiction over the case; his investigative gaze could not be impartial and objective. In a plot twist borrowed subsequently by Agatha Christie in *The Murder of Roger Ackroyd,* at the end of the novel it is revealed that not only was the narrator far from impartial, but also he was himself the murderer. If his position as court investigator has been corrupted by his involvement in the matter under investigation, then, this is no less true of his position as the narrator of a "true crime" tale: in this memoiristic first-person narrative, the reader's seeing turns out to have been deceived in the most unexpected way precisely because of the fictional author's emotional involvement in what is being related.

Motifs of seeing and being seen pervade *The Shooting Party* and contribute to expressing the psychology of the novel's characters. From the start Kamyshev and Ol'ga—a precocious femme fatale dressed in the exhibitionistic color bright red—engage in a play of gazes. At their first meeting, Kamyshev recalls, "her eyes looked off somewhere to the side, but I, as a man who knows women, felt her pupils on my face [. . .] I looked back . . . The red spot didn't move and watched us proceed" (S 3:265). When later the same day Kamyshev and the count who is hosting him take refuge from the rain in Ol'ga's father's hut, Ol'ga watches the visitors "boldly, staring, as if we weren't people new to her but zoo animals" (S 3:270). Ol'ga tells Kamyshev about her fantasy of an exhibitionistic death: she dreams of being struck by lightning atop the local hill while everyone watches (S 3:272). During the debauch of the narrator and the count, Ol'ga watches (S 3:284–85); at her own wedding she is ashamed to kiss her groom in front of Kamyshev (S 3:322); and when Kamyshev seduces her shortly thereafter, the two are observed by a peeping Tom who then applauds them (S 3:325). Long after the events described in his tale took place, Kamyshev looks at Ol'ga's photograph while writing his memoir (S 3:265–66). This is but a sampling.

These motifs of seeing and being seen allow the narrator to lay out what the count calls "a conversation with eyes," the first step in his usual program of seduction (S 3:341). They also express the novel's very Dostoevskian theme of pride: thus Ol'ga's shame when Kamyshev and the others see her demented father (S 3:273–74), her concern about rank (*mestnichestvo*), as indicated by the place she occupies in church (S 3:297), and her betrayed husband's injured pride. These motifs are also motivated by the novel's mystery plot, for detective stories tend to require moments of peeping and overhearing to advance the action; in this tale, however, where the investigator turns out to have committed the crime, what is learned through peeping and overhearing deceives the reader: these are false leads playing on the conventions of the genre. Perhaps the most important generic connection reaches back to that greatest and most paradoxical of all detective stories, whose distinctive mix of blindness, insight, sexual passion, and rage finds echo in Chekhov's novel: this is of course *Oedipus Rex,* in which, however, not only the reader but also the criminal discovers only at the end that he has committed the crime for which his nation is paying the price.

The narrator-investigator will not be gouging out his own eyes, however; insofar as he makes a spectacle of his crime, he takes care to mask his self-exposure, appearing in his own memoir under the pseudonym Sergei Petrovich Zinov'ev. "My role in this story is rather scandalous," he explains. "It would be awkward under my own name . . . " (S 3:245). The official's colossal irresponsibility as both court investigator and narrator, the full dimensions of which emerge only at the novel's end, is perhaps connected with this notion of living under an assumed identity, which in Kamyshev's case includes living in the rooms of his predecessor without changing anything—furniture, family pictures on the wall, pet parrot. Meanwhile the fictional author Antosha Chekhonte actually enters the novel as a character in the frame situation.

The Shooting Party is one of those works by the early Chekhov that are not often read, and even more rarely read seriously. From all evidence, little planning went into its composition—certainly nothing on the scale of the mature Chekhov's failed efforts to write a novel. Nevertheless, this potboiler is a remarkably original work, and its originality derives from Chekhov's handling of seeing and being seen, hiding and showing, as thematic material and stylistic device.

A very short Chekhonte piece from 1885 similarly exploits the juridical setting, though without the melodrama and mayhem of The Shooting Party. In "A Cultured Log" ("Intelligentnoe brevno"), a judge must try his neighbor for hitting a servant on the nose with a comb. The accused, incredulous that he is to be tried for such a matter—by a friend, no less—will not accept the authority of the court. The judge not only arranges a settlement of ten rubles but also pays the fine himself, since his friend refuses; thus is resolved the dilemma of maintaining an impartial and professional perspective on a case in which he is emotionally involved. "God save me from having to sit as judge over acquaintances," he exclaims (S 4:36); his friend, disappointed that the judge did not punish the servant for daring to file a complaint, considers him incompetent.

The positions of servant and master also appear in Chekhov as defined by the dynamics of seeing and being seen. In "A Big Commotion" ("Perepolokh," 1886), servants in a landowner's home are strip-searched after a brooch worth two thousand rubles goes missing. The young governess of gentry origin, who has just finished school and started working in the home, observes the uproar and the tears and humiliation of the servants, but she does not quite understand what is happening until "for the first time in her life she had to experience at its sharpest the feeling so familiar to people who are dependent, without recourse, living on the bread of the rich and the powerful" (S 4:331): she returns to her room to find it being searched by the lady of the house, who is tossing her personal possessions.

Here the vectors of power that traverse the field of relations between mistress and servant in predictable ways are associated too with the vector of a particular kind of gaze. All employees are reduced to passive objects for the examining eye of the master, and this eye observes no boundaries: the examined are presumed to have no private selves into which that gaze may not peer. Although the governess is not strip-searched, the inspection of all her personal possessions is an invasion analogous to the treatment of the other servants. Having been insulted by their suspicions, she finds it impossible to sit at the dinner table with her employers while they discuss the theft. She returns to her room, and there begins the process of recuperating her dignity, righting her damaged self. First, she indulges in fantasy: she imagines that she has inherited a large sum of money, bought the most expensive brooch available, and thrown it in the face of the mistress; her employers have been reduced to beggary and she offers them charity; she has bought a fine, expensive carriage and passes by the landlady's windows, arousing her envy. That is to say, she fantasizes about being seen—but being seen as the poor see the rich. Next, the governess decides on a practical step: she will leave this house and return to her parents. While she is packing, the master of the house enters her room and attempts to persuade her to stay. He apologizes and begs forgiveness for his wife's offensive behavior, but to no avail. Finally, he offers to humiliate himself in exchange for the humiliation she has suffered: he confesses to having stolen the brooch himself. And then, aroused by the governess's pride, he makes his own offensive proposal: "God, you ought to stay. In the evening I'd drop by your room . . . we'd talk" (*S* 4:337). The title of this tale soon found application with regard to Chekhov himself. A few months after publishing this story in the *Peterburgskaia gazeta* (under the Chekhonte pseudonym), Chekhov wrote his brother Aleksandr that the (first) five stories published under his true name in *Novoe vremia* had created "a big commotion" (*perepolokh*) that poisoned him "as by fumes" (10 May 1886).

The most significant of Chekhov's mature stories in which peeping is the central plot device also involves the relations between master and servant. The narrator of Chekhov's lengthy "Story of an Anonymous Man" ("Rasskaz neizvestnogo cheloveka," 1893) is a spy posing as a butler, who becomes deflected from his mission; not surprisingly, motifs of seeing and being seen overtly define the overarching plot. But in addition to the motifs of peeping, eavesdropping, and hiding one naturally associates with spying, this story presents virtually all of the key components related to the thematic complex of seeing, being seen, hiding, and showing: anonymity and pseudonymity; the implications for professional identity; and (in anticipation of the following chapters' foci) tuberculosis and degeneration, the peculiar erotic position of the voyeur, and the activities of reading and writing. Such an inventory makes "Story of an Anonymous Man" appear paradigmatically Chekhovian.

Nevertheless, it has long been considered one of its author's oddest works. Readers have been distracted by the hero-revolutionary, the Petersburg setting, and the aristocratic milieu—all uncharacteristic of the mature Chekhov. And as a first-person narrative in the form of notes or a diary written by an anonymous author, the story is something of a throwback to the poetics of an earlier time.[33] The ideologically oriented readers of Chekhov's day focused on political content, and objections arose from both left and right. Tolstoy, always an idiosyncratic reader of Chekhov, lauded the hero's conversion to nonviolence, but this positive evaluation was possible only through a skewed reading of the story that willfully overlooked the motifs of impotence and illness which accompany that turn, not to mention its insidious results.[34] Overt allusions to Turgenev and the traditional theme of the "superfluous man" create yet another frame of reference for reading the story, and commentators have found several possible real-life prototypes for the anonymous hero, including a former naval officer and revolutionary who had repented and written a memoir.[35]

All of these interpretive paths have diverted most readers from what this story has in common with other of Chekhov's works—in particular, its genetic connections with early material—as well as from the story's autobiographical implications. To reorient our reading in such a direction, it is enough to consider that the former naval officer who narrates "Story of an Anonymous Man," as a sailor, voyeur, and dreamer telling a story involving peeping, pseudonymity, triangular desire, and revolt against paternal authority, rearticulates the central motifs of "At Sea."

The plot of the story is as follows. The nameless hero recounts how, "for reasons about which now is not the time to speak in detail," he entered into service as the lackey of a middle-aged Petersburg official, Orlov, whose father held high governmental office: "I figured that, living with the son, overhearing conversations and reading papers and notes left on his table, I would be able to learn in some detail the plans and intentions of the father" (S 8:139). But something goes amiss, causing the hero to abandon his espionage mission. Instead of learning about the father (who in fact is all but absent from the son's life "as though his father had died long ago" [S 8:144]), the spy focuses on the son, and in particular on the son's amorous involvement with a married woman named Zinaida. When chance offers an opportunity to assassinate the father and make a clean getaway, the spy finds he has lost interest. A new feat beckons instead: he will expose the son's betrayal of his mistress and whisk her away to Venice in a rescue mission. Zinaida admires him as a revolutionary who will "bring down [his] heel on the vile serpent's head and crush it" (S 8:200), and participating in his activities appeals to her. But in the very process of exposing his true identity to her and recounting his past exploits, he is becoming someone else. Her admiration devolves into contempt, precisely because he has devoted himself to her alone rather than to the cause. She poisons herself after delivering Orlov's child, and the story ends with the mortally ill narrator returning to Orlov for a man-to-man talk to ensure the child's future.

The narrator's troubles began, it appears, with the onset of illness, "consumption, and with it something rather more serious" (S 8:139). That "something rather more serious" is the change in personality that coincides with the onset of illness, and perhaps issues from it. The revolutionary hero becomes passive and a dreamer; he begins to enjoy his watching activity. Like the customs inspector who, in Chekhov's later notebook jotting, searches passengers with a zeal that "makes even gendarmes indignant" because he so enjoys his work[36]—and like Chekhov's own brother Aleksandr as a customs officer (see this section's epigraph)—this professional spy's gaze has degenerated into a kind of peeping.

As both a lackey and a spy, the anonymous man is defined professionally in large measure by his looking. The lackey is to remain himself unseen while keeping watch over his master in order to satisfy the latter's needs and wishes. Thus the anonymous man describes his usual morning duties, the first of many instances in which his apparent transparency is remarked: "I would help him dress, and he submitted to me, keeping silent and not noticing my presence" (S 8:139). As in "The Daughter of Albion" and the cartoon "A Classical Woman," the master's lack of embarrassment before a servant even when undressed is a socially appropriate sign that "he didn't consider me a person" (S 8:141); he is not a person precisely insofar as his gaze is powerless and without consequence across the boundaries of social hierarchy.[37] Keenly sensitive to the social semiotics of seeing and being seen, the chambermaid Polia—of equivalent status to the anonymous man in his role as lackey—pretends to a superior position by appearing before him in various states of undress: "Like the Roman matrons who were not ashamed to bathe in the presence of slaves, she sometimes wore only a slip in my presence" (S 8:144). The narrator once responds to Orlov's late-night bell only partially dressed, and this provokes a sharp rebuke; but it also causes Orlov to notice the lackey's sick body and, for the first time, register the person behind the lackey's role. This so disarms Orlov that he addresses the narrator with the inappropriately polite "vy" (S 8:167).

The interplay of gazes between master and servant is conditioned by and sustains a hierarchical social relationship requiring utter subservience from the lackey. Nevertheless, there is also a sense in which the lackey's behavior, and in particular his seeing, can be understood as a professional characteristic: "Two grown persons were supposed to watch, with the most serious attention, while a third drinks tea and chomps biscuits" (S 8:139). The lackey must observe with detachment, and this detachment is not unlike the putative objectivity on which is grounded the professional identity of a physician, judge, detective, or scientist. Though called upon to facilitate the activity of his master (by delivering letters and deceitful messages, for example), he nevertheless remains outside the scene. In his scripted role he is entirely his master's agent; he does what his master has told him to do and says what his master has told him to say. If he were to become involved in the scene he is observing—if, as he says, he were to attempt to enter a conversation between Orlov and his friends—his master would not simply fire him, but consider him mad.

The narrator asserts that his position as a lackey "is probably funny and barbarous, but I didn't see anything humiliating for myself" (S 8:139). There is nothing humiliating in this position for the narrator because he occupies it with a certain professional detachment—all the more so, since he is simultaneously fulfilling a second role, that of spy, in which his looking is in fact a kind of aggression, a means of accumulating knowledge and power over his object. In this respect as well he remains unseen, masked by a false name and servant's livery, but he can look forward—like the inspector traveling incognito in "The Truth Will Out" ("Shilo v meshke")—to the moment when he will stun his master by revealing his true identity. He will make a point of doing so in the denunciatory letter he leaves for Orlov, which he signs with his real name (S 8:191).

But from almost the very start of the narrative, the anonymous man's vision becomes invested with libido and fantasy and, as a consequence, is de-professionalized. This he explains by the tuberculosis that began to manifest itself just as he took on this mission, and which, he says, has transformed him into a dreamer: "I wanted to experience once more that inexpressible feeling when, strolling in a tropical forest or watching the sunset in the Bay of Bengal, you are both dumbstruck with rapture and at the same time pining for your homeland. I dreamed of mountains, women, music, and with the curiosity of a boy I peered into faces, listened carefully to voices. And when I stood by the door and watched Orlov drink coffee, I felt not like a lackey, but like a man for whom everything on earth, even Orlov, is interesting" (S 8:140). His first contact with Orlov's mistress engages the anonymous man even more deeply: "Returning home on foot, I recalled her face and the scent of subtle perfumes and I dreamed" (S 8:143).

Becoming implicated in the scenes he has been observing means failing in both his roles, as lackey and as revolutionary. Correspondingly, the anonymous man's own description of what he has been doing and why changes. Consider the letter he leaves for Orlov when he abandons his dual post: "To steal into a house under an alien name, to spy on your intimate life from behind the mask of a lackey, seeing and hearing everything, in order to make revelations afterwards of lies no one has asked for—all this, you'll say, is akin to thievery" (S 8:188). This account of his motivations—the "in order to"—diverges greatly from the one laid out in the story's opening paragraph. It characterizes not his original mission, but his immediate emotional response to the situation in which, instead of dispassionately observing, he found himself involved.

But this is not my interpretation alone. When the narrator returns to Russia at the story's end to make arrangements for Orlov's daughter's future, the two men talk about that letter. Ironic distance is Orlov's distinctive personality trait; he accepts the narrator's critique of his personality and habits but denounces the narrator's emotional involvement in the matter:

> "Yes, my life is abnormal, rotten, worthless, and it's cowardice that keeps me from starting a new life—here you're entirely right. But the fact that you take this so dearly to heart, get upset, and even reach despair—that's not rational; here you are entirely incorrect."
>
> "But a living person cannot help getting upset and despairing when he sees himself and others around him perishing."
>
> "Who says! I am by no means preaching indifference; I want only an objective relationship to life. The more objective, the less the risk of falling into error." (S 8:212)

Orlov proceeds to invoke the theory of degeneration to explain both his and the anonymous man's failures in life. Arguing along lines that resemble the positions of Laevskii in "The Duel" and Dr. Ragin in "Ward 6" (see chapter 3), he invokes an extreme biological determinism to excuse his own detached ethical stance and passivity: "In nature and in the human environment nothing just happens. Everything has prior bases and is inevitable. And if this is so, then why should we get so upset and write despondent letters?" (S 8:212–13). Orlov advocates a maximally detached, distant, and putatively objective point of view not just on himself but on the whole "human environment" as the only sensible way of seeing the world. Not surprisingly, he is most uncomfortable in situations where his humanity interferes with this stance: he collapses when faced with Zinaida's tears, and he stumbles when he suddenly realizes that his lackey is mortally ill.

Precisely in regard to their modes of seeing, then, the narrator and Orlov represent a pair of complementary opposites—so much so that it makes sense to speak of them as doubles. In fact, the narrator's letter to Orlov, having begun with Orlov, takes the remarkable turn of speaking about the two of them, Orlov and the narrator, jointly. Following the paragraph that ends "You are a weak, unhappy, and unlikable [nesimpatichnyi] person," the letter asks, "Why have we become worn out?" (S 8:190; emphasis added), and continues in the same vein. This connection between Orlov and the narrator was even more heavily underlined in the original version of the story, from which Chekhov excised during revision a whole series of remarks indicating the closeness between the anonymous man and Orlov.[38]

A number of previously unexplored interpretive possibilities follow from considering the narrator and Orlov as doubles. For instance, the revolutionary's plot against the government minister becomes a plot against the father, which, from a psychoanalytic perspective, would in turn help explain why the anonymous man forgoes the opportunity to assassinate this figure: his hesitations echo those of Hamlet in Freud's Oedipal interpretation. More interesting, perhaps, is the way this psychological closeness between the observer and the observed becomes also a connection between the one who writes and the one who reads. As such, this doubling provides a point of access to the metapoetic and autobiographical dimension of the story.

Savely Senderovich has delicately broached the possibility of identifying Chekhov with the story's hero. In addition to drawing the obvious conclusion regarding the anonymous narrator's tuberculosis, he reads the story's uncharacteristic first-person narration as a defensive attempt at distancing the author from his text, a way of asserting, "I have nothing to do with this story—it was communicated to me by a certain person and belongs to him." The intuition that Chekhov felt a particular need to distance himself from the narrator is supported by the afterword Chekhov claimed to have written for the story, and planned to publish in the book version (but did not); in it the author was to explain how he came by the anonymous man's manuscript. Senderovich also interprets the narrator's facelessness, his anonymity, in a psychoanalytic key, as an "oneiric property of the text," betraying the repression of an identification.[39]

If we are justified in considering the narrator and Orlov as doubles, however, then Chekhov's identification extends also to the aloof and ironic bureaucrat. Certainly Orlov's distance, self-control, and handling of women are more reminiscent of the impression Chekhov made on others than the behavior of the moony anonymous hero. In the letter expressing the anonymous man's critique of Orlov's character, one might very well detect echoes of the reproaches Lika Mizinova frequently launched at Chekhov: "I can't do as you do, relate to everyone evenly and the same [odinakovo i rovno]. Perhaps that's a major failing, but I nevertheless prefer to be that way; for me at least there is something precious, while for you, there's never anything."[40] Chekhov himself connected this story with Lika by calling it, in a letter to her of 28 June 1892, "that liberal story I started in your presence." Was this perhaps an invitation for Lika to read herself into the tale, as she would later with Seagull and "Ariadne?"

"Anonymous Man" belongs to the series of stories involving peeping revealed by Marena Senderovich to have metapoetic significance. Indeed, as a narrative that emanates from a spying situation, "Anonymous Man" realizes Chekhov's metaphor of writing "through a crack in the wall." This configuration is replicated even more literally in the denunciatory letter the narrator leaves for Orlov. But when he visits Orlov at the end of the story and the two discuss that letter, a new dimension is added to this peculiar communication situation. Now the author confronts his reader directly to contest the meaning of what he has seen and written. Ultimately the anonymous man asks for his letter back. He takes a step that can never be taken by an author who has dared to publish: he asserts rights over uttered words and, in spite of the Russian proverb "A word is not a bird: once escaped, you'll never catch it," removes them from circulation. (And yet, as the anonymous implied author of the narrative in which this letter is embedded, he will give these words even wider distribution.)

If the anonymous man is the story's implied author, then, both Orlov and Zinaida are associated with the activity of reading. A voracious and somewhat indiscriminate, but highly critical reader, Orlov approaches texts as he approaches people—holding them at arm's length while reading, maintaining great ironic detachment, "like a savage's shield," and with a reflexive expression of mockery on his face that separates his self from the scene (S 8:140). Zinaida is a naïve reader in the tradition of Madame Bovary and Don Quixote; her romanticization of Orlov's passion and political ideas, as well as the narrator's revolutionary plans and convictions, are repeatedly attributed by Orlov to the models she has assimilated from Turgenev, and she quite characteristically couches her decision to depart St. Petersburg in a citation from the end of Balzac's *Père Goriot*. Once she has gone abroad, her conflation of life and literary models accelerates toward an inevitable and tragic denouement: "When she sat like that, clasping her hands, stony and pained, I would have the impression that we were both playing roles in some sort of old-fashioned novel titled 'An Unfortunate Woman,' or 'The Abandoned Woman,' or something of the sort. Both of us—she, the unfortunate and dropped one, and I, the true devoted friend, a dreamer and, if you like, a superfluous man, a failure capable of nothing any longer except coughing and dreaming, and perhaps also sacrificing himself . . . but who now needed my sacrifices, and for what?" (S 8:199). The relationship between the narrator and Zinaida thrives only so long as it functions as a kind of *Arabian Nights,* in which the narrator regales Zinaida with tales from his past and plans for the future. When Zinaida realizes that her storyteller is himself no longer invested in his stories, she becomes disenchanted: "Vladimir Ivanych, for the love of God, why have you been dishonest? All these months, while I was dreaming aloud, raving, delighting in my plans, turning my life around, why didn't you tell me the truth, but rather kept quiet or encouraged me with tales, acting as though you sympathized with me completely?" (S 8:205). She accuses him of adopting a false narratorial stance, of telling stories as a kind of seduction: "And all your fine ideas, I see, come down to one inevitable, necessary step: I am supposed to make myself your lover" (S 8:206).

If the narrator was showing a fake self in the tales he told to divert Zinaida, then his narratorial authenticity as implied author of the larger narrative is underwritten, strange as this might seem, precisely by his anonymity and pseudonymity. These motifs, apparently well motivated at the level of plot by the exigencies of underground activity, lose that purpose by the end of the narrative. The narrator remains unnamed for the reader, even though an amnesty or pardon has permitted him to emerge from underground and return to Russia. He signed his letter to Orlov with his true title, name, and surname, and he has returned to see Orlov. Why then must the reader remain in the dark? Meanwhile, the anonymous man ignores the convention of using false names or initials to refer to the "real life" subjects of his story; he alone remains protected by the cloak of anonymity. In his letter to Orlov, the anonymous man characterizes himself as having assumed a false name in order to write about what he has seen—in order, that is, to "expose lies" ("chtoby potom neprosheno izoblichit' vo lzhi" [S 8:188]). The verb here translated as "to expose," *izoblichit'*, recalls the literary generic term for fiction that exposed social ills, "literature of indictment" (*izoblichitel'naia literatura*). By the end of "Anonymous Man," anonymity's function has become literary rather than seditious.

But it is not only the anonymous narrator who operates under a false name. The precarious and painful situation of Zinaida's orphaned daughter is discussed precisely in terms of her name. By law she is the daughter of Zinaida's husband, and so bears his surname (and, in her patronymic, his first name); but in fact she is the offspring of Orlov. In short, the child Sonia is a work sent out into the world under another's name, a work produced pseudonymously by Orlov.

The anonymous man approaches Sonia as if he were her real father: "I loved this little girl madly. I saw the continuation of my own life in her, and it seemed—no, I sensed, almost believed—that when I finally divest myself of this tall, bony, bearded body, I'll live on in those light blue little eyes, in her silky blond hair, and in those plump pinkish hands, which so lovingly stroke my face and embrace my neck" (S 8:209). It is hard to say which is sadder at this point— the thrice-fathered child's fatherless situation, or the narrator's improbable expectation of living on in the memory of a two-year-old child. The anonymous man's paternity is at once the most real and the most false: only he cares for the child, but he has no legal or blood connection to her, and he is unlikely to be recalled by her after his imminent death. How does this child address the anonymous man? As "Daddy"? This most heartfelt and genuine relationship cannot but be founded on posturing and pseudonymity, as though the anonymous man has come to stand for pseudonymity itself.

Janet Malcolm calls this story "a strange, febrile work that reads as if it had been written nonstop in the heightened state of consciousness that tuberculosis has been said to induce in artists." According to her, it suffers a serious structural flaw: "For reasons that one can attribute only to Chekhov's own lack of enthusiasm for revolution, the narrator loses interest in his cause, becoming exclusively preoccupied with the predicament of Orlov's beautiful young mistress."[41] Chekhov's illness and personal political views interfered with his writerly duties, she argues, and this is reflected in a plot twist by which the entire narrative goes awry and fails. Without quite understanding the story, she has put her finger on what is most important about it, what it is in fact about: not revolution but the hazards to the self resulting from changes in the vicissitudes of seeing and being seen in which the detached observer becomes a part of the scene.

The Stories of a Difficult Case: Dr. Chekhov in His Art

> Medicine is my lawfully wedded wife, and literature is my mistress.
> —Chekhov to Aleksei Suvorin (11 September 1888),
> and repeated many times

The preceding examples are but a sampling of how Chekhov handles the thematic complex of seeing, being seen, hiding, and showing, in its connection with representations of professional identity. The theme is psychological, to be sure, but what invests these facts about his texts with psychobiographical significance? As in the previous chapter, it proves possible here to move beyond a circumstantial and associative argument and to demonstrate an existential connection between the appearance of these motifs in Chekhov's texts and in his biography.

Chekhov graduated from the faculty of medicine at Moscow University in June 1884. During the summer holiday with his family in a small town west of Moscow, Voskresensk (now Istra), where his brother Ivan had a position as a schoolteacher, he managed a two-week stint as a locum tenens in nearby Zvenigorod. His career as a physician got off to its genuine start only upon his return to Moscow, and in September he hung a sign on his door, "Doctor A. P. Chekhov."[42] In December of the following year he was caring for the mother and three sisters of an art school colleague of his brother Nikolai, Aleksandr Ianov.[43] The mother and one of the sisters died of the typhus that was afflicting them—the latter while holding Chekhov's hand. The surviving Ianov sisters became good friends of the Chekhov family and frequent guests at their table.

According to Chekhov's brother Mikhail, this episode gave Chekhov a decisive push away from medicine and toward literature: "Feeling himself completely impotent [bessil'nyi] and guilty, and for a long time sensing the pressure of the departed's grasp on his hand, Anton Pavlovich decided right then to drop medicine entirely and, subsequently, went over definitively to the side of literature."[44] As Mikhail well knew, Chekhov never did "definitively" drop medicine; only his own severe illness finally put an end to his practice. But this fact does not discredit the brother's account of the death of the Ianov women as a traumatic blow to Chekhov's confidence as a physician, and to the sense of potency that had come with a solid professional identity.[45]

What may be most interesting about this sad incident, however, is how not the person of Chekhov but his traumatic experience itself "went over to literature," how it came to be worked into fiction. Readers of Chekhov might anticipate a discussion of the 1887 "Typhus" ("Tif"), which scholars associate with the Ianov family tragedy (among other of Chekhov's encounters with typhus) and rate a Chekhonte masterpiece.[46] But what I have in mind is two stories published (also under the Chekhonte pseudonym) a year apart, "The Mirror" ("Zerkalo," 1885) and "A Work of Art" ("Proizvedenie iskusstva," 1886). While the tone, timing, and subject matter of "The Mirror" make reading it in the light of the Ianov tragedy a rather obvious move, this is hardly the case with the amusing and lighthearted "Work of Art." Nevertheless, both bear the deep imprint of Chekhov's guilt and sense of professional impotence in regard to the Ianov women.

"The Mirror" appeared at the very end of December 1885, while Chekhov was still caring for the Ianovs. In this New Year's story, reminiscent of the fortune-telling episode in Tolstoy's *War and Peace,* a young noblewoman, Nelli, is attempting to divine her future husband in a fortune-telling device consisting of two mirrors. She sees her "fated" one (*suzhdenyi*), and blissfully watches months and years of their future life together unfold before her eyes in "picture after picture" (*S* 4:271). This takes up one paragraph of Chekhov's tale. And then, as the magic lantern show proceeds, the arc of a plot becomes discernible: her husband is gravely ill with typhus, and she is banging at the door of the district doctor late one winter night. She goes straight to the doctor's bedroom, but the doctor, who has just returned from a series of calls, is himself down with the fever and barely coherent, and he refuses her summons. After threatening to sue—the doctor is legally obligated to respond—and pleading "like the lowest beggar" (*S* 4:273), she rouses the man, and they begin the forty-verst (twenty-seven-mile) ride back to her estate. By the time they arrive, however, the doctor is delirious, and she must set out to find another, distant physician. Then, as she sees in the mirror the illnesses of her children, the death of one, old age, and the death of her husband, "all the preceding life with her husband seemed to her just a stupid, unnecessary preface to this death" (*S* 4:275). She drops the mirror, and the story ends.

The biographical context for this story is quite suggestive. It was apparently written during the period when Chekhov was caring for the Ianov women. Like the doctor in "The Mirror," Chekhov was himself undeniably ill by now: in addition to his frightening encounter with typhus, since the previous year he had suffered episodes of blood-spitting, early symptoms of the tuberculosis that would kill him. Nine months later, in a letter to Mariia Kiseleva that he begins by telling her that the two surviving Ianov sisters are present as he writes, Chekhov complains about his own health and remarks: "I still haven't had the doctor's sign hung out yet, but I nonetheless have to practice! Brrr . . . I'm afraid of typhus" (21 September 1886).[47]

At this time, too, Chekhov was edging close to marriage with Dun'ia Efros: within a few weeks of this story's publication, he writes his new Petersburg friend V.V. Bilibin, a minor author and secretary at *Oskolki,* that he has become engaged. This marriage would never take place, but there is good reason to believe that, at the moment, Chekhov was projecting a future for himself not only as an ill physician, but also as an ill husband; and he had fears of falling short in both roles. As we shall see, "The Mirror" manifests a self-reflexive and defensive tendency that one often finds in Chekhov's handling of illness.[48]

There is yet another important context for this story, however: it came out shortly after Chekhov's trip to St. Petersburg at the end of 1885. It thus belongs together with the great number of stories in this period, discussed in the previous chapter, that involve imposture, peeping, and debuts, and like them responds to Chekhov's new visibility as an author with a metaliterary plane of meaning.

In "The Mirror," this metaliterary dimension is evoked by the initial situation of Nelli, reading her future in mirrors. Chekhov's reader embarks on a story depicting a parallel, if rather peculiar, act of reading. While the story's title refers to only one mirror, Nelli's divination procedure actually involves two; nevertheless, to the extent that it refers to Nelli as a mirror of the reader's position in the text, the singular title does apply. Indeed, while divining her future, Nelli is "pale, tense, and immobile, *like a mirror*" (*S* 4:271; emphasis added).[49] Consider, too, that the mirror has long served as a conventional figure for narrative self-reflectivity or, in Lucien Dällenbach's discussion, "mise en abyme."[50] And Charles Isenberg reminds us that frame tales are always implicitly metaliterary and mirroring in that they thematize the situation of narrative transmission.[51] But just what sort of reading is reflected here? In Nelli's desire to see the future, she sees the end; and having seen the end, she no longer cares for all that will transpire between now and then. The end of the story is a shocking disillusionment for Nelli; this was even further underlined in the original version of the story, which closed, "Going to bed, she no longer dreamt of marriage" (*S* 4:434). As will be the case for Dr. Ragin in "Ward 6," as well as for the student in Chekhov's philosophical story "Lights" ("Ogni," 1888), such an "ends" perspective proves dangerously depressive. And might this short-circuiting and collapse of desire not also apply to the reader of "The Mirror"? For what reader does not immerse himself in a narrative with an "ends" perspective, or as Peter Brooks calls it, "reading for the plot"?

Chekhov's visibility in this text is multiple and quite teasing. One catches sight of him as a shadowy figure emerging in and disappearing down the infinitely regressing reflection set up by the two facing mirrors. Chekhov appears not only in the sick doctor but also in the husband, particularly if we follow Radislav Lapushin's interpretation of the two ill men as doubles.[52] As the story's author, he is also the source of the future that Nelli and the reader seek to divine as the story begins: he is the keeper of that mystery.

The young woman engaged in divining her future poses a question to the author of her fate; and insofar as this motif of divination (*gadan'e*) constitutes a frame for the narrative to follow, her question is replicated on a variety of ontological planes. The character demands to know: What will my future be? The patient asks the doctor: Will I live? And every reader embarks with and is propelled forward by the question: How will the story end? Each of these questions articulates a desire that, in this story about seing the unseen, knowing the unknowable, is ultimately directed to the self of the author, to Chekhov. The reader desires not just an ending but the author himself; the patient desires a cure, which transfers onto the person of the doctor; and a would-be fiancée desires Anton Pavlovich, who will, however, escape this trap, as well as all those set for him over the next fifteen years.

If Chekhov is visible in this story, it is because he simultaneously stimulates the desire to see him (he has seduced us into reading), acknowledges it, and flees from it into that space beyond the mirror's surface. You can have it all, Chekhov says, but in the end all you get is the ending: death.

"A Work of Art" was published a year after "The Mirror," in December 1886. As we shall see, though the Ianov deaths were now well in the past, there remained constant reminders of the episode in Chekhov's life, and this story bears signs pointing to it as well.

"Work of Art" begins with the visit of a grateful widow's only son to the doctor who has saved him from typhus. The family is poor, he says, so instead of money he has come with a gift: a "valuable" antique bronze candelabra "that came to us from my late papa."[53] The youth only regrets that he cannot offer a matching one to make a pair. Unfortunately, the narrator says, the bronze is of two female figures "in the costume of Eve, and in poses I cannot describe for lack of boldness and appropriate temperament." As a "family man" the doctor cannot possibly keep the object, but unable to persuade the former patient to take it back, he does the next best thing: he gives it to a lawyer friend as compensation for professional help. The lawyer then unloads the bronze on a comic actor, and the actor sells it to the very same woman who sent it to the doctor in the first place. The former patient returns to the doctor in delight: now he can complete the pair.

The most obvious links between this story and Chekhov's care of the Ianov women a year earlier are the gifts he received afterwards. Like the youth's family in "Work of Art," the Ianovs were not well off; perhaps for this reason, or perhaps because monetary compensation would have been awkward, Chekhov was presented with a gold Turkish coin, which, as ultimately occurs with the candelabra in "Work of Art," he pawned.[54] But there was also a second gift: at the beginning of 1886, one of the surviving Ianov sisters, Mariia, brought him a hand-sewn photograph album inscribed as an offering "in memory of my deliverance from typhus."[55] Less than a year passed between Mariia's presentation of the gift and the publication of "Work of Art." Mariia Ianova's album and the candelabra function as substitute payment for the same medical service, and they are akin in other respects as well: both are affect-laden personal mementos of a professional service, and both are objects that are meant to be gazed upon. The pleasure of owning them is a pleasure of seeing; and because they commemorate moments of professional practice—a significance anchored, in the case of the album, by Mariia's inscription—they are objects the viewing of which facilitates contemplation of one's own accomplishments, in essence, one's self. That scholars have failed to connect the two is surprising.[56]

Within two weeks of receiving the present, Chekhov wrote a letter (18 January 1886) reminding V. V. Bilibin of his promise to send a photograph: he planned to place it in the album. Chekhov cited Mariia's inscription ("in memory of my deliverance") not, he told Bilibin, "to boast, oh no! (even without that you can guess that I'm a great physician)." Where in this letter can we find traces of the trauma his brother Misha ascribed to Chekhov? Chekhov's self-praise, joking or not, sounds oddly unreflective in the context of a case in which two of his patients died. If on the surface of it Chekhov's recovery appears rather too complete, however, a closer reading reveals otherwise: "The album is typhoidal, but I give you my word, you won't get infected—a witticism that I send you for free. You can print it . . . I wrote you [Chekhov is summarizing the contents of a previous letter that did not reach Bilibin] about how all my fish in my aquarium died as a result of a cigar tossed into the water . . ." Traumatic death mutates into humorous verbal art, a printable witticism; and, as in "Work of Art," a professional service is given away for free, though something is expected in return (Bilibin's photograph). The gift itself, though meant as a tribute to professional success, is "typhoidal," that is, contaminated by failure and death. And the paragraph ends by further undercutting Chekhov's boasts of therapeutic prowess: the casually murdered fish signal that Dr. Chekhov is quite likely to deliver creatures under his care *to* death rather than *from* it. All this occurs with an accent of humor, in a letter to the up-and-coming author's recent acquaintance and editor, which is to say, in a carefully shaped document that, like much of Chekhov's voluminous correspondence, deserves to be read as an epistolary work of art.

"Work of Art" is even more perceptibly haunted by the Ianov catastrophe than this letter. The interpretive key to the story, I believe, is to be found in the bronze itself, in both the ambivalent and revealing contextual or metonymic associations that accrue during its circulation and its iconic representation of female nudes.

The Work of Art as Metonymy

The gift in "Work of Art" is offered as a tribute to the physician's success, and the package delights the recipient as such; that is, until just what is wrapped in number 223 of the *Stock Exchange Gazette* (*Birzhevye vedomosti*) is revealed (more about the wrapping later). The doctor explains his reaction to the bronze by twice protesting, "Children run around here, and ladies visit." For his lawyer friend, a "bachelor and frivolous minded," possessing and viewing the bronze might be appropriate—but not for him. The grateful patient entreats the doctor to rise "above the crowd" and perceive the pornographic bronze with artistic detachment. Part of the humor here derives from opposing the youth's refined aesthetic approach to the female body to that of more mature men, who giggle and blush like adolescents. But the boy's remarks cast his own reaction to the piece in physiological imagery suggestive of an upwardly displaced male orgasm (and reminiscent of imagery associated with the sailor's erotic fantasies in "At Sea"): "Why, it's an artistic thing, just look at it! So much grace and beauty that it fills the soul with a feeling of reverence and tears come up to your throat! When you see such beauty, you forget everything earthly . . . Look at it."[57] The doctor responds; "I have an excellent understanding of all that," though just what "all that" refers to remains ambiguous: is it aesthetics, the phenomenology of male sexuality, or both?

In this context the value of the sculpture is determined by the subjective sensations aroused in men through its viewing. What matters is its effect (emotional, physiological) on male viewers, certainly much more than the women it depicts. Indeed, the narrator, in his own professional capacity, declares himself unable actually to show us this sculpture; to describe it would make him a pornographer rather than an author. Even the doctor calls it "unliterary." The figures of the women are all but blotted out as soon as the candelabra is unwrapped: they signify less through their bodily shapes than through the distress and chain of suppressions those bodies trigger.

If the bronze appears a shame-provoking invitation to voyeurism, it is certainly no surprise that the prospect of sexualized seeing disconcerts the doctor: his professional capacity demands examining the body with detachment. We have seen the widespread treatment of this theme in Chekhov's fiction, but there is also an instance when Chekhov commented directly on the topic. In a letter to his protégée Elena Shavrova, Chekhov objected vigorously to Shavrova's fictional characterization of gynecologists as "skirt-chasers and cynics," writing: "Gynecologists deal with an atrocious prose you've never even dreamt of [. . .] He who constantly sails the sea loves dry land; he who is eternally immersed in prose passionately longs for poetry. All gynecologists are idealists" (16 September 1891). Among Chekhov scholars, for whom the private Chekhov's inner life and intimate relations with women (including Shavrova) have remained an irresistible mystery, this outburst has been discussed as a sign of neurotic squeamishness or gynophobia, or, alternatively, as the understandable reaction of a clinician to the severe conditions with which a peasant population receiving little health care might present itself.[58] I read the intensity of Chekhov's reaction quite differently, as issuing from the challenge to his professional identity in Shavrova's indictment. I am particularly struck by Chekhov's oddly generalizing defensive response, which speaks of "all gynecologists," and I suspect that his reaction issues chiefly from the psychic appeal and corresponding threat of sexualized seeing itself. For to indulge in the seductive pleasures of voyeurism while on the job—to sexualize overtly his most important tool—risks undoing a physician's professional identity. This is precisely the logic argued against in the first notebook entry Chekhov eventually used in *Seagull,* regarding the character who would become Dr. Dorn: "Lokidin lived it up and chased a lot of women, but this didn't prevent him from being a fine obstetrician" (*S* 17:29, 272–73).

Here we might do well to return to Vikentii Veresaev's scandalous disclosure of the pleasures medical students derive from examining disrobed female patients. Veresaev emphasizes the anxiety that accompanied this pleasure, as well as the shame and suffering of the patients. His exposé condemns himself and his male colleagues for their eroticized, unprofessional seeing, but it also presents mastering the inner tension between pleasure and shame provoked by the professional privileges of a physician's gaze as a general and unavoidable aspect of becoming a doctor. What Dr. Veresaev presents as a more or less normal struggle between pleasure and its suppression appears from the evidence to have been, in Dr. Chekhov's case, acutely felt; or so the mass of material explored in this book would suggest. It follows that Shavrova's ogling physician might well have disturbed Chekhov not only because of the injustice of her depiction but also— perhaps even more so—because of the way that depiction resonated with his own psyche. Chekhov clearly identified with Shavrova's character; his letter begins, "So, we old bachelors smell like dogs?"

When the youth in "Work of Art" exhorts the doctor to "rise above the crowd," he is in essence saying, "Sublimate!" The irony is that his pornographic gift simultaneously incites a radical de-sublimation of the doctor's seeing. In presenting the gift, the youth praises the physician's powers—which are powers of sight—and provokes an access of pride in the physician; but when the gift's wrapping is removed, that sight is suddenly sexualized. Engorgement of self becomes engorgement of another kind, and this lays bare the libidinal component of activities defining the doctor's professional identity. Such sudden exposure might well frighten and shame.

Viewing the bronze facilitates engorgement of self because the bronze, in commemorating the physician's therapeutic success, becomes also a metonymic sign of that professional's self, and a sign whose contemplation paves the way for feelings of pride. When the bronze comes to two other professionals (the lawyer and the actor), it does so again in recognition of professional abilities. The bronze's value for the youth presenting it has to do with the object's patrimonial status—it "came to us from my late papa"—and it thus also represents the deceased father and dealer of bronzes. And of course it is given in a kind of exchange for the life of the "only son," which the doctor has saved.

In all of these contexts the bronze acquires a symbolic value of masculinity and professional potency: it stands for the doctor's therapeutic power, the lawyer's acumen, and the actor's talent. Adopting the language of psychoanalysis, we might say that the bronze, as the sign of the father, stands for the phallus. Indeed, how better to describe the sense of self-importance displayed by the mother's beaming and proud "only son"—this fact is remarked five times, once by the narrator and four times by the son—than to say, again in the figurative language of psychoanalysis, that he has become the phallus of his mother, even more so now that he has conquered death itself to take his late father's place. For each of the men who receive it, then, the bronze stands for a part of the self, a part on which a very positive, even infantile-grandiose self-image is based. And it stands for the very possibility of gaining pleasure from viewing oneself through that part's exposure, which has its source in infantile sexuality.[59] If the bronze invites a voyeuristic male gaze, it also provides a temptation for male exhibitionism.

For all three men, then, the bronze offers the possibility of reveling in one's sense of professional ability. It involves an infantile and autoerotic sexualization of professional pride, pleasure from the proud exposure of oneself: exhibitionism. This temptation makes the doctor and the lawyer somewhat uneasy, however; the comic actor, by contrast, a professional exhibitionist, does enjoy the piece. In the psychoanalytic idiom, one could say that the comic more nearly approaches the bliss of perversion, while the doctor and lawyer remain inhibited perverts or neurotics.

It is because the dangers of enjoyment edge out the pleasures that the bronze circulates like a hot potato. Each recipient worries above all that women might see the bronze, or far worse, witness his eying of it. Even the actor indulges in the pleasure offered by the bronze only among other males, and behind locked doors, fending off women knocking at his door with the remark (substituting his own nakedness for the bronze's): "No, no, Ma [matushka]! I'm not dressed!" But whence this fear of being observed? If the paradigmatic exhibitionist's pleasure results from exposing himself to another, why does the bronze, once unwrapped, transform nascent bliss into anxiety and shame? Could this be because both anxiety and bliss share a common font? I am suggesting that the sexualization of professional identity and ability, the phallic (and ultimately autoerotic) nature of professional pride is laid bare, so to speak, by the iconic signification of the bronze.

Even the bachelor lawyer declines to possess the bronze: "My mother comes here, and clients, and I'd be ashamed before the maid." Let us consider for a moment this notion of shame. Whereas guilt has to do with transgressions real or wished, and in the psychoanalytic frame of reference pertains to Oedipal dynamics, shame has to do with who one is: it results from a blow to the self-image, a disruption of the necessary narcissistic processes regulating self-esteem which derive from the pre-Oedipal period of development. As one of the founders of shame theory has written, "Shame is about the self; guilt is about things done or undone."[60] For the doctor, the gift's bestowal comprises two moments: receiving the admiring regard of the other (the gift is still wrapped), then exposure of the bronze. The first moment raises pride to dangerous heights, thereby paving the way for an access of infantile grandiosity, which involves sexual pleasure from being seen and seeing oneself. Such regression has its dangers, however, and here the metaphor of height is less than adequate. It is not just a question of excess pride; the bronze incites repression because, once it is unwrapped, the revelation of its erotic qualities makes overt this sexualized and infantile self-regard. The resulting rejection of both the gift and the pleasures it entails can thus be understood as ego defense.[61]

For these professional men, then, to be seen as the subject who derives his pleasure from seeing and being seen—to be caught in this narcissistic and autoerotic moment—threatens a catastrophic collapse of professional identity, especially before such inferiors as women, children, and servants. The bronze renders the professionals' superior social positions precarious because it reveals something infantile and sexual about status itself.

The Work of Art as Metaphor

The embarrassment generating the action of "Work of Art" derives from the candelabra's representation of female nudity. This nudity and the provocative pose prove unspeakable for the narrator, however, so that to discuss them here risks indulging in fantasy rather than reading, if one can deploy so naïve a distinction. But there does remain something textual to talk about: the bronze is also an iconic sign of duplication, in that it comprises two nudes. Moreover, the youth presenting it laments his lack of a matching candelabra: this doubled sign apparently requires duplication to be complete. And when at the story's end the bronze returns to the doctor, it does so in the guise of such a second, identical bronze completing a pair. Thus Savely Senderovich has identified this story as a metapoetic treatment of the device of reduplication, which he considers central to Chekhov's poetics, and in demonstration of which he could hardly have chosen a better work.[62] But this leaves open the question of how to interpret reduplication in this particular story, a question that takes us, first, back to the Ianov catastrophe.

For there were four women in the Ianov family. Since two died and two survived, the two female figures of the bronze could stand for either pair of women. In its initial presentation, the bronze—like Mariia Ianova's album—would refer to the two surviving sisters, whose photos are in fact displayed on the album's first page, in which case the youth's regret that he cannot offer a matching candelabra might simultaneously lament the absence of the two deceased Ianov women. Here indeed was a pair of women requiring another pair to be complete. When, at the story's end, such completion seems to have been achieved as the second bronze is brought to the doctor, it is a spooky moment, as unwelcome as a return of the dead. This undesired return of the bronze transforms it from a sign of the doctor's potency into one of helplessness, and thus a reminder of failure, an allusion to the pair of women Chekhov lost. The story ends with a motif of organ loss—"The doctor dropped his jaw; he was about to say something, but said nothing: he had lost his tongue [*u nego otnialsia iazyk*]"—which the figurative language of psychoanalysis would trope as castration.

Unlike Mariia Ianova's gift to Chekhov, the fictional bronze is presented to commemorate an unambiguous therapeutic success, one without the painful associations attached to the Ianov album. It is only through the plot mechanism of a return *against the doctor's will* that the bronze can serve to express as well the unsuccessful repression and return of troubling thoughts about the Ianov deaths. How could the album commemorating Mariia Ianova's deliverance from typhus not have simultaneously reminded Chekhov of the two women who died? All the more so, since the signature below the inscription identifies her in the context of her larger family: "Mariia Ianova, 1886, Ianovs, first daughter."[63] No doubt the pair of Ianov women, often dining with the Chekhov clan, were accompanied, for Chekhov, by the specters of his two lost patients. To "right" his damaged sense of self, as Helen Block Lewis puts it, he might well have wished

for those who survived to vanish and so let him forget about the dead—an aggressive wish that could in turn generate additional guilt. In fact, when Chekhov
mentions the Ianov sisters in his letters, it is often in irritated and demeaning
tones: he calls them "whorelets";[64] he says that his youngest brother, Misha, is
chasing after one of them; he names them "Iashen′ka" and "Iaden′ka," the latter nickname evoking the Russian for "poison" or "venom."[65]

Seeing and Gender: A Theoretical Digression

> In the morning, when I've risen from sleep, and am standing in front of the
> mirror and putting on my tie, my mother-in-law, wife, and sister-in-law
> come in, quiet and demure. They stand in a row and, smiling respectfully,
> wish me good morning. I nod to them and give a speech in which I explain
> to them that it is I who am the head of this household.
> —Chekhov, "My *Domostroi*" (1886)

At this point the gender component to the scopic thematic complex in Chekhov demands attention. As Chekhov reveals in "My *Domostroi*"[66] and as the
next chapter demonstrates in detail, Chekhov was clearly working through the
vicissitudes of seeing in connection not only with professional identity but with
the category of gender as well.

The classical Freudian treatment of exhibitionism, scopophilia, and scopophobia relates them to the threat of castration that arises in the Oedipal complex. The reality of the threat is based on the male child's viewing of the female
body, and his understanding of it as the body of a castrated male. The exhibitionist and the voyeur both seek "reassurance against castration," the former by
gaining proof of his possession of the member through the victim's reactions,
and the latter by seeking to view "screen experiences" that repeat (in the hope
of mastering) the "experiences that aroused his castration anxiety, either primal
scenes or the sight of adult genitals."[67]

The shadow of Oedipal dynamics, so defined, does indeed fall across "Work
of Art." The youth, in triumphing over death and supplanting his father in possession of the bronze and his mother, has bypassed the Oedipal problematic, or
at least emerged from it as a triumphant phallic victor: not for him the usual
path of acquiescence and identification. But for the other male characters—the
lawyer who fears that his mother will see the bronze, the actor who addresses
all the actresses as "Ma" or "Mother dear" (*matushka*), and especially the doctor—the phallic, infantile-grandiose fantasy of Oedipal immunity that the
bronze arouses immediately provokes a defensive reaction.

The candelabra's oxymoronic gender significations support such a line of interpretation. In "The Uncanny," Freud's influential reading of E.T.A. Hoffmann's tale "The Sandman," reduplication as a plot function is linked with the notions of castration anxiety and issues of looking and showing.[68] The conflation of the phallus with the female body that occurs in regard to the bronze has been treated in psychoanalytic theory as a neurotic representation of and an attempted solution to castration anxiety; among Freud's writings this is seen most clearly in his brief "Medusa's Head," where the Medusa is read as a contradictory condensation of the feminine and the phallic.[69] So too may be the visual image of the bronze nudes and the phallic candle(s). Just as professional pride may be associated, in psychoanalytic terms, with exhibitionism, so may failure and shame be understood through the trope of castration.

Luce Irigaray has argued that the psychoanalytic discourse surrounding sexual difference, in which "the gaze is at stake from the outset," belongs to a distinctively male "libidinal economy" in which the figuration of woman as a castrated man sustains the construction of a phallic and narcissistic male identity. Woman exists in this economy only as fetish, a kind of negative *mise en abyme* of man, whose self-image depends on the perpetual mirroring of his phantom possession of the phallus by woman's lack of it: "But finally, in Freud, sexual pleasure boils down to being plus or minus one sex organ: the penis. And sexual 'otherness' comes down to 'not having it.' Thus, woman's lack of penis and her envy of it *ensure the function of the negative,* serve as representatives of the negative, in what could be called a *phallocentric*—or phallotropic—dialectic."[70] Chekhov's story reads well as a parable illustrating the French feminist's argument: the bronze would then trouble the doctor because of its metadiscursive laying bare of how the female body, constructed according to phallocentric notions of sexual difference, sustains the fiction of a phallic masculine identity, a prideful self immune from the laws of castration and death. And this occurs just at the moment when the doctor is primed for a full and triumphant accession to that imaginary self. The phallocentric language of psychoanalysis works so well in Chekhov precisely because he writes about men constructing gendered professional identities through viewing the female body; when the focus of his narrative is a woman, she typically either vacates her self as the abject captive of that process or shamelessly exploits it with an exhibitionistic posture associated with prostitution or acting on the stage.

Back to the Text(s)

Perhaps the single greatest weakness of most psychoanalytic approaches to literature is their casual dismissal of the surface—as Freud does with manifest content in regard to dreams—while granting genuine significance only to latent or symbolic content. And all too often the operation results in finding only what theory put there in the first place. If my reading suffers a similar fault, it seems fair to note that the story itself begins by depicting such a gesture. What does become of the *Stock Exchange Gazette* (*Birzhevye vedemosti*) in which the bronze was wrapped?

Indeed, the discarded wrapping itself requires reading, and not only because of the lovely irony by which a substitute for monetary payment arrives wrapped in a newspaper dedicated to finance.[71] As the editors of Chekhov's collected writings have noted, Émile Zola's novel *L'oeuvre* (*The Masterpiece*) was being se-rialized in the *Stock Exchange Gazette* during the period when issue 223 was printed. And it just so happens that the very title of Chekhov's short tale could serve to translate that of Zola's weightier narrative into Russian.[72]

Zola's novel chronicles the decline of a young artist, Claude Lantier. Recog-nized by all to be of outstanding talent, Claude alternately struggles either to capture in oils or to rid himself altogether of an obsessive vision involving fe-male nudes and, in its final variant, a hellish cityscape of Paris. The closer he comes to creating his masterpiece, which should bring recognition, the more he is derided by the public and his peers. Thus his colleague Dubuche tells him: "The Public won't understand that. . . . They'll think it's just smutty. . . . And it is smutty!"[73]

The trajectory of Claude's fate as artist and man in large part follows the li-bidinal vicissitudes of his seeing. And this takes place in conjunction with his great ambition to be exhibited, that is, a powerful drive to exhibitionism. The plot begins with a voyeuristic moment: Claude, prone to a kind of obsessive and excessive sublimation, happens to observe a cab driver attempting to rape his young female passenger; when the woman, Christine, falls into Claude's hands, he conceives the contrasting (and yet not unrelated) passionate desire to paint her in the nude. She eventually submits to his distinctive sort of seeing: "Chaste as he was, he had a passion for the physical beauty of women, an insane love for nudity desired but never possessed, but was powerless to satisfy himself or to cre-ate enough of the beauty he dreamed of enfolding in an ecstatic embrace. The women he hustled out of his studio he adored in his pictures. He caressed them, did violence even, and shed tears of despair over his failures to make them ei-ther sufficiently beautiful or sufficiently alive."[74] Nevertheless, the two eventu-ally become lovers, and a radical de-sublimation takes place: "Henceforth, all his fondness for female beauty, all the desires he used to work out in his painting, were concentrated in the one warm, living, supple body he had made his own."[75] But everything changes when Claude's artistic ambition is rekindled and Christine, now his wife, once again poses for the masterpiece-to-be:

6. *Stock Exchange Gazette* (*Birzhevye vedomosti*), front page of no. 223, mentioned in Chekhov's "Work of Art." Zola's novel *L' oeuvre* (*V mire khudozhnikov—roman iz parizhskoi zhizni Emilia Zolia*) was serialized in the paper.

She knew everything now, so what more was there to hope for? Her body, which once he had covered with his lover's kisses, he now viewed and worshipped merely as an artist. Now it was the delicate colouring of her breast that fired his imagination, some line of her belly that brought him to his knees in worship. His desire was blind no longer; he did not crush her whole body against his own, as he used to do, without even looking at her, in an embrace they hoped might fuse them into one.

No! This was the end.

She had ceased to exist, since all he could find to adore in her now was his art, and nature, and life.[76]

She has been sublimated out of her own fleshly existence.

In "Work of Art," Chekhov responds to the psychological, sexual, and aesthetic problematic elaborated in Zola's novel. Perhaps he even steals from Zola, though he certainly makes no secret of it. But there is an additional sense in which "Work of Art" echoes *The Masterpiece*. As Claude sinks, the career of his friend, the author Sandoz, ascends. The relationship between these two characters was known to be loosely based on that between Zola and his friend Paul Cézanne.[77] Indeed, the Russian subtitle of the serialized novel, "A Novel from the Parisian Life of Émile Zola," marketed the work as a roman à clef. As we have seen, in "Work of Art," Chekhov follows Zola in the methodology of incorporating a profoundly autobiographical dimension into his fiction.

Chekhov's Two Identities

In a moment of dissatisfaction with his canvas, Zola's obsessed artist vows to begin again. "I'm going to start afresh!" Claude repeats. "It can kill me, it can kill my wife, it can kill my child, it can kill the lot of us, but this time it'll be a masterpiece, by God it will!" The next morning Claude's son—unloved, malnourished, deformed, and, in terms of the medical discourse of the day, to which Zola more than any other European author gave literary expression, a "degenerate"—is found dead. Claude responds the only way he can: "He tried to resist it at first, but the attraction grew stronger and stronger to the point of obsession, until at last he gave way, fetched out a small canvas and set to work on a study of the dead child." Soon he is working with great enthusiasm and a "vague smile" on his lips; what results, in the view of Sandoz, is a "masterpiece."[78] This is precisely where the segment published in issue 223 of the *Stock Exchange Gazette*—the issue named in Chekhov's text—begins: Claude takes his *Dead Child* to the Palais de l'Industrie and submits it in competition for inclusion in that year's salon. The first of the three chapters appearing in the paper tells of the painting's painful reception by judges, colleagues, critics, and the public; the "work of art" in this segment is in fact Claude's dead child made into art, *The Dead Child*.[79]

So too, in "Work of Art," Chekhov turns deaths for which he feels himself responsible into art, though far less directly and in a humorous key. Indeed, the story may exemplify how the superficial and comic works of the early Chekhov could have the most profound and troubling emotional roots. Everything is on the surface here, as though psyche were turned inside out, transforming the unconscious mechanisms of defense into those of plot construction, and the most troubling secret obsessions into overt thematic material. The result is something of a farce. Or perhaps farce is less the result than a facilitator of the creative process, with laughter, a diacritical sign of insignificance, providing the conditions under which such sensitive material might emerge.

Zola's novel shows how such sublimation can in turn be an act of cruelty: Claude's behavior verges on a kind of criminality, both against others and against himself, since by the end of the segment excerpted in issue 223 (chapters 10–12), which is the end of the novel, Claude has hanged himself. And there is at least a hint of such aggression against self and others in Chekhov's use of the Ianov material in his lighthearted "Work of Art." But now we are in a position to see how such transgression can also facilitate the exit from one damaged professional identity and entry into another. In lampooning the physician, Chekhov becomes a writer. One can observe this translocation of the self in Chekhov's letter to Bilibin about Mariia Ianova's typhoidal album; it happens, too, in the very writing of "Work of Art," where a doctor is made the butt of a comic writer's joke; and more familiarly, this is the possibility Chekhov affirms in his often-repeated witticism, "Medicine is my lawfully wedded wife, and literature is my mistress." The rhetorical operation here is very much like those working on the bronze in "Work of Art": a male's professional identity is represented by, and therefore conflated with, his female erotic objects and, as a consequence, is sexualized. Wife and mistress become figures of speech for separate aspects of a dual self.

CHAPTER 3

Self and Other through the Lens of Science

"Listen, in our society nowadays there are two predominant attitudes toward women. Some measure female skulls so as to prove that woman is lower than man, they search out her imperfections so as to deride her, to appear original in her eyes and justify their own bestiality. The others try with all their might to raise woman to their own level, that is, force her to learn 35,000 species, to say and write the same inanities that they say and write themselves. . ."

Likharev's face darkened.

"But I'll tell you, woman has always been, and always will be, the slave of man."

— Chekhov, "On the Road"

"I'm reading Darwin. What luxury! I love him terribly," Chekhov wrote his friend and the secretary at *Oskolki,* Ivan Bilibin, in a rambling 1886 letter chiefly about literary matters (11 March 1886). This was no new attachment. Chekhov's admiration for Darwin, entirely characteristic of his educational background and social and professional class, was already long-standing at this point and would continue until the end of his life. But just as the legacy of Darwin took some problematic turns in the last decades of the nineteenth century, giving rise to the racist, classist, and misogynistic discourses of degeneration theory, Chekhov's own deeply personal engagement with Darwinian thought became increasingly complicated and ambivalent.[1] Although he never ceased thinking about his own body and those of others in evolutionary-biological terms, he also quite evidently became troubled by the problematic ethics issuing from the peculiar visual rhetoric and practical application of this body of

99

knowledge. As a budding medical professional, Chekhov had reveled in the powers this knowledge seemed to promise, and the superior position it assigned him, particularly in regard to women and to his own tainted family heritage. Only a few years later, however, sobered by the experience of medical practice, his journey to Sakhalin, and his own illness, Chekhov began dismantling such perspectives both in overt statements and in his art. The story of his involvement with the ideas of evolution and degeneration emerges most clearly in an ephemeral social Darwinist dissertation project Chekhov conceived as a medical student, and the post-Sakhalin stories "Duel" (1891), "Ward 6" (1892), "Black Monk" (early 1893), and "Three Years" and "Ariadne" (both 1895).

"A History of Sexual Dominance"

When Chekhov was still a medical student publishing under a variety of pseudonyms, he looked forward to attaching his real name to the serious medical studies that it was, he thought, his vocation to write.[2] One idea for a dissertation project that took shape then was provisionally titled "A History of Sexual Dominance" ("Istoriia polovogo avtoriteta"). We know of the project from a single source only, a letter Chekhov wrote to his eldest brother, Aleksandr (17 or 18 April 1883). The project never progressed beyond the outline articulated in this letter; nevertheless, this document—all the more revealing for having been written while Chekhov was tipsy[3]—is enormously useful as an open declaration of Chekhov's professional and emotional investment in the scientific theories of his time. An ambitious Chekhov envisioned utilizing his newfound scientific and writerly knowledge to assist Nature in raising the female sex to intellectual levels on a par with man's. He shows euphoric confidence in the powers this new knowledge puts into his hands—or, perhaps we could say, into his gaze, into his professional capacity to examine and understand others who, by definition, occupy a lower intellectual level—and this confidence extends beyond the sphere of the medical in ways that are also evident in this letter.

Chekhov's prospectus alternately cites the English historian Henry Thomas Buckle (1821–1862), the biologist and social theorist Herbert Spencer (1820–1903), and Charles Darwin (1809–1882), bespeaking an entanglement of the biological with the social-historical very much in the spirit of the second half of the nineteenth century. While Spencer and Darwin remain well known, and much has been published on Darwin's reception in Russia, Buckle passed quickly into obscurity (though less so in Russia than in his native England). His meteoric career derived from the project of placing historiography on scientific grounds: Buckle sought to establish the "laws" of historical development; he based these laws on material environmental conditions (heavily emphasizing statistics); and he defined progress in terms of intellectual advancement. These three men were idols of nineteenth-century Russian positivism and intellectual beacons for the men and women often grouped under the heading of "men of the sixties," as well as for subsequent generations; this was especially true for those of Chekhov's social and educational background.[4]

Chekhov's strong link with that tradition is manifest in the many pithy, aphoristic passages in his letters defending the hard sciences and medicine, as well as in his book on Sakhalin, with its heavy emphasis on the effect of environment on the population's evolutionary progress or degeneration. Nevertheless, Chekhov reached maturity at a time when even some of the most ideologically committed materialists of the previous generation had come to question their assumptions. Thus, in 1879 the radical critic Nikolai Shelgunov wrote: "Let us admit that in the 1860s there were made overly courageous generalizations and conclusions from Darwin; let us agree that we were mistaken [to think] that the [physiologist's] frog would save the world—all this was unfounded and laughable."[5] In 1890 Chekhov wrote Suvorin, "If I were offered a choice between the [positivistic] 'ideals' of the celebrated sixties and today's poorest *zemstvo* hospital, I'd take the latter without the least hesitation" (24 December 1890).[6] While Chekhov would remain devoted to the writings and achievement of Charles Darwin, in later years his attitude toward Buckle became somewhat ironic. Buckle's name always appears in passing in Chekhov's works, as a signal that the character who has read him is, should be, or pretends to be modern, intellectual, and liberal. We see this, for example, in "The Man in the Case" ("Chelovek v futliare," 1898): "Yes. These are thinking, upright people, they read both Shchedrin and Turgenev, and various Buckles and so forth, but here they were submitting, putting up with it" (*S* 10:44); in the remarks of Epikhodov in *Cherry Orchard* (*S* 13:216); and in *Seagull,* where Dr. Dorn reproaches the schoolteacher Medvedenko: "You all read Buckle and Spencer, but you have no more knowledge than a watchman" (*S* 13:262).

At this early moment in his medical career, however, while Chekhov is still a student absorbing the thought of these figures, his attachment to these thinkers and the science of his day emerges clearly from this letter. The argument in Chekhov's prospectus begins with the observation that domination by males is not universal; in lower life forms there is none, or even "negative" domination (i.e., submission). As one moves up the evolutionary chain, egg-laying species begin to show a marked superiority in males; but nature, "not supporting inequality," created mammals, among whom this inequality is weaker. The most important premise of Chekhov's argument is this: "Nature herself does not tolerate inequality. Given the chance, she corrects her departures, made out of necessity." Eventually nature will also eliminate sexual inequality, but at the present moment "in *homo* there is dominance—the male is superior." Chekhov's emphasis on the beneficent and harmonious principles at work in nature—nature's bent toward equilibrium—departs from orthodox Darwinian principles, but it is very much in keeping with the Russian reception of Darwin, which in the earlier years especially tended to ignore or reject the notion of intraspecies "struggle for existence."[7]

Buckle was wrong, Chekhov continues, in claiming that women and men have different aptitudes. In "The Influence of Women on the Progress of Knowledge," Buckle had theorized that women were more deductive, romantic, and idealistic, while the minds of men were inclined to operate inductively, in a scientific, rationalistic, and materialistic manner. The influence of women—especially "remarkable mothers"—has "tended to raise us into an ideal world, lift us from the dust in which we are too prone to grovel, and develop in us those germs of imagination which even the most sluggish and apathetic understandings in some degree possess."[8] For, he writes, "we are too apt to speak as if we had penetrated into the sanctuary of truth and raised the veil of the goddess, when in fact we are still standing, coward-like, trembling before the vestibule, and not daring from very fear to cross the threshold of the temple. The highest of our so-called laws of nature are as yet purely empirical."[9] Chekhov disagrees: "Buckle says that [woman] is more deductive . . . etc. But I don't think so. She's a good doctor, a good lawyer, etc., but in the field of creative work she is a goose. A perfect [*sovershennyi*] organism creates, but woman has never created anything." The ideal and the empirical, creativity and its lack—these are some of the key semantic oppositions aligned with gender difference in the discourses Chekhov is engaging. Chekhov borrows the terms from Buckle, even if he reverses their values.

Chekhov then tells his brother that nature intends woman to be man's equal; what is more, "nature must be helped," and it is to this end that a scientific understanding of sexual inequality is to be developed. Such optimism is made possible by "the passionate belief in social progress and a preoccupation with designs for the improved quality of human life" that define the young Chekhov's scientific and social milieu.[10] A sharp formulation of this faith can be found in Nikolai Chernyshevskii's inspirational and resoundingly influential *What Is to Be Done?* (*Chto delat'?* 1863), where the heroic "new man" Rakhmetov indicts Vera Pavlovna's plan to leave her sewing cooperative: "You could have harmed the cause of all mankind and betrayed the idea of progress! That, Vera Pavlovna, in ecclesiastical language is called a sin against the Holy Spirit."[11]

Chekhov's scientific faith in the spiraling progress of the species over time manifests an adherence to the Lamarckian notion that features acquired by one generation as a result of environmental pressures can lead to phylogenetic change; that is, they can be inherited by the next generation. In the prospectus Chekhov cites with approval Spencer's *Education: Intellectual, Moral, and Physical,* in which this perspective is resolutely transferred from the biological to the social.[12] As ontogeny repeats phylogeny in biological development, so it is assumed to do in social history. Chekhov goes so far as to assert that the manuscript of his study "is unlikely to come out thick: there's no need, since natural history repeats itself at every step, and history at every third."

In addition to the scientific and ideological background sketched above, Chekhov's letter outlining his "History" also betrays a personal emotional investment in the topic of sexual dominance. This is what most interests us here: not the consciously held ideological program, but the way the very self changes, more or less unconsciously, as it assumes a system of knowledge, and the powers presumed to follow from a new way of seeing others. Chekhov's research project (which he outlined, to repeat, while "under the influence") has in addition the status of a wish, a fantasy. At once ethically commendable, politically progressive, and megalomaniacal, this prospectus presents a precocious therapeutic fantasy situating the entire female sex as Dr. Chekhov's patient.

How strange that Chekhov's letter, though very often remarked (it is the only place where the "History" is described, and comes up in treatments of Chekhov's relations with women),[13] has never been read in its entirety. For in it the young and sanguine medical student is confident of much more than his superiority over the females of his species, the scientific laws of evolution that will raise the female's intellectual level, and his ability to help this process along. Chekhov revels in his mastery of several areas, but most especially in his success in the field of "creative work," which has already made him his large family's chief breadwinner, and it is precisely that area which distinguishes woman from man: "To work on *Oskolki* means having graduated [*imet' attestat*] . . . I have the right to look down on *Budil'nik,* and now it's not likely that I'll work someplace for a nickel: I've become more expensive." And there is his assertion, cited earlier, that a woman can be "a good doctor, a good lawyer, etc., but in the field of creative work she is a goose."

All this emerges in a letter to his eldest brother, also an author, whom Chekhov has in all respects decisively surpassed. The letter begins with an instruction in the poetics of stories likely to appeal to the publisher Leikin, and it ends with assurances that Aleksandr could be of help in this scientific project in spite of his "lack of knowledge." In short, Chekhov makes quite an assertion of dominance in this letter about "sexual dominance." The letter's postscript, more about the brother he is inciting to creative work than about women, places Aleksandr into the position of woman: "Remember that a perfect organism *creates.* If woman doesn't create, then it means that she remains further from the perfect organism, and consequently, is weaker than man, who is closer to such an organism." To the extent that Chekhov's scientific project in social engineering is meant to raise woman up, in the best tradition of the 1860s, the letter in which it appears is meant to raise up his brother; when Chekhov dismisses woman as "weaker than man," he likewise feminizes his elder brother, telling him, "You are weaker than me." The double agenda of this letter could be derived from a cheap pun between *avtor* (author) and *avtoritet* (authority, dominance), while the association of Aleksandr with woman, a "goose" in creative activity, is further reinforced by Chekhov's nickname for him: "Gusev."

The letter is thus but one of several documented moments marking Chekhov's patriarchal ascent to the head of his family.[14] We witness the conjunction of Chekhov's bold optimism and confidence in himself and the scientific method, the rather unproblematic objectification of the female sex as a patient for whom he knows the cure, and his sense of alliance with the forward movement of time: "If you want to take it up, then at leisure, not hurrying, after maybe ten years we'll be able to gape at the result, not useless, of our labor." And yet Chekhov is still a medical student producing, for the most part, trifles for the popular press. Might not a proportionately exaggerated perspective on "weaker" woman play a fundamental role in the intoxicating psychological dynamic of self-aggrandizement at work in this letter?

The project went nowhere. Chekhov, with his keen autoanalytic sensibility, realized the troubling implications of the position he had taken in that letter and soon moderated the exuberantly self-assured tones expressed in it. In the 1890s the thin ethical ice on which one objectifies and categorizes another human being as "degenerate," or inferior on the evolutionary scale, would become the central theme of his major post-Sakhalin works.[15] There is evidence, furthermore, that Chekhov was in at least equal measure alarmed by the danger to one's self that inhered in observing others from such a perspective. Chekhov the playwright came to view the stage as an "execution block" and an invitation to *mania grandiosa,* because writing for the stage made the playwright part of the scene, unsettlingly visible to others; for Chekhov the physician enticed by the sociobiological perspective, a particular kind of professional seeing threatens to inflate the self, rendering it vulnerable to megalomania.

In the interval separating the early dissertation proposal for a history of sexual authority and the post-Sakhalin stories, to which we turn shortly, Chekhov's evolutionary outlook acquires darker shadings as he grapples with ascendant theories of biological and cultural degeneration and his own ill body.[16] At issue in large part was the turn Darwin's legacy had taken by the end of the century, with the natural law of "survival of the fittest" and Lamarckian ideas regarding the inheritance of acquired features leading to social Darwinism and theories of degeneration (for example, Lombroso and Nordau).[17]

Fundamental to the theory of degeneration was a pioneering emphasis on the visual. According to Sander Gilman, the "first documented use of clinical photography in the recording of the physiognomy of the insane to illustrate a medical text appeared in the atlas to B. A. Morel's 1857 *Traité des dégénérescences physiques, intellectuelles et morales de l'espèce humaine et des causes que produisent ces variétés maladises.*"[18] From its earliest articulation, a central feature of the theory of degeneration was that the malady's signs were visible and apparent to a properly trained eye, and could moreover be codified with the assistance of the objective and scientific tool now available in the new art of photography. There was nothing metaphoric about the scientific gaze in the theories and practice of the French psychiatrist Jean Martin Charcot (1825–1893) or the Italian Cesare Lombroso (1836–1909). Gilman tells us, "It was in psychiatry, an area which on the first glance would seem singularly unfruitful for the use of the camera, that the first systematic theory and practice of clinical photography were undertaken."[19]

Both Chekhov's explicit remarks on the theory of degeneration as Max Nordau and others elaborated it and his literary treatments of the topic indicate considerable critical distance. But as is vividly apparent in Chekhov's remark to Elena Shavrova that "there's very little in life that might not be harmful and passed on by heredity" (28 February 1895), Chekhov's thinking was nonetheless profoundly conditioned by the theory of degeneration, and the ideas underwriting it most certainly continued to have a deep and disquieting resonance for his sense of self. As the grandson of a serf, the son of a bankrupt failure, the brother of two alcoholics, one consumptive, and as himself a consumptive, could he have helped considering what this theory had to say about *himself?* One of Chekhov's joking pseudonyms, "Brother of My Brother" (*brat moego brata*), emphasizes the hereditary and familial component to the self: we can indeed say, "He is the son of his father" or "brother of his brother" and convey information despite the phrase's circularity.

Even after the bacillus causing tuberculosis was discovered by Robert Koch in 1882, heredity continued to play a considerable role in scientific thinking about predisposition and susceptibility to the disease. Thus in 1891 a Petersburg organization known as the Russian Society for the Protection of Public Health (Russkoe obshchestvo okhraneniia narodnogo zdraviia, or "Roonz") officially recognized tuberculosis as an infectious disease, but nonetheless also considered prohibiting marriage for consumptives and their relatives down to the third generation. Cognizant of the fact that there was no scientific evidence for the role of inheritance in tuberculosis, Roonz set that proposal aside, and yet it still recommended that tuberculars avoid marriage so as not to "pass on to their descendants a predisposition to consumption."[20] Scientific evidence to the contrary notwithstanding, then, the body of the tubercular patient continued to be perceived as degenerate and dangerous to the hygiene of the species. We can only speculate about the extent to which this fact contributed to Chekhov's reluctance to have himself examined by another physician or to enter into marriage, but there is ample evidence that Chekhov thought of himself in such evolutionary biological terms.

Chekhov's friend and literary colleague Vladimir Giliarovskii, who was renowned for his strength, recalled that in the 1890s Chekhov joined the gymnastics club of which Giliarovskii was then the chairman; he did so only to please Giliarovskii and had no intentions of working out. Chekhov joked about how inappropriate such muscular ambitions were for himself, but he added: "There will come a time—perhaps in about a hundred years—when everybody will be strong, and there will be a lot like you [. . .] That time will come!"[21] Chekhov told Leikin that the hemorrhoids from which he suffered were a result of the inherited tendency for his veins to widen (22 May 1887); he explained seasonal sleep disturbances among his family members as an "atavism," the phylogenetic memory of their serf heritage;[22] and in a letter to Aleksei Suvorin he expressed befuddlement at his two elder brothers' chronic problems with alcoholism precisely because there had *not* been a history of alcoholism in the family (10 October 1888). Chekhov even applied the logic of evolutionary biology to poetics, telling his brother Aleksandr that the latter's nefarious literary tendency to subjectivity was correctable because "you weren't born a subjective writer . . . It's not an inherited trait but an acquired one . . . " (20 February 1883). When in March 1897 Chekhov was stricken with a lung hemorrhage while dining at the Hermitage Hotel in Moscow, he soberly pointed out to Suvorin that his brother Nikolai and his cousin Elizaveta Mikhailovna, née Chekhova, both of whom had died of consumption, had suffered the same sort of hemorrhage from the same (right) lung.[23]

The famous letter to Suvorin in which Chekhov told how a "young man," meaning himself, "squeezes the slave out of himself drop by drop" (7 January 1889) should probably be taken quite literally. Chekhov's personal history then becomes an evolutionary leap, a heroic battle against biological determinism; his illness and death, from a disease understood to be hereditary, appear as biology's revenge.[24] The "intimations of mortality" that, according to scholars,[25] became a central theme in the mature Chekhov must have been intimations of the workings of heredity as well, a questioning of the self's place in the schemes of

7. Vladimir Giliarovskii demonstrates his strength, Melikhovo, 1892. Chekhov center front, his brothers Mikhail behind him and Ivan on the right. Photograph by Isaak Levitan. Reprinted courtesy of The State Literary Museum (Gosudarstvennyi literaturnyi muzei), Moscow.

evolution and degeneration. If the theory of degeneration offered a ruthless scientific-ideological lens for looking at others, for Chekhov it could not but raise the question of how he was to look at himself.

"Duel"

Most scholarly discussions of Chekhov's attitude toward the theory of degeneration center on the summer of 1891, when, having moved from an unsatisfactory dacha to Bogimovo, the estate of E. D. Bylim-Kolosovskii, Chekhov made the acquaintance of a fellow *dachnik,* the eminent zoologist (and founder of Russian zoopsychology) V. A. Vagner. The two discussed the theories of evolution and degeneration at length. According to Chekhov's youngest brother, "Vagner would assert: once there is evidence of degeneration [*vyrozhhdenie*], then, of course, there's no way back, for nature doesn't joke around; but Chekhov would object: no matter how great the degeneration, it can always be conquered by will and education."[26]

This Bogimovo association is credited with leading directly to two of Chekhov's works, one journalistic and one a major story. The feuilleton "Fokusniki" ("Conjurers"), composed with Vagner's assistance, denounces the unscientific and inhumane conditions at the Moscow Zoo.[27] "Duel," also written in Bogimovo, is often read as asserting the same position Chekhov maintained when discussing the dogma of degeneration with Vagner: in discrediting both the social Darwinist position of one protagonist and the fatalistic acceptance of the imprint of degeneration by that character's opponent, Chekhov clinches his argument with Vagner.[28]

The central conflict of "Duel" arises from the personal animosity of a zoologist, von Koren, toward a dropout university student of philology, Laevskii. Von Koren is conducting marine research at a Caucasus Black Sea town while planning an expedition to the Arctic; the disillusioned Laevskii came to the romantic south to create a new life with his mistress, another man's wife, but now regards those dreams as unrealistic and the mistress a millstone around his neck. Chekhov's dual professional identity as physician and author is implicated in the narrative's ambiguous, agonistic juxtaposition of the discourse of science (associated with von Koren) with that of the Russian literary tradition (Laevskii). This major story—one of Chekhov's longest—denounces the "extreme epistemological hubris"[29] with which the theories of evolution, social Darwinism, and degeneration armed scientific seeing. "I am a zoologist, or a sociologist, which comes to the same thing" (S 7:393),[30] the character von Koren announces, in a revealingly concise formulation of the scientistic overreaching of Russian Spencerians.[31] The zoologist goes so far as to dispute ascription of "moral law" to the realm of theology with his friend the deacon, asserting the biological grounds and evolutionary function of morality and thereby laying claim to it as a domain of science: "I don't say that it will one day be seen under a microscope, but its organic connection has been manifestly proven: serious affectations of the brain and all so-called mental diseases show themselves first, so far as I know, in a perversion of the moral law" (137; S 7:430). In condemning the relations between Laevskii and his mistress, Nadezhda Fedorovna, von Koren tells Dr. Samoilenko that "the repugnance of the masses for illicit love and licentiousness" is "the only thing that has survived from natural selection, and if it were not for this obscure force regulating relations between the sexes, the Laevskiis of the world would be showing you how to live and the human race would degenerate within two years" (119; S 7:412). Von Koren's medico-scientific knowledge authorizes him, he asserts, to rid the world of the "pernicious" Laevskii, who is "as dangerous to society as the cholera microbe," concluding, "It would be doing a service to drown him" (76; S 7:369). Speaking of "the drones, who ought to be killed" (138; S 7:431), he applies an analogy between the sociobiology of bees and human social organization that had been current in Russian thinking for decades.[32]

But how will this act of social hygiene be accomplished? Through a duel, the paradigmatic plot situation of an entirely different discourse, that of Russian romantic literature. There the fatal contest often occurs in exotic southern tales whose settings are replicated in "Duel"; but rather than an artificial selection furthering the species and so benefiting the larger social entity (as von Koren would have it), the romantic duel stages a clash between the colossal egos of romantic heroes and superfluous men.[33] Indeed, von Koren's knowing eye and aggressive stance toward others is part and parcel of a personal psychology remarkable for its narcissistic self-satisfaction; how he sees others feeds a self-aggrandizing self-regard:

> [Von Koren] would sit down in the drawing room without a word, take an album from the table, and carefully examine the faded photographs of unknown men in full trousers and top hats and ladies in crinolines and lace caps [. . .] When he had gone through the album, von Koren would take a pistol from the shelf, screw up his left eye and take deliberate aim at a portrait of Prince Vorontsev, or he would stand before the mirror studying his swarthy face and big forehead, his black hair, kinky as a Negro's, his shirt of dun-colored cotton printed with huge flowers like a Persian rug, and the wide leather belt he wore instead of a waistcoat. This contemplation of his own image gave him almost more satisfaction than examining the photographs or the expensively mounted pistols. He was quite pleased with his face, his beautifully trimmed beard, and his broad shoulders — unmistakable evidence of his excellent health and strong constitution. He was satisfied, too, with his dashing get-up. (74; S 7:367)

Laevskii, by contrast, associates himself with the character type of the superfluous man, the Russian Hamlet: "'My indecision reminds me of Hamlet,' thought Laevskii [. . .] 'How true Shakespeare's observations! Ah, how true!'" (73; S 7:366). But Laevskii's is a distinctively fin-de-siècle and medicalized Hamlet, as his litany of excuses (cited by von Koren) shows: "'I'm a failure, a superfluous man,' or: 'What do you expect from us, old man, the dregs of the serf-owning class?' or: 'We're degenerating. . . .' Or [Laevskii would] start a long rigmarole about Onegin, Pechorin, Byron's Cain, Bazarov, of whom he would say: 'They are our fathers in spirit and in flesh'" (77; S 7:370). At one point Laevskii employs the rhetoric of degeneration to explain an embarrassing outburst of hysterics: "In our neurotic age we are all slaves to our nerves; they are our masters, and do as they will with us. In this respect civilization has done us a disservice . . ." (130; S 7:423). Thus the dueling discourses of science and the

Russian literary tradition—tools by means of which the two key characters view and judge each other—prove terribly confounded: von Koren applies literary stereotypes to Laevskii and, in his putatively scientific reasoning, makes no ontological distinction between data drawn from literature and those drawn from life (Anna Karenina's suicide is adduced as proof of the innate instinct for sexual morality in humans [S 7:119]); the philologist manqué Laevskii explains himself with the rhetoric of degeneration. There is remarkable consonance between the worldviews of these two men.[34]

In fact, the arsenal of scientific and literary notions mobilized by von Koren and Laevskii vanishes after the duel. These ideas turn out not to have been the focus of Chekhov's tale, which concludes with agreement between the two: "Nobody knows the real truth" (159; S 7:454–55). This remark is uttered three times, lest the reader miss the point: first by von Koren, after which it is immediately echoed by Laevskii, who then repeats it in his final musings. In "Duel," attention is drawn to the intersection of personality and knowledge, with the former revealed as more fundamental. How one individual sees another is a function of who one is in a psychological sense rather than the knowledge one wields; a work that began with striking portrayals of "epistemological hubris" closes with a no less remarkable assertion of epistemological modesty.

We are reminded of Aleksandr Chudakov's sage formulation of the function of ideas in Chekhov's poetics: "In Chekhov's world the idea does not strive to the realization of its existence in and of itself; it is always fixed within the incidental circumstance of its worldly existence. An idea cannot be extracted from that empirical existence into which it is submerged [. . .] An idea in Chekhov's world is not brought to a dogmatic conclusion in its internal development."[35] One key aspect of the "empirical existence" of the ideas of evolution and degeneration in Chekhov's world is the author's sense of his own place in regard to these scientifically postulated processes. The consumptive Chekhov could not help but struggle with the logic of metaphor at work in von Koren's claim that "the tubercular and the scrofulous are recognized by their diseases, the immoral and the insane by their acts" (138; S 7:431).

But if the ideology behind a certain kind of scientific seeing peters out in this story rather than arriving at "a dogmatic conclusion in its internal development," this is not true of the motif of seeing itself. Indeed, the story ends with a veritable bonanza of scenes of seeing, and in them the very nature of the act undergoes transformation. One might even say that seeing in the story has come to a "dogmatic conclusion": it is now both self-reflective and empathic. Laevskii's moment of conversion, the start of a new life for him, begins not with the conventionally climactic duel but as a result of catching sight of his mistress in bed with another man. In other words, the culminating moment of this seaside story, like that of Chekhov's early "At Sea," stages a kind of "primal scene," but with this important twist: Laevskii had himself already displaced Nadezhda Fedorovna's husband, so that this episode constitutes his translocation from actor to observer of a scene in which he too is depicted. It is, as in "At Sea," an accidental version of Hamlet's "mousetrap." Having witnessed this scene, Laevskii suddenly understands something about his own and Nadezhda Fedorovna's positions; he resolves to change, and most remarkably, he does.

For von Koren, similarly, observing the change in Laevskii means recognizing his own errors. In the story's final episode, von Koren, on his way to meet the boat that will take him north, peers through a window at Laevskii, now married to Nadezhda Fedorovna and hard at work at his desk. The scene transfixes him (S 7:451–52). Von Koren has been "surprised" by Laevskii, and he accedes to Samoilenko's urgings to stop in, make it up, and part with Laevskii in person (though, ever vain, he cannot help wishing he had left "witnesses" to this humbling scene outside [S 7:452]). The story ends with Laevskii watching as von Koren is rowed in heavy winds out to the steamer: "The boat is thrown back; she makes two paces forward and one back, but the oarsmen persevere, they row indefatigably and are not afraid of the high waves. The boat goes on and on; now it's out of sight, but in half an hour they'll be alongside its ladder. So it is in life . . . In the search for truth men make two paces forward and one back. Mistakes, suffering, and the tedium of life forces them back, but the thirst for truth and a stubborn will drives them on and on. And who knows? Perhaps they will arrive at the real truth . . . " (161; S 7:455).

As von Koren embarks on his lengthy and difficult voyage of exploration, and Laevskii, on a life of genuine labor, a new metaphor for progress and regression displaces the evolutionary biological model that had been articulated by both characters in the past. Like von Koren, Chekhov deliberately expunged the self-aggrandizing component to his own seeing that the bio-evolutionary perspective offered him as a physician; and far more concretely than the character Laevskii, Chekhov also had to struggle against the implications of that perspective for his own degenerate body.

"Ward 6"

Chekhov's major story of the following year, "Ward 6," grows out of the same concerns that produced "Duel," though in it the theme of degeneration is not so overtly stated. Central to "Ward 6," too, is the trope of seeing, which becomes concretized in opposing motifs: on the one hand, a cold, ostensibly objective official gaze; on the other, the understanding eye of a co-sufferer. As mentioned in chapter 2, the overarching plot structure of the story is also best described in terms of the vicissitudes of seeing. The story begins with a narrator, directly addressing the reader, inviting us to "have a look" at what is happening inside the hospital's psychiatric wing (*S* 8:72); the handling of narrative point of view in the story subsequently manipulates the reader into the position of the trapped object of others' gazes. Of the five inmates of the ward, the only character whose biography we learn and who acquires a significant role in the story, Ivan Gromov, suffers from paranoiac delusions; that is to say, he is obsessed with the question of how others see him. And most significantly, the story's chief character, Dr. Ragin, abandons his professional position as the one who sees, avoiding his doctorly responsibilities: he cannot stand to conduct physical examinations, and he neglects to oversee matters at the hospital where he is chief. When his friend Mikhail Aver'ianych takes him on a therapeutic journey to Moscow and Warsaw, Ragin begins to pretend that he is ill and, rather than touring the sights, lies on the sofa in his hotel room, "facing the sofa back"—so as not to see (*S* 8:112). Eventually Ragin is himself examined by others, assigned a pathology, and committed to the hospital's psychiatric wing. In other words, the trajectory of Ragin's fate as a character is from seeing to being seen, and this latter position very quickly leads to death.

Much as in "Duel," the two chief protagonists of "Ward 6," Ragin and Gromov, who slug it out in verbal arguments, represent opposing ethical positions that come to be tested by the author's plot design. The history of the story's reception includes many complaints by readers and critics unsure of which side the author wishes his reader to take, but most who have written on the tale see Chekhov as negating Dr. Ragin's quietism, the stoic position of mind over matter, in favor of the ethical activism and sensitivity to pain expressed by the lucid madman Gromov.[36] Ragin's intellectual position has been associated with the thought of Tolstoy, Schopenhauer, and Marcus Aurelius (there are some more or less direct citations from the last two, though Chekhov does diverge from the originals),[37] and the story is read as an argument against philosophizing, generally speaking.

In "Ward 6," however, it is a matter not just of philosophizing but of doing so in a madhouse. By situating the arguments of Gromov and Ragin in a psychiatric ward, Chekhov invites evaluation of these characters' utterances on grounds other than their coherence and verity; they are also psychopathological symptoms. As was the case in "Duel," words become symptomatic behavior, signifiers on the plane of personality rather than—or, better, in addition to—elements of a philosophical argument. Readers who adopt the interpretive tactic of refereeing the debate between Ragin and Gromov are operating at the same level as Chekhov's characters and miss this essential aspect of Chekhov's project. And they are diverted from the story's polemical orientation toward fin-de-siècle theories of degeneration, and from Chekhov's thematic and stylistic reflection on the eye with which such putative pathologies are viewed.

Chekhov's fundamental strategy is to present the madman Gromov and the eccentric Dr. Ragin as highly understandable, to make their words and perspectives maximally *resemble* those of his readers. Thus, apart from Gromov's delusions of persecution, his thinking is remarkably cogent, as the doctor discovers; and for Gromov as an inmate of the hospital, even his persecution delusions acquire sad validity. What Ragin discovers in his turn, having entered the space of the ward and into dialogue with a madman, is exceptionally mundane and self-evident: it is painful to be abused.

The overall narrative strategy of the story is calculated to achieve a similar effect of discovery on readers. The most notable technique for achieving this aim is Chekhov's careful manipulation of how we see his characters through a crafty handling of narrative point of view and voice. The story opens with a distinct narrator, the oddness of which at this stage of Chekhov's career surely signals that something special is taking place.[38] This I-narrator expresses his own likes and dislikes, for instance, of Gromov: "I like his broad pale face with high cheekbones [. . .] I like the man himself" (9; S 8:74);[39] he addresses a "you," the reader, in a perpetual present tense, and he invites this reader to take a risky expedition into the ward, where "we" will see "them," the madmen.[40] But while presenting the case history of Gromov, the narrator shifts into a free indirect discourse representation of this madman's thoughts, so that the narrator's perspective and voice merge with Gromov's, as in this passage:

He knew of no crime in his past and was confident that in the future he would never be guilty of murder, arson, or theft, but was it not possible to commit a crime by accident, without meaning to, and was not calumny too, or even a judicial error, conceivable? Not without reason does the age-old experience of the people teach that no one is safe from the poorhouse or prison. And, legal procedures being what they are today, a miscarriage of justice is not only quite possible but would be nothing to wonder at. People who have an official, professional relation to other men's suffering—judges, physicians, the police, for example—grow so callous in the course of time, simply from force of habit, that even if they wanted to they would be unable to treat their clients in any but a formal way; in this respect they are not unlike the peasant who slaughters sheep and calves in his back yard, oblivious to the blood. (12–13; S 8:77–78)

The same occurs with Ragin. First his physical appearance is described, and then his biography, after which the narrator shifts to free indirect discourse: "Yes, and why keep people from dying if death is the normal and lawful end of everyone?

What does it matter if some trader or functionary lives an extra five or ten years? If you see medicine's goal as lessening suffering with medicines, then willy-nilly you have to ask: why lessen them?" (*S* 8:85). Beginning with the ninth chapter (*S* 8:94), the narration attaches to Ragin's point of view, where it remains until the very end, when two short paragraphs tell how the doctor's corpse is disposed of after his death (*S* 8:126).

"Ward 6" has always been considered one of Chekhov's most powerful works; its devastating effect on the reader has been attested to by, among many others, Lenin.[41] Might not this potency issue from Chekhov's handling of narrative point of view and voice, from his trick of beginning the story with a chatty narrator who distances himself and the reader ("we") from the madmen ("they"), but subsequently merges the narrator's and the reader's perspective with that of the madmen? Just as the doctor enters the asylum and begins speaking of himself and Gromov as "we," the reader is slotted into Ragin's perspective in a process that culminates with the shocking experience of his beating and last moments from the internal point of view.

This formal aspect of the story is well suited to the theme, expressed in virtually identical comments (cited previously) by both Gromov and Ragin, of the injustices that occur as the result of how people in responsible positions *see* others. To be seen, they know, whether by physician or judge, results in a selfhood fatally overwhelmed by the pathological identity attributed by that professional's system of knowledge; to repeat Ragin's formulation, it is "a vicious circle you'll never get out of" (*S* 8:119). The entire project of degeneration theory and the new discipline of criminal anthropology were epitomized by just such a deterministic labeling of subjects: certain physical characteristics and modes of behavior marked subjects as *essentially* criminals and madmen. Supported by photographic tables of degenerate types, it was a discourse in which the visibility of pathology to the trained eye was key, and which provided the professionals wielding it extreme distance from and mastery over those they studied.

Chekhov clearly saw the dangers of this attitude in medical practice, as indicated in his autobiographical statement to Grigorii Rossolimo: "If I were a teacher [at a medical school], I would try to draw my students as deeply as possible into the realm of the patient's subjective feelings, and I think that could really be of use to the students."[42] His understanding of how it feels to be ill, Chekhov explained to Rossolimo, comes from his own bodily ailments, which cause him sufferings "rarely comprehensible to a doctor." To make them comprehensible to students, Chekhov proposes applying in the medical sphere techniques he has developed as an author of prose fiction, and the way he conceives using subjective narration in medical education tells us something about the special value he understands it to have in his narrative poetics. It also defines

Chekhov's narrative strategy in "Ward 6," where the official attitude in ethical life is associated with third-person impersonal narration. This handling of narrative point of view provokes a slight digression regarding the story's connection with Tolstoy.

"Ward 6" is often viewed as a polemic with Tolstoy, in which the failure of Ragin's quietism indicts Tolstoy's doctrine of non-resistance to evil. But Chekhov's aim of inoculating against the "official attitude" by drawing the reader "as deeply as possible into the realm of the patient's subjective feelings," and his narrative strategy for doing so, are borrowed directly from Tolstoy and are entirely consonant with the latter's thought. "Ward 6" recalls Tolstoy's story "The Death of Ivan Il'ich" ("Smert' Ivana Il'icha," 1886) precisely in its dramatization of this theme through manipulation of narrative point of view. There too the reader begins with maximum distance on Ivan, who has already died: the story opens with Ivan's colleagues learning this fact from a newspaper. But the narration circles back in time and gradually assumes the point of view of Ivan, whose consciousness is then followed into death. In "The Death of Ivan Il'ich," as in "Ward 6," this formal device drives home the central theme of the difference between seeing others from the outside, officially, with a cold objective eye — as Ivan Il'ich used to do in his juridical profession, and as happens to him as a patient — and from the inside, with empathy. Here it is worth recalling from the preceding chapter that finding a path between these two poles of seeing was a central theme of Veresaev's memoir of a physician's education.

Chekhov's biographical digressions regarding both Gromov and Ragin further condition how the reader understands their psychopathologies. In terms of the fundamental opposition between "nurture" and "nature," Chekhov lays the groundwork for an environmental rather than a hereditary understanding of the psychopathology of both Gromov and Ragin.

Ragin was forced into medicine by a domineering father, a man of the positivistic 1860s; his own strongly felt vocation was for philosophy and theology, pursuits far more representative of the cultural values dominating the last decade of the century. If Ragin is in no sense *like* his father — there is no evidence of hereditary influence — his whole life has nevertheless issued from the will of his father; he has accepted the father's authority and assumed his professional identity. His quietism, his acceptance of what life has dealt him, follows from this initial breaking of his character. In this sense Gromov's accusation that Ragin has never experienced pain is shortsighted, and Ragin's own mistaken acknowledgment of this as fact betrays repression. Ragin, like all the characters shut away in Ward 6, has indeed suffered a debilitating loss, and the peculiarities of his lifestyle, read as symptomatic behavior, might be understood as belated defenses against it. His acceptance of the will of the city fathers derives from the lesson he learned in regard to his own; and the philosophy of stoicism might well appeal to him because it promises that he will never again suffer the pain that resulted from the contest with his father. Having been coerced out of the religious sphere into the scientific one of his father and the generation of the 1860s, Ragin responds by shaping his life into a private ritual of reading, alcohol consumption, and repetitive thoughts and utterances.[43] The conduct of his professional life as a physician constitutes a kind of passive resistance to the will of his father: he is not responsible to his duties, nor does he advance financially, as did his father. If his father has ordered him to be a physician, so be it, but as a physician he will be a failure.

It is remarkable how often students (and the occasional scholar) will speak of Ragin as having gone insane simply because he lands in a psychiatric ward.[44] But one can talk about psychopathology in the doctor's case, and it seems quite clear that Chekhov—who made it a point of pride to construct his characters in harmony with a medically verisimilitudinous psychological code—has provided cues to make sense of that pathology in terms not of heredity but of personal history, and in particular as that relates to the father.

This is not to define Ragin's passivity as a strictly psychological fact. There is also an insidious complicity between the scientific doctrines of evolution and devolution, so central to the discourse of Ragin's profession, and Ragin's personal inclinations. In theory, the prospect of degeneration provided a powerful theoretical argument against therapy. Thus Veresaev devotes a chapter in his memoir to the ambiguous evolutionary function of medicine:

> Already we have to hear more and more often the cry raised amongst doctors and anthropologists, that medicine is terribly one-sided and that its usefulness to mankind is open to grave question. "Medicine benefits the individual at the expense of the type." Mother Nature is prodigal and careless: she casts numberless creatures upon the world, not caring much as to the perfection of each specimen; the task of weeding out and destroying the unsuccessful and unfit is left to merciless life. And it is here that medicine appears upon the scene and strains all its energies to frustrate this work.
>
> A woman in child-bed may have narrow hips and she cannot give birth; she and her child must perish; medicine steps in and saves both, and thus enables women with bad, narrow hips, unadapted for childbirth, to multiply. The higher the infantile death-rate, which medicine so energetically combats, the surer is the next generation of being purged of all weakly and sickly organisms. The syphilitic, tuberculous, rickety, mentally infirm and nervous individuals, cured through the good offices of medicine, breed and produce a puny and nervous degenerated posterity. All these weaklings who, although they have been preserved, are rotten to

the core, mix and cross with the healthy and thus conduce to the rapid impairing of the race in general. And every new success of medicine will accelerate this downward progress of deterioration.[45]

Ragin has it both ways at once: he entertains progressive visions of a bright distant time when there will be no more madhouses, prisons, barred windows, or hospital gowns, but meanwhile he acquiesces to an immutable, deadly nature. This works because his perspective is scientific and theoretical to such a degree that everything temporal and of this world—in particular, the realm of the ethical—dissolves before the eternal laws of nature. And just as the elaboration of the law of tooth and claw in human society allowed the British to justify exploitation of colonized peoples and withhold social aid from their own lower classes, the principle of natural selection facilitates Ragin's dismissal of patients' (and his own) sufferings; it is a clinician's excuse. In this sense the character of Dr. Ragin greatly resembles von Koren in "Duel," with the difference that Ragin neither second-guesses nor pretends to execute nature's will.

What Ragin cannot dissolve in scientific abstraction, however, is precisely that with which he has always most sought to come to terms—the cruel awareness of his own eventual extinction, prefigured in the painful loss of his forcibly abandoned vocation, and accepted prematurely when he agrees to enter the asylum at the story's end:

> Oh, why is man not immortal? he thinks. Why these brain centers and their convolutions, why vision, speech, feeling, genius, if all this is destined to go into the ground, ultimately to grow cold together with the earth's crust, and then for millions of years to whirl with it around the sun without aim or reason? Surely it is not necessary, merely for the sake of this cooling and whirling, to draw man, with his superior, almost godlike intelligence, out of oblivion, and then, as if in jest, to turn him into clay.
>
> The transmutation of matter [*obmen veshchestv*]! But what cowardice to console oneself with that surrogate for immortality! The unconscious processes which take place in nature are beneath even human stupidity, for in stupidity there is at least consciousness and will, while in these processes there is absolutely nothing. (25; *S* 8:90–91)

Ragin's musings raise questions that cannot be answered outside theological discourse; indeed, they provide that discourse's raison d'être. But he meditates in an altogether different language. Although Chekhov's commentators identify this rejection of immortality as a polemical allusion to the Roman stoic Marcus Aurelius (*S* 8:448), the notion of "transmutation of forms" also echoes contemporary scientific ideas on the propagation and evolution of species. In personal-psychological terms, Ragin's compulsively repeated posing of questions in a language in which the possibility of an answer is already foreclosed verges on masochism. Since he has been barred in a sense by his father from the notions of immortality offered by religion and transcendental philosophy, and has rejected that offered, in its own limited way, by biology, the constant horizon of his thoughts and worldview is all the more so death—the end not just of any individual but of life as such.

Indeed, Ragin's whole life is oriented toward ends; he even reads his medical journal from the back first.[46] Such an "ends" perspective would have been appropriate had Ragin pursued his vocation for theology and the life of the mind; for a physician, however, it proves disastrous. After Ragin loses his position and descends into poverty, imagining that the end no longer serves to shut out the present moment's suffering, "in an effort to stifle his contemptible feelings he [. . .] tried to imagine some spirit flying through space a million years hence, passing over the globe, looking down and seeing nothing but clay and bare rocks. Everything—culture and moral law—would have vanished, leaving not so much as a burdock growing. Of what consequence then was the insignificant Khobotov, the oppressive friendship of Mikhail Averianych, or his shame before a shopkeeper? It was all trivial, mere nonsense. But such reasoning no longer helped" (49–50; S 8:116).

This thematic node juxtaposing time, progress, and subjectivity with their negation is reflected in the story's ironic plot structure. When Ragin is committed to the ward, where time is irrelevant, his own personal history may be said to have come to an end. But only now does the doctor begin to appreciate the meaning of the time he has been living through. Hitherto, in keeping with his apocalyptic perspective, he had been living outside of it, according to a routine composed of present-tense imperfective (in this case, iterative, which is to say ahistorical) verbs: "His life passes thus" (S 8:85–93). The very narrative of "Ward 6" begins, as it were, twice, first in a passage framed in the present tense of the reader, where the narrator invites us to follow him into the hospital, and once again when it is revealed that the doctor has been visiting the psychiatric ward. Aside from the brief anamneses of Gromov and Ragin in the exposition, narrative structured by consecutive time and reported in the past tense truly commences with Ragin's accidental visit to the ward, where he meets and becomes interested in Gromov. This is the plot's *zaviazka,* or complication; at this moment the temporal movement of the narrative converges with a chain of causes and effects ending in the doctor's commitment and death.

In Chekhov's treatment of Gromov, too, illness, worldview, and politics are all correlated with a personal history in which relations to the father are key. First, there is a hereditary disjunction: whereas Gromov's father was a "solid and prosperous man" (*S* 8:75), Gromov "never, not even in his early years as a student, struck one as a healthy person. He was always pale, thin, subject to colds, he ate little and slept poorly" (*S* 8:76). Since Chekhov always insisted on the mutual implication of the physical and the psychological,[47] Gromov's frail constitution might be adduced as a source of his mental illness. But this proves something of a red herring, since in the physical sense Gromov turns out to be the fittest of his family; he survives conditions that kill the rest of them, and the robust Ragin as well.

If heredity explains nothing here, as with Ragin the key to Gromov's psychopathology appears to be a dynamic of identification with his father. Gromov's paranoid delusions hinge on the obsessive thought that he will be considered guilty of a crime he has not committed. This idea takes hold of him after seeing many shackled prisoners escorted by guards: "Previously Ivan Dmitrich very often encountered prisoners and every time they aroused feelings of sympathy and awkwardness, but this time the meeting produced some sort of special, strange impression. For some reason it suddenly seemed to him that they might put him in leg irons and lead him to prison through the mud" (*S* 8:77). Gromov's illness is connected with a faculty for seeing that facilitates empathy for and even identification with the person observed. He takes to an extreme the viewpoint that Chekhov would have taught to medical school students; his psychopathology is a more ineluctable version of the hypochondria that, for a brief period, gripped Veresaev as a medical student. It does not help that Gromov is acutely aware of how the official gaze functions, and the way he imagines himself seen with this official gaze—the core of his paranoiac delusions—is supremely realistic, all the more so since Gromov's own father was a criminal who perished as a result of his indictment for forgery and embezzlement (*S* 8:75). Gromov's very natural identification with his father thus paves the way for seeing himself in the criminals he sees.

The point here is not to introduce some variety of psychoanalytic theory to account for these characters. One would rather ask: What is the nature of the psychological code with which Chekhov is operating? Since the writing of a case history already inevitably involves a process of selection guided by theoretical considerations, we can learn much by the way Chekhov associates a particular psychopathology with a particular history. Chekhov conspicuously grounds illness in a personal-historical way rather than a biological-deterministic one.

In sum, the rhetoric and imagery drawn from the theory of degeneration clearly serves a polemical purpose in "Ward 6": Chekhov invokes that discourse only to undermine it. This was to be expected, given his overt statements on the subject. "I'm tired of listening to disquisitions, and reading phonies like Max

Nordau makes me sick," he wrote Suvorin (27 March 1894). A similar parodic strategy can be found in Chekhov's epistolary description of his dinner with one of "the most committed Lombrosians on the Russian medical scene," Dr. Praskov'ia Tarnovskaia.[48] His evaluation of this woman was remarkably nasty: "If she were stripped naked and painted green, she'd be a swamp frog. After a chat with her, I mentally crossed her off my list of physicians" (letter to M. P. Chekhova, 22 July 1888). Laura Engelstein cautiously suggests, "Perhaps Chekhov, himself a physician, projected his distaste for her view of human nature onto her physiognomy";[49] and the language Chekhov uses proves her correct. He "crossed her off" after talking with her, so it was clearly Tarnovskaia's ideas that rankled him. And in stripping this woman and calling her a "swamp frog," he does more than remark her obesity: he categorizes this person's inner qualities on the basis of her physical characteristics, as per the Lombrosians, and he associates this theorist of degeneration with amphibians, lowly creatures on the evolutionary scale. In short, Chekhov cuts to the dehumanizing heart of Tarnovskaia's ideas by assuming their very language.

So too in the 1894 story "On the Country Estate" ("V usad'be"), the "incorrigible Darwinist" Rashevich, who considers himself, as a nobleman, the peak of evolutionary progress, observes "strict sexual selection" in the choice of a husband for his daughter. When lower classes reach into the spheres of arts and sciences unsuited to them, he argues, then they become ill and degenerate, and the level of culture falls. But it is Rashevich who, virtually bankrupt and disliked by all, is the degenerate; his neighbors (and, at the story's end, even his own daughters) refer to him as "the toad" (*zhaba*).

"The Black Monk"

Chekhov's deeply personal engagement with the legacy of Darwin continues in the 1894 story "The Black Monk" ("Chernyi monakh"). One of Chekhov's oddest texts and among the most resistant to interpretation,[50] "Black Monk" has often been understood in connection with Chekhov's biography; in it readers who were close to Chekhov presumed to glimpse his inner life. One such intrusion provoked a defensive explanation of its origin, with Chekhov writing Aleksei Suvorin, whose wife had seen the work as evidence of its author's ailing psyche: "It seems I'm mentally healthy [. . .] I wrote 'Black Monk' without any despondent thoughts, in cold meditation. The desire to depict a case of megalomania [*maniia velichiia*] just came to me" (25 January 1894). It is more than a little ironic, however, that Chekhov's attempt to deflect the lay diagnosis of Suvorin's wife reveals that the image of the black monk floating across a field had come to him in a dream: his disavowal of the personal significance of the tale in fact suggests quite the contrary (even if we accept his explanation that he dreamt the black monk because "he eats too much at dinner"). His brother Mikhail, to whom Chekhov reported the dream immediately afterwards, recalls him as having been quite shaken by it; Mikhail also associates the theme of the garden in "Black Monk" with Chekhov's ambitious and painstaking horticultural efforts at Melikhovo.[51]

What truly allows us to see Chekhov in this story, however, is its link with his proposal a decade earlier for a "History of Sexual Dominance." "Black Monk" is structured around the same terms and oppositions that shaped the early Chekhov's thoughts on nature, gender difference, and progress, as documented in the letter to his brother Aleksandr. In "Black Monk" the grandiose projects and the very selves of two high-achieving male characters—one an agronomist, the other a philosopher—inflate preposterously and collapse, and this fatal dynamic is associated with how each sees the feminine in its embodiment as the young woman they both love (as daughter, sister, and wife) and the trope-laden object of their professional gazes: nature, the realm of the ideal.

Much of the story's rhetoric derives more or less directly from Buckle's essay "The Influence of Women on the Progress of Knowledge." Chekhov's method is to confound the opposite extremes of what Buckle called distinctively male and female, subverting the English theorist's gender associations and optimistic view of their interaction. This is not surprising, since Chekhov already disagrees with Buckle in his outline for a history of sexual dominance. But this story's encounter with the feminine also reevaluates Chekhov's own early scientific theories, and, significantly, his ambitions as well. His exploration of the theme of degeneration—the negative side of evolutionary theory's consequences for humanity—retroactively ironizes the self-aggrandizing faith in natural law and the scientific approach, fed by a particular view of the opposite gender, expressed in his plan for the truly megalomaniacal "History."

The story begins with the return, after five years' absence, of the scholar Kovrin to the estate of his guardian, the noted horticulturist Pesotskii. The visionary and ecstatic Kovrin falls in love with and marries Pesotskii's daughter, who as a little girl was like a young sister to him; the results are catastrophic. The story's gothic subcurrents involving incest and the devil, and its play with the "paradise lost" theme have not gone unnoticed.[52] But if Pesotskii's garden recalls others of literary—especially romantic—tradition, what really distinguishes this garden is its positivistic, late-nineteenth-century twist. Chekhov's presentation of the garden—indeed, the whole story—is structured around the oppositions between woman's idealism and man's materialism, between the romantic, philosophical, and timeless, and the positivistic and historical; between

Mother Nature and the science of man. Pesotskii's garden is an apotheosis of the male scientific gaze, and it is also an artificial paradise, a technological feat of extremely ambivalent meaning. It is for good reason that Pesotskii, who has mastered Mother Nature, feels that disaster menaces his garden at every moment (S 8:230): the artificial paradise is always on the verge of apocalypse,[53] and the otherworldly overtones pervading Pesotskii's estate should be interpreted in this context.

The estate comprises three gardens. The ornamental and commercial gardens are surrounded by a "gloomy and severe" English garden, which ends at a "desolately [*neliudimo*] glistening" river's "precipitous, steep, clayey bank, on which grew pines with bared roots looking like shaggy paws" (those of Cerberus?); here "there was always the feeling that if you just sat down you'd write a ballad." The other two gardens appear as man-made freaks of nature. "The decorative part of the garden, which Pesotskii himself scornfully called trifles, had produced a fairy-tale impression on Kovrin back in his childhood. What oddities, refined monstrosities [*urodstva*], and mockeries of nature! Here there were espaliers of fruit trees [. . .] arches, monograms, candelabras, and even '1862' in plum trees—a cipher standing for the year when Pesotskii first took up gardening" (S 8:226). This multiply signifying date represents an intrusion of historical time that is entirely out of place in the garden of Judeo-Christian tradition, which is before time, and to which, in the Christian millennial context, man and woman will return only when "time shall be no more."[54] The ornamental garden is a Disneyland construction of nature, a projection of human whims and fantasies of form realized through technological manipulations—an anti-Eden. The commercial garden, by contrast, which "every year brought Egor Semenych [Pesotskii] several thousand in clear profits," is Eden as an industrial hell, a terrible perversion of nature. Kovrin finds it filled with a "black, thick, acrid smoke" protecting the fruit trees from frost, and he encounters workers "who were wandering in the smoke like shades" (S 8:227–28; similar visions of hell will be addressed in the next chapter).

When one thinks of a nineteenth-century industrial hell, one thinks of England, home to Darwin, Spencer, and Buckle. But the Pesotskii estate is both scientific and English in yet another sense: not only does Pesotskii put the principles of Darwin to work in his scientific and commercial activities, but also the very space in which he lives is emblematic of the argument of Darwin's *Origin of Species*.

Thus, the division of the estate into areas of artificial cultivation and natural development—the ornamental and commercial gardens in the first instance, and the surrounding English garden—reflects the key analogy drawn by Darwin between artificial selection in the breeding of plants and animals and natural selection in the wild. The "monstrosities" of Pesotskii's ornamental garden echo the "monstrosities" Darwin discusses in the opening chapters of *Origin,* "Variation under Domestication" and "Variation under Nature." Just as these "trifles," as Pesotskii calls them, constitute a final proof of the horticulturalist's powers, Darwin's approach to questions of species definition, variation, and evolution focused attention on monstrosities rather than dismissing them as incomprehensible aberrations, or as otherworldly, as had essentialists since Aristotle.[55]

Moreover, the space of Pesotskii's estate ends precisely where Darwin's *Origin* ends: at a riverbank that symbolizes, also, an epistemological boundary, the limit beyond which scientific seeing gives way to the theological. In Chekhov's story the transcendent vision of the black monk appears from across this boundary to Pesotskii's scientistic world, while the very last paragraph of *Origin of Species* begins: "It is interesting to contemplate a tangled bank, clothed with many plants of many kinds, with birds singing on the bushes, with various insects flitting about, and with worms crawling through the damp earth, and to reflect that these elaborately constructed forms, so different from each other, and dependent upon each other in so complex a manner, have all been produced by laws acting around us." The paragraph concludes: "There is grandeur in this view of life, with its several powers, having been originally breathed by the Creator into a few forms or into one; and that, whilst this planet has gone cycling on according to the fixed law of gravity, from so simple a beginning endless forms most beautiful and most wonderful have been, and are being evolved."[56]

The peculiar juxtapositions of nature and science, Eden and apocalypse, in "Black Monk" both rely on and problematize the Darwinian, Bucklean, and Spencerian terms that had structured Chekhov's projected "History of Sexual Dominance." The discourses that empowered the young medical student's professional seeing—in particular with regard to a feminine object—achieve an uncanny concreteness in this story, as the rhetoric of Darwin's argument transmutes into the spatial setting of Chekhov's fictional text, and the individual psychological dynamic accompanying such seeing becomes a case history in megalomania.

For example, the young Chekhov viewed socioeconomic, intellectual, and creative inequalities or asymmetries as departures from nature's impulse toward equilibrium; in Pesotskii's commercial garden, where the trees are arrayed with perfect symmetry "like ranks of soldiers," and in the geometric shapes of the ornamental garden, symmetry has become a sign of nature's corruption. As Pesotskii's former ward, Kovrin is himself a product of this estate, an unnaturally cultivated human being, a hothouse flower.

Buckle asserts that a penchant for the ideal can be the gift of heredity and rearing by a "remarkable mother."[57] Kovrin had such a mother, and Pesotskii traces Kovrin's genius to her talents. "Blood means a lot," he remarks (S 8:246). But Kovrin's physiological predisposition to tuberculosis proves a far more significant inheritance, though even here assumptions about heredity mislead: after his first hemorrhages Kovrin "was not particularly frightened," because his mother had lived more than ten years from the time she first displayed such symptoms. Nevertheless, he will die within a few weeks.

In Buckle's scheme, women are more "deductive," and their influence on coldly inductive males is held to offer positive benefits. But the black monk, a projection of Kovrin's mind, pushes deductive logic to such an extreme that it can no longer conceivably engage in dialogue with positivistic thought: "I exist in your imagination, and your imagination is a part of nature, which means I exist in nature as well" (S 8:241). This syllogism appears well crafted and succinct, but because of shifty premises it arrives at a conclusion so sharply opposed to the empirical approach that its logic takes precedence over its conclusion; it is a model of deductive reasoning, and of its hazards.

At the university Kovrin lectures on psychology, which in the Russia of his time was becoming a hard (inductive) science, in effect a branch of physiology. His vocation, however, and his own research are in the area of philosophy, so that his professional identity involves a contradictory mixture of Buckle's key terms.

As a young natural scientist Chekhov wrote that only males create; Buckle's argument had proclaimed "the intention of combating this proposition,"[58] of showing that woman's superior deductive capabilities and instinctive connection with the realm of the ideal provide a necessary ingredient for the creative intellectual progress of innately inductive man (never mind for the moment that such progress occurs exclusively in men, in whose thought the influence of remarkable women merely provides a necessary supplementary factor). "Black Monk" undermines both positions, insofar as it frames Kovrin's creativity—deriving, according to Pesotskii, from his mother—as a psychopathological symptom. When Kovrin sees the black monk he says, "I didn't know that my imagination was capable of creating such phenomena" (S 8:241). Kovrin's hallucination demonstrates his triumphant grasp of the transcendent and ideal: it is inspired by the serenade of Gaetano Braga (1829–1907) about a *girl* of "morbid imagination" who perceives a "divine harmony incomprehensible to us mortals" in sounds she hears in the garden at night (S 8:232). The black monk tells Kovrin that he likes him because "you serve eternal truth" (S 8:241); and when Kovrin dies, it is because "his weak human body had already lost its balance and could no longer serve as an envelope [*obolochka*] for his genius" (S 8:257).

Kovrin's very name—from *kovër*—seems connected with this idea of *obolochka*, or, to stretch the point, the "veils" (*pokryvala*) before which, in Buckle's phrase, positivistic man trembles: "We are too apt to speak as if we had penetrated into the sanctuary of truth and raised the veil of the goddess, when in fact we are still standing, coward-like, trembling before the vestibule, and not daring from very fear to cross the threshold of the temple. The highest of our so-called laws of nature are as yet purely empirical."[59] The Pesotskii family name, by contrast, conjures up the irreducibly material: sand (*pesok*), gravel, and dust. In Buckle's terms it recalls that very "dust in which we are too prone to grovel," and out of which woman's natural tendencies of mind can help raise humanity.[60]

The year Pesotskii began his vocation (and inscribed into his ornamental garden), 1862, marks the gardener as a "man of the sixties," that generation distinguished by its faith in the material and the practical, and by its attachment to Buckle, Spencer, and Darwin. Still a year before Darwin's *Origin* would be published in Russia, knowledge of it was nevertheless already widely disseminated. And it is perhaps more than coincidence that 1862 is the year in which Buckle met a premature death: he succumbed to typhoid fever in Damascus, after a journey through Egypt and Palestine—precisely that region where Kovrin's legendary black monk first appeared—and so left unrealized his monumental project of a history of civilization, just as both Kovrin's and Pesotskii's ambitions come to naught. If there is something of the shade of Buckle in the black monk, no figure could better convey both the seductive promise of genius and fame (especially in progressive circles) and the eventual catastrophic collapse of this promise.

Pesotskii is an agribusinessman who has put Mother Nature to work and is profiting handsomely through the cult of labor inaugurated by Chernyshevskii's Rakhmetov and the "men of the sixties." In his anti-Eden all toil in the garden, especially Pesotskii: in spite of his many laborers, he himself "does everything. I work from morning to night" (*S* 8:236). Like Kovrin he writes scholarly articles, but their titles betray a practical, materialist orientation: "On Catch Cropping," "A Few Words on the Remarks of Mr. Z. Regarding Respading the Soil for New Gardens," "More on Dormant Bud Grafting" (*S*8: 237). In the context of the story's play around the opposition between materialism and philosophical idealism, the Russian term for catch cropping, *promezhutochnaia kul'tura* (literally, "intermediate" or "in-between" culture), appears as an oxymoronic pun on the word "culture," a materialist abnegation of the continuity of transcendent cultural values, "eternal truth." Moreover, the idea of intermediate forms was precisely what various essentialist critiques of Darwin's theory found unacceptable—and unproved.[61]

Pesotskii inveighs against theorists, the "scholarly ignorance of our patented gentlemen gardeners, who observe nature from the heights of their academic departments" (S 8:238). Kovrin is just such an academic, and when he dies, it will be on a balcony, overlooking the sea from the heights.

The influence of Tania Pesotskaia, the story's chief female character, proves directly opposite to that attributed to women by Buckle; indeed, as the daughter of a remarkable positivist father, she already inverts Buckle's terms. And it is she who insists that Kovrin return to reality through medical treatment, reversing the gender positions in the grandiose fantasy scenario of the therapeutic encounter which animates Chekhov's "History of Sexual Dominance." (In this sense Tania is doubled by Suvorin's wife, who, having read "Black Monk," urged "poor Anton Pavlovich" to see to his mental health [P 5:265].) Kovrin's last visual image of Tania is as "walking, living relics [zhivye moshchi]." If at the end Kovrin dies because his body can no longer contain the soul of his genius—a genius in quest of that ideal expressed in the millennial legend of the black monk and Braga's serenade—Tania lives on as a soul-less body; she has been reduced to a *material* essence. Whereas the term *moshchi* is most often associated with a saint's relics, that bodily remainder whose whole function is to signify the spiritual and so offer worshippers a connection between the material and the ideal, between earth and heaven, for Kovrin, Tania as *moshchi* is reduced to a nagging, unpleasant memory. The monk, then, as a phenomenon immaterial and beyond the everyday bounds of time and space, is Tania's antithetic double. Kovrin starts seeing him at the same time he falls in love with Tania; and he loses all affection for his wife when the monk's visits cease.

The legend of the black monk presents itself to Kovrin's consciousness as a memory of something that never happened: he cannot recall reading or hearing of it anywhere. Indeed, Kovrin lives outside of time. He is not worried about when he will die (ten years seems more than ample), and he revels in his insomnia, that is, he does not accede to nature's most fundamental alternation of night and day. His delusions of grandeur and hallucinations regarding the monk, who is supposed to appear at intervals of one thousand years, are structured by millennial time and borrow from the Book of Revelations. In this sense he lives in the same chronotope as Pesotskii, who feels his garden constantly threatened by apocalypse.

Tania, by contrast, comes to stand for memory as the linkage of matter in mundane time and space. At the story's beginning it is she who knows precisely how long it has been since Kovrin last visited her family estate; at the end, when her letter of indictment reaches Kovrin in the Crimea, "the handwriting on the envelope reminded him how, two or so years ago, he was unjust and cruel." Thereupon follows a whole chain of unpleasant recollections ending with a repetition: "All of this came to memory upon glancing at the familiar handwriting" (S 8:254). Kovrin reads the letter, tears it up, and throws the pieces on the floor, then begins working to calm himself. The bright white scraps of the letter on the floor bother him, so he gathers them up and throws them out the window, only to have the sea breeze return them to his feet. It is as though there were an irreducible materiality to both Tania and her message; and if the shredded letter can no longer contain the message, just as her body as a living mummy no longer appears to contain a soul, this only emphasizes its signifying function as a material, or metonymic, connection with a real history Kovrin would rather forget.

Chekhov too had something to forget. In alluding to the scientific authorities he had cited in his "History of Sexual Dominance," and reversing the values of the key terms and oppositions derived from those thinkers, he recalls and dismisses the scenario that gave life to the early Chekhov's therapeutic fantasy. There is insight in Mme. Suvorin's psychobiographical interpretation of the story, and significance beyond the physiology of digestion, too, in the fact of the story's source in Chekhov's troubling dream. Chekhov operates beyond the ideological plane in addressing Darwin, Spencer, and Buckle; he seeks above all to sever something of his own previous emotional investment in their ideas.

Chekhov wrote Suvorin that the story was about a case of megalomania, but it in fact depicts two: both Kovrin and Pesotskii suffer delusions of grandeur, even if Pesotskii's do not lead to a psychotic break with reality. And yet, these two could indeed be one insofar as they are both partial autobiographical projections of Chekhov: as the physician who wrote about the "music" he had heard in the lectures of his favorite medical professor;[62] the new landowner and active gardener; the creative artist who, unlike the author of a prospectus on sexual dominance, has really made a name for himself in the literary world; the pride of his family; the doted-upon older brother of remarkably close relations with his sister. Both Pesotskii and Kovrin experience dizzying heights and then collapse, essentially as a result of initially triumphant confrontations with that which is figured as feminine: Nature, Tania. The encounter proves calamitous because the two men cannot modulate their sense of self before an imaginary other who appears so promising a subject for their impulse to mastery.

Chekhov saw this dynamic at work in himself, perceived it as dangerous, and exorcised it in his autoanalytic response to the dream of the black monk. What Chekhov once acted out in the letter to his brother containing a proposal for a social Darwinist research project, "Black Monk" depicts with critical distance. As is most apparent in "Duel" and "Ward 6," Chekhov relentlessly frames ideological positions in an individual psychological context. If his projected "History of Sexual Dominance" provided a good example of gender polarities projected from within one individual in accord with that individual's needs, under the cover of scientific verity, then "Black Monk" shows Chekhov reflecting critically on this problem, and on its implications for himself as a creative artist, physician, and man.

"Three Years"

The theme of degeneration plays out in a merchant milieu very close to the Chekhov family's own in the 1895 "Three Years" ("Tri goda"), Chekhov's second-longest narrative.[63] Here is a work in which motifs of seeing and being seen—though occurring overtly and with great prominence—acquire no apparent structuring role. On the contrary, it is their strangeness, their lack of integration into the larger whole that attracts attention. In a narrative that was initially conceived as the subject for a novel, then very deliberately trimmed to *povest'* (long story) scale, these motifs of peeping and peering strike the reader as extraneous and supplemental; they tip us off to undercurrents of meaning that do not fall under the rubric of what has been called the story's central theme, "the sad story of a 'false' [*nenastoiashchego*] capitalist who does not care for his business."[64]

As the title suggests, the key structuring feature of "Three Years" is time. The temporal framework of three years arose at the very start of Chekhov's planning and never changed, even as the novel became a story.[65] If Chekhov's first major story, "Steppe," covered three watershed days in a child's life, these three years reflect a middle-aged appreciation of and resignation toward the ongoing experience of time and loss; thus the story's last words, "We'll live on a bit, and we'll see" (*S* 9:91). What does happen in the course of the three years is handled with a minimum of dramatic tension. The central male character, Laptev—the son of a wealthy Moscow merchant and, like Chekhov, grandson of a serf—falls in love with and marries a woman, Iuliia, who does not share his affection. He becomes accustomed to the rutted life of a marriage without love, then grows detached from his wife as she grows more fond of him. At the end of the story, the pair's initial positions have reversed, though the last lines suggest that Laptev is not entirely indifferent: he voyeuristically observes his close friend Iartsev staring at Iuliia's "beautiful neck" and wonders what further trials the future holds for him (*S* 9:91).

It is over time, too, that Laptev's siblings and father are attacked by grave, slow-acting diseases that, it is emphasized, manifest themselves only with the passage of years: his sister dies of breast cancer after surgery and a period of remission; Laptev's brother undergoes a perplexing personality change, but only toward the end of the story clearly succumbs to mental illness, perhaps as the result of a brain tumor (Laptev expects him to die in a few months); and Laptev's father is gradually going blind. In the story's handling of the characters' diseases, as well as in its final passage, the trope of sight is central: the invisible, unnoticed, or merely hinted at becomes manifest, overt, seen. But the motif of seeing and being seen occurs in far more literal and interesting ways as well.

The character most closely associated with such motifs is Kostia Kochevoi, orphaned at seven, raised by the Laptevs, and in effect their adoptive younger sibling. Trained as a lawyer and working as a barrister's assistant, he first appears in the narrative engaged in his morning routine of lifting weights and peeping at the apartment of a French family across the way (*S* 9:49). "What did you see today through the binoculars?" Iuliia Sergeevna later asks Kostia. "Today, nothing, but yesterday the old Frenchman himself took a bath" (*S* 9:53). Kostia subsequently takes up photography with a passion that moves him to take pictures of his friends daily and causes him to lose weight from anxiety over the difficulties of mastering this craft (*S* 9:79). And Kostia is a sightseer who travels to the world's fair in Chicago that Chekhov himself had hoped to attend.[66]

Kostia's drive to see is at once an individual character trait and a motif associable with a broader pattern in the story. This active variant of the drive to see is in consonance with a personality that—in an echo of Chekhov's autobiographical remark about "squeezing the slave" out of his own veins—endeavors to overcome the conditions of his birth, early upbringing, and inheritance; for Kostia's father had been an impoverished, alcoholic minor official who drank himself to death when his son was only seven. Kostia's peeping occurs hand in hand with his morning gymnastics and the "fifteen drops of some sort of medicine" he takes daily with a "worried face" (*S* 9:49), all part of a regimen for mastering his own body, and the world around him, in a heroic struggle to defeat his degenerative inheritance. Kostia persistently aspires to the position of observer, a position whose meaning lies in its opposition to that of the passive object of the other's gaze, the body on which signs of degeneration manifest themselves. So he takes up photography; so he travels to Chicago for the world's fair, a spectacular event that offers fair-goers a vantage point from which they might *see* the whole world. Wanderlust is encoded in Kostia's surname, Kochevoi, which translates as "nomad."

When Kostia does attract the eyes of others, he does so as an aggressive and exhibitionistic subject: the Laptevs are diverted for a day by watching him perform successfully as defense counsel in court (*S* 9:66–67), and "when tipsy he was always very agitated, hollered, gave policemen and cabbies a hard time, sang, and laughed furiously" (*S* 9:70). Kostia has also authored unpublished novels and aspires to fame. But what does he write, and how? "In his novels he described only the countryside and landowners' estates, though he had seen the country

very rarely, only when he would visit acquaintances at their dachas; and he only
once in his life had been to a landowner's estate, when he had traveled to Voloko-
lamsk on legal business. He avoided the element of love, as though he were
ashamed by it, and in his frequent descriptions of nature he loved to use such
expressions as the whimsical outlines of the hills, the odd forms of clouds, or the
chord of mysterious accords" (S 9:51–52). Kostia writes through binoculars, as
it were, avoiding material that might expose his own world and the affective dimensions of his own life. Unlike the early Chekhov, who spoke of masking the
writing self as a means, paradoxically, toward safe self-exposure, Kostia removes
his self from his writing altogether. Writing for him is but another sphere in
which he might appear—if he were to be published—as a commanding perspective on others. His gymnastics, medicines, peeping, and novel writing are at
bottom all of a kind; in him the story's theme of degeneration and its metapoetic reflections on art intersect.

Chekhov told Ivan Bunin that peasants and merchants were particularly susceptible to degeneration, and he directed him to "Three Years" for elaboration.[67]
The central character Laptev understands the illnesses, self-doubt, and general
unhappiness that assault his clan over the course of the story as clear signs of degeneration. He attributes his own timidity, lack of confidence, and pervasive
feeling of guilt to the fact that "I am a slave, the grandson of a serf" (S 9:75), and
he explains the vast constitutional difference between his formidable father and
himself as resulting from the inheritance of acquired characteristics: his young
mother conceived and gave birth to him when she was "already exhausted by
constant fear" (S 9:39), utterly beaten down by life with the family's patriarch.
"What sort of nerves and what sort of blood have we inherited?" he asks his
brother. "You and I will do well if we don't have children. Oh, if only God would
grant this distinguished merchant clan to end with us!" (S 9:80–81).

The tale of the family's decline includes odd digressive discussions between
characters about the possibilities for human agency in progressive social evolution, which recall Chekhov's early project for a "History of Sexual Dominance."
In one instance Iartsev utters, with slight variation, words that Chekhov had
written in his notebook during the Bogimovo summer (1891):

> As a consequence of differences in climates, energies, tastes, ages, equality among
> people is physically impossible. But a cultured person can make those inequalities
> harmless, just as he has already done with swamps and bears. One scientist man-
> aged to train a cat, a mouse, a pigeon hawk, and a sparrow to eat from one dish,
> and we must hope that education will accomplish the same with people. Life
> marches ever forward, culture achieves huge triumphs before our eyes, and obvi-
> ously there will come a time when, for example, the current situation of factory

workers will appear as much an absurdity as now does serfdom, when girls were traded for dogs. (S 9:56)

Chekhov's notebook entry includes the further remark: "Equality among people will never be possible. It therefore follows that inequality is an immutable law of nature" (S 17:9). The key premise of Chekhov's early social Darwinist thinking—nature's penchant for equality—now appears to have been abandoned. In both Chekhov's notebook entry and the remarks of his fictional character, the focus is no longer on seeing biological differences but on how difference is seen culturally; and it is in the latter realm that inequality is to be addressed. But even if we are to accept this view as Chekhov's own in the early to mid-1890s—a provisional assumption at best[68]—such optimistic reflections on the evolutionary potential for human beings is more than balanced in "Three Years" by evidence of regression.

The Laptev patriarch, even as he goes blind, boasts of his lifelong vigor (he never had to visit a doctor) and wonders at his children's feebleness (S 9:84). Blindness is perhaps the dominant motif of the Laptev family: their warehouse is dark; their affairs move forward almost of their own volition; Laptev himself would prefer to turn a blind eye to his past and the commercial enterprise he is inheriting, "to walk away, and never return here" (S 9:90). When at the end Laptev takes control of his father's business, he accepts this legacy as though it were an inherited disease, and is certain that "the millions and the business [. . .] will ruin his life and make a slave of him" (S 9:89). Light allows Kostia to peep at neighbors and snap pictures; in the dark, a damaging past returns to afflict the present. Laptev's childhood memories of oppression and cruelty paralyze and repress him; his mentally ill brother Fedor has been "seeing" their dead sister (S 9:82); while walking through the dark from a dacha outside Moscow toward the city, Iartsev (who has been contemplating writing a historical drama) imagines the forest he is traversing to be inhabited still by figures from centuries past, and he is seized by the hallucinatory image of a Polovets raider kidnapping a young Russian girl. This vision is an atavistic throwback or phylogenetic memory, a projection onto historical seeing of the processes of biological degeneration. "Moscow is a city that will have yet much to suffer," he remarks without thinking, seized by the vision of a historical future haunted by returns of the past (S 9:70).

If in "Three Years" the hidden and hereditary becomes visible, this motif of seeing also intersects—though in an odd and rather localized way—with the story's theme of art. Laptev is an amateur painter, Kostia writes novels of peasant and landowner life for the desk drawer, and Iartsev is working on a historical novel as the story ends. At times the characters discuss art in ways that clearly reflect on the narrative encompassing them. Thus Kostia calls for literature to have a "serious social objective," continuing, "Those novels and tales where it's all alas and alack, and she fell in love with him, but he fell out of love with her—such works, I say, are worthless and the devil take them all" (S 9:55); but just such a falling in and out of love defines the overarching plot line of "Three Years."

There is also the visit of the Laptevs and Kostia to an exhibition at the school of painting, where Iuliia is taken by a painting that has been identified as recalling Isaac Levitan's *A Quiet Place* (*Tikhaia obitel'* [S 9:457]). The Levitan connection has diverted readers, however, from what the passage appears to say about the seeing of art.

> Iuliia Sergeevna looked at the pictures, like her husband, through her fist or through binoculars, and wondered at how the people in the paintings were as though alive, and the trees, like real ones; but she didn't understand it, it seemed to her that a lot of the paintings at the exhibit were the same, and that the whole aim of art was precisely that the people and objects in paintings, when you looked at them through your fist, stood out like real ones [. . .]
>
> When they were all tired and Laptev went to find Kostia, so as to go home, Iuliia stopped before a small landscape and looked at it indifferently. In the foreground was a little river, across it a timber bridge, and on the other bank, a path that disappeared in the dark grass, a field, and then on the right a bit of woods, and beside it a campfire: it must be the night watchmen. And in the distance, the sunset was burning out.
>
> Iuliia imagined herself walking along the little bridge, then the path, farther and farther, and all around it's quiet: sleepy crakes are calling, in the distance the fire twinkles. And for some reason it suddenly began seeming to her that she had long ago and many times seen these very clouds, which stretched across the red part of the sky, and the forest, and the field, and she suddenly wanted to walk and walk and walk along the path; and there, where the sunset glowed, there rested the reflection of something unearthly, eternal.
>
> "How well this is painted," she said, wondering that the painting had suddenly become comprehensible to her [. . .]
>
> She tried to explain why she liked this landscape so much, but neither her husband nor Kostia understood her. (S 9:65–66)

What is the difference between the way Iuliia and Laptev view the canvases at first—through fisted hands or binoculars—and Iuliia's subsequent experience of the Levitan-like landscape? Their initial postures as consumers of art parallel that of Kostia Kochevoi as producer: they employ a technology of seeing to gain critical distance from and mastery over the object of their viewing. Laptev measures the right and left arms on a painted figure, finds them unequal, and does not hesitate to pronounce critical judgment: "Generally timid in life, he was extremely bold and self-confident at painting exhibitions" (S 9:65). Furthermore, the "binocular" perspective loses sight of the painting's assembly as a whole. While amplifying and replicating the frame separating an aesthetic object from its surroundings—and defining it as a whole from the perspective of its author—they impose arbitrary sub-frames around elements observed through the clenched fist, cutting them off from the rest of the painting.

Standing before the Levitan-like painting, by contrast, Iuliia becomes drawn into the scene she is viewing. It would not be correct to say that she sees the work as a whole, because she also loses sight of the frame separating it from the space in which she is standing. She finds it impossible to articulate why she likes the piece and, having abandoned critical distance, instead projects herself into the painting. Afterwards she sees the rest of the paintings in the exhibit with new eyes, and when she returns home with altered taste, the paintings on the walls of her home no longer please her (S 9:66); that is to say, this experience of art has changed her. To be sure, Levitan was Chekhov's favorite painter and a close friend, and Iuliia's response to the landscape pays tribute to Levitan's talents and impressionist style; it might also be interpreted characterologically as expressing her desire to escape the circumscribed life into which marrying a wealthy Moscow merchant has cast her. But these interpretive matters are ancillary to the bipolar patterns of seeing that Chekhov presents in this passage about consuming art.

The two opposing approaches to art portrayed here find correlation in two different kinds of poetics. And what we learn in the painting exhibition holds no less true for the poetics of fiction.[69] Iuliia's experiencing of art is diametrically opposed to the poetics employed by Kostia as novelist. Read as a mirror in the text (mise en abyme) for Chekhov's own narrative, this episode suggests a desire on Chekhov's part to draw readers into the inner worlds of his characters, as he proposed teaching medical students to enter the subjective worlds of their patients; this would entail rendering, rather than realistic indications of three years' passage, the lived experience of time. But such a programmatic interpretation appears hasty. Seeing is always problematic in Chekhov, and there are vulnerabilities—indeed, a loss of self—associated with Iuliia's position before the landscape. Her ability to so thoroughly enter the scene she is seeing may well be connected with her femininity and her lack of occupation; it invokes the dangers of being seen, or of being overwhelmed by what one sees, that play out in Chekhov's verbal art and life, especially in connection with themes of degeneration.

"Ariadne"

The intersection of evolutionary biology, sociology, and gender first charted in Chekhov's dissertation prospectus appears yet again, and quite overtly so, in the 1895 story "Ariadne" ("Ariadna"). The titular character is a coquettish and manipulative woman, whose trampled and ruined lover, Shamokhin, tells his story to a frame narrator. Although the male is clearly dominated in this tale of sexual inequality, Shamokhin arguably regains the upper hand—or at least attempts to—in the very act of relating his story. The social Darwinian analytic tools deployed in his layman's rhetoric assign him a superior and comprehending view of the phenomenon of Ariadne.

Shamokhin regards Ariadne, and "urban, bourgeois, educated woman" in general, as a degenerate breed: having been largely relieved of the struggle for existence, she is "returning to her primeval condition, already halfway to a human animal, and thanks to her a great deal that has been conquered by human genius has already been lost" (S 9:130). It is not quite accurate to say, however, that she has been relieved of the struggle for existence; rather, that struggle has been reduced to attracting a mate, which, Shamokhin argues (very much along the lines of Pozdnyshev in Tolstoy's "Kreutzer Sonata" of 1889), in effect breeds women for the trait of coquettishness. Shamokhin's collapse before the wiles of this woman, his unmanning, becomes less an individual failing than an inevitable sociobiological consequence of the current social and cultural order.

Scholars have had some difficulty defining Chekhov's position on his character Shamokhin's amorous travails and patently misogynistic theories. Shamokhin's argument regarding woman's backwardness very much resembles Chekhov's own in the dissertation prospectus on sexual inequality, as well as scattered remarks elsewhere.[70] Moreover, suppositions about the story's roots in Chekhov's own relations with Lika Mizinova or Lidiia Iavorskaia have swirled around "Ariadne" from the time of its first publication.[71] The situation is further complicated by an extremely noteworthy narrative structure, in which the persona of the frame narrator is indistinguishable from—indeed, invites conflation with— the person of Chekhov.[72] This insertion of Chekhov's authorial persona into the narrative frame, reminiscent of his handling of the editor figure in the early *Shooting Party,* is utterly uncharacteristic of the late Chekhov and, as we have seen, rather odd for Chekhov at any stage in his career. What are we to make of such an anomaly?

On the face of it, the presence of a stand-in for Chekhov who reacts critically to Shamokhin's tale would seem a distancing device: the frame narrator finds Shamokhin dull, turns away from him, and falls asleep in the midst of the latter's ranting; at one point he even dismisses Shamokhin as a "convinced misogynist" (*S* 9:131), addressing the reader in a way that presumes consonance of values between the frame narrator and the tale's readers and a shared perspective on Shamokhin. In other words, these reactions model the reader's response to Shamokhin and his tale, and they suggest a negative authorial evaluation.

And yet, the stylistic evidence also submits to quite the opposite interpretation. Why, one wants to ask, did Chekhov apparently feel the need to put his figure into the frame while simultaneously distancing himself from what that frame encloses? In other words, rather than a presentation that is neutral or unmarked for personal significance, we have here a narrative in which a personal connection is both suggested and denied. The extraordinary need to assert distance—to represent *his very self* turning his face to the wall and away from his fellow traveler's social Darwinist discourse—might well betray, to borrow from Savely Senderovich's treatment of "Story of an Anonymous Man," "the repression of an identification,"[73] a disavowal of the self who had in fact given voice to these same notions. Indeed, among Chekhov's late works, "Ariadne" shares much stylistically with "Anonymous Man." This commonality goes beyond the first-person narration: Chekhov's plans for the latter story at one time involved the title "Story of My Patient," and called for an epilogue that explained how the frame narrator, not distinguishable from Chekhov himself, came into possession of the anonymous man's manuscript. In short, we see here a stylistic pattern for the handling of particularly sensitive and personal material on Chekhov's part, peculiar conditions under which Chekhov makes his self visible in a fictional narrative.[74]

The Cherry Orchard

The discourse of degeneration, directly countered in many of the late Chekhov's statements on the topic and in his narratives, nevertheless becomes embodied in Chekhov's own speech in some curious and rather ambivalent ways. While he overtly rejected the Lombroso-Nordau camp on scientific and ethical grounds, Chekhov's thinking about his self remained deeply conditioned by the notion of degeneration: recall his characterization of the specific manifestations of his tuberculosis as an inherited trait, or of his brother Misha's sleeplessness during the spring and at summer's end as an atavistic throwback to the time when their ancestors worked in the fields. This is, quite literally, the blood Chekhov had to squeeze out of his veins drop by drop.

By the time Chekhov wrote *Cherry Orchard* (*Vishnevyi sad,* 1904), however, further such self-discipline was futile. Biology had settled the score; his own fatal illness had reached an acute phase. Traditional interpretations of the play understand it as depicting the degeneration and virtual extinction of the entire landowning class. If the work as a whole falls easily under the rubric of degeneration, it is also the case that the theory of degeneration enters this play more subtly, through echoes of the European novelist who is most tightly connected with the theory of degeneration and fin-de-siècle syndromes: once again we encounter the influence of Émile Zola.[75]

Cherry Orchard appears to echo central themes and specific imagery from Zola's *Dr. Pascal* (1893), which Chekhov read and commented on at some length in a letter to Suvorin (11 November 1893). Chief among them is the garden of a family estate, whose trees are cut down and land sold off in small parcels. The study of heredity and degeneration has been the life's work of the eponymous hero of Zola's novel. Data for this study come from Pascal's own family, the Rougon-Macquart clan (which Zola had been chronicling in a series of novels capped by this one), and are elaborated in files on family members, a genealogical tree, and theoretical writings. All this material is kept in a massive oak cupboard, "a period piece from the previous century."[76] This cupboard and its contents, a metaphor also for Zola's own collected writings on the theme of degeneration, is the novel's central image. Described with florid rhetoric, it is directly addressed by the narrator in odic tones, and the novel's culmination involves its emptying out and the burning of its contents by the deceased doctor's mother, who seeks to protect the family's good name.

Zola's cupboard, I would suggest, is echoed in the hundred-year-old *shkaf* (bookcase) so amusingly addressed by Gaev in act 1 of *Cherry Orchard*. In Zola the cupboard is a synecdoche for a degenerate family history, and for the history of France as well; in Chekhov, it has been convincingly argued, the *shkaf* stands for the legacy of Russian literary history and its impact on Gaev's family and on Russia.[77] Gaev salutes this bookcase: "For more than a hundred years directed toward the bright ideals of virtue and justice; your silent summons to fruitful work did not weaken over the course of one hundred years, supporting courage and faith in a better future in our family, and instilling in us the ideals of virtue and social self-consciousness" (*S* 13:207–8). Given the actual situation of Gaev and his family, however, these words acquire a thoroughly ironic accent: his remarks about the progressive ideals embodied by this bookcase must be read with a negative sign, so that instead of a symbol of progress, this *shkaf*, like Zola's, serves as a symbol of degeneration. At times Chekhov used *shkaf* as a metaphor, too, for his own declining body.[78]

There are some striking resemblances between Zola's physician-hero and Chekhov himself; according to Chekhov's biographer Donald Rayfield, "Anton's life at Melikhovo seemed to outsiders an idealization of *Dr. Pascal*."[79] Dr.

Pascal's niece, who eventually becomes his mistress, incarnates the fantasy ad-
dressee of Chekhov's early projected "History of Sexual Dominance" when she
tells her uncle:"I want to thank you . . . Master, you and you alone have made
me what I am. As you have explained to me, so clearly and so often, you have
corrected my hereditary tendencies."[80] Over time both doctors—Chekhov
much more quickly—tempered their lust for such remarkable therapeutic
power, their faith in the possibility of its acquisition through scientific research
into evolution and heredity, and, most important, their pretension to a position
that would not be implicated in the pathology under study: whereas Pascal embarks on his research with the "belief that the title 'Doctor' can displace the surname, freeing the subject from the psycho-pathological inheritance of the
family," his "*hubris,* after all, is exposed by heredity itself—*dégénérescence* brings
him down."[81] One of Dr. Pascal's final acts is to inscribe his own death on his
family tree:"Dies, of heart disease, November 7, 1873."[82] Was not the same impulse to witness and declare one's own death (rather than leave that position to
others) expressed in Chekhov's famous penultimate words in Badenweiler:"Ich
sterbe"?[83] Interestingly, Chekhov speaks of his own ill health in the same letters to Suvorin commenting on Zola's *Dr. Pascal* (24 August 1893, 11 November 1893).

   To be sure, Chekhov disagreed with much he found in Zola; when it came
to the medical (in particular, sexological) and scientific side of things, he said,
Zola "understands nothing and makes it all up by himself in his study."[84] And
one can hardly conceive an enterprise more repellent to the private Chekhov
than Zola's subjecting himself to a medical investigation of the relationship between "intellectual superiority" and "neuropathy." In 1895 Zola had allowed the
psychiatrist Édouard Toulouse and other medical specialists to conduct several
months of examinations—including photographic studies—that resulted in a
book-length monograph on Zola. In his foreward to the volume, Zola proclaims
his love of the truth. "I have never hidden anything, and have had nothing
to hide," he asserts. "My brain is as though in a skull of glass, and I don't fear
those who come to read it."[85] For Chekhov, this would have been the stuff of
nightmares.

   Still, the death of Zola in 1902 was a painful shock to Chekhov, who wrote
his wife that he "didn't much care for him as a writer, but on the other hand, as
a man, these past years during the tumult of the Dreyfus affair [. . .] valued him
very highly" (18 September 1902). As a physician and scientific thinker and, simultaneously, an author of fiction and drama, Chekhov was clearly engaged with
the work of the author of *Le Roman expérimental.*[86]

   Dr. Pascal was a work of great autobiographical significance to Zola, who actually registered at hotels under the pseudonym of Pascal.[87] Any such personal

meaning of *The Cherry Orchard* for Chekhov remains far more oblique, and yet a strong case has been made for reading the play as a deliberately composed "last testament."[88] Both pieces sum up the meaning of a life's work; both do so in an atmosphere charged with notions of degeneration; and both contemplate the rebound of this powerful paradigm for seeing others onto the self.

CHAPTER 4

Erotic and Mythic Visions

NINA: "It's hard to act in your play. There are no live characters in it."
TREPLEV: "Live characters! We need to depict life not as it is, and not as
it should be, but as it presents itself in dreams."

—Chekhov, *The Seagull*

In Russian, rather than "having" dreams (as we say it in English), you "see"
them. For the physician and author who staked his professional identity on a
putatively objective vision, dreams and hallucinations were of particular interest. This is seeing at its most subjective and solipsistic — the limit case of the unscientific gaze. Chekhov himself slept poorly and was frequently troubled by
dreams (as well as a nervous twitch); but he also sought to apply scientific understanding to such visions.[1]

Like Freud, Chekhov was prepared to generalize on the basis of self-observation. In a letter to Dmitrii Grigorovich regarding the latter's story "Karelin's
Dream" ("Son Karelina"), Chekhov wrote, "Of course, a dream is a subjective
phenomenon, and its internal aspect can be observed only by the individual
himself, but since the process of dreaming is the same in all people, it seems to
me that every reader can measure Karelin by his own yardstick and every critic
must willy-nilly be subjective. I'm judging on the basis of my own dreams,
which I see often" (12 February 1887).[2] In his ensuing discussion Chekhov emphasizes the role of physical discomforts in provoking dreaming; the specific imagery staged for the mind's eye he characterizes as but accidental, lent by the
immediate environment: "It seems to me, if I lived continuously in Petersburg
I'd dream of the banks of the Neva, the Senate Square, massive fundaments . . ."
In terms of the master distinction informing dream thinkers since antiquity,

what Chekhov describes is *enūpnion,* "the nonmeaningful dream, [which] is meaningless because it simply reproduces, in sleep, the daytime preoccupations of the dreamer. In Artemidorus' succinct definition, an *enūpnion* (literally, 'something in one's sleep') is 'a dream that has no meaning and predicts nothing, one that is active only while one sleeps and that has arisen from an irrational desire, an extraordinary fear, or from a surfeit or lack of food."[3] But another side of dreaming—one open to deep psychological and mystical approaches—pervades Chekhov's texts and is discernible in his life as well: the dream as *oneiros,* which offers a unique and profound source of information about self and destiny for interpreters with the proper hermeneutic tools.

Recall Chekhov's own dream of a black monk. According to the memoir of Chekhov's brother Mikhail, the vision that inspired the story was preceded by a discussion between Chekhov and others at Melikhovo of mirages. They theorized that, just as light from the sun can be seen after it has dipped below the horizon, an optical illusion might be refracted through the prism of the atmosphere and reproduced "ad infinitum." This discussion is echoed in "Black Monk" by Kovrin's recollection of the "strange" legend of the chimerical monk, replicating across continents and through many centuries, which he relates to Tania before he actually has the delusion of seeing and conversing with the monk (*S* 8:233). In other words, the imagery of both Chekhov's own dream of a black monk and his character's hallucination has been planted beforehand by accidental circumstances. As for the stimulus or psychic mechanism that used these "day's residues" (as Freud would soon call them)[4] and generated the actual dream, Chekhov attributed his own dream of the black monk to having overeaten, thereby reducing the meaning of his vision to a somatic source. Kovrin's hallucinations in "Black Monk," by contrast, were psychopathological symptoms in a case study of megalomania, and in no way pertained to the story's author (or so he wrote in the letter responding to the worries of Suvorin's wife on that score).

And yet, as I observed in the previous chapter, the textual cues for reading both Kovrin's hallucinations and Chekhov's dream remain quite ambiguous. The story's hellish dimensions—as well as details associating the monk with Henry Buckle and the Pesotskii estate's topography with Charles Darwin—make this dream figure more than an index of the character Kovrin's demented mind: they are signs of an author's hand; they emanate from a viewpoint apprehending the narrative's whole design. With regard to Chekhov's own siesta nightmare, Mikhail Chekhov's account suggests implications beyond indigestion: "Once I was sitting on a bench right by the house after lunch, and suddenly out runs my brother Anton, who in a kind of a strange way started to pace and wipe his forehead and eyes [. . .] 'Did your twitching wake you up?' I asked. 'No,' he answered, 'I just saw a horrifying dream. I dreamt of a black monk.'"[5] Surely only a dream of portent can so upset its dreamer, even if our post-Freudian definition of what is "meaningful" in dreams no longer matches that of late antiquity.

The oneiric (loosely speaking) has increasingly become the focus of scholarship on Chekhov's texts, in spite of a critical tradition viewing his oeuvre as the acme of realism. Just as the legend of Chekhov's objective eye has dissuaded readers from pursuing a psychobiographical understanding of the author through his works, so too has there been a broad bias against reading Chekhov esoterically. In recent years, however, scholars have begun excavating deep symbolic planes of meaning in Chekhov's verbal art—what the psychoanalytic tradition of dream interpretation would call latent content. Most notable among their findings are Savely Senderovich's revelation of a Saint George complex in Chekhov, and Julie de Sherbinin's complementary unveiling of a widespread thematic complex involving the two Marys—the virgin and the whore.[6]

This material dovetails with Chekhov's consistently ambivalent treatment of the erotic in ways that invite psychological interpretation. In Chekhov's articulations of the Saint George masterplot, the female object as a virginal creature—whose rescue from the beast, a *podvig* or hero's feat and triumph of the spirit, would win her as a bride for the hero—becomes, more often than not, conflated with the devouring beast of hell itself; in the Marian complex that plays out in Chekhov, she is the virgin and the whore. According to object relations and self-psychological psychoanalytic theories, such splitting of the erotic object into ideally good and bad figures characterizes the pre-Oedipal or narcissistic psychodynamics I have broached in previous chapters. It harks back to developmentally primitive mechanisms of psychological defense, "gives rise to repeated, intense and convincing oscillations of self-esteem," and contributes to a sense of "life lived in pieces," an inner world "populated with caricatured part objects."[7] If I suggest associating such symptomology with the Marian and Saint George complexes in Chekhov—or with his handling of pseudonyms, his split professional identity ("wife and mistress"), his struggles to maintain a sober and measured self-esteem in certain arenas (the theater, or as a scientific researcher with woman as his object of study), or with features of his own erotic life that will be taken up in this chapter—then this is to be taken not as a lay diagnosis but as an extremely tentative and heuristic insight into the psychological processes that might be involved in such an assemblage of facts. It would be utterly preposterous to speak of a severe personality disorder in regard to Chekhov.

What is more, these symbolic dimensions of Chekhov's oeuvre lead beyond the person of the author to broad cultural and historical vistas, for the stories and iconography of Saint George, the dragon of hell, the Mother of God, and the Marian harlots to which Chekhov alludes represent models for seeing the world that have had the widest conceivable distribution and influence in Russian religious and secular culture. In other words, these mythologemes (in Senderovich's terminology) can be both symptomatic formations emanating from an individual psyche and cultural paradigms of cognition.

Ultimately, the precise connections between these deep structures in Chekhov's poetics and those of Chekhov's own psyche cannot help but remain speculative and disputable. Whereas in previous chapters I offered readings of Chekhov's texts that were anchored in existential or genetic connections with Chekhov's life, here the discussion of two dreamlike dimensions to Chekhov's life and works boasts few such arguably causal connections. Instead, the case will rest on structural analogies and the broad recurrence of certain patterns of imagery. In fact, I rather mirror Chekhov's position as critic of Grigorovich's dream story: even with the theoretical apparatus of psychoanalysis at our disposal, we must also "willy-nilly be subjective," and rely on our own experience of how dreams work to identify features as such.

Seeing and the Erotic in Chekhov

In Chekhov's writings the erotic is most often treated ironically, and is perhaps better called the anti-erotic. But there is also a strain of the overtly erotic that appears very much like the manifest content of overtly erotic dreams: it is immediate and explosive, and it is first and foremost visual, about seeing and being seen.[8] In Chekhov's life, too, the erotic appears to have been chiefly connected with seeing. Indeed, there were instances when Chekhov was not overly shy about portraying this dynamic of arousal in himself. In an 1887 letter to his family sent from Taganrog during his journey south, for instance, he relates his observations while strolling the platform during a train stop at Khartsyzskaia: "Young ladies. In the last window of the second floor of the station there sits a young lady (or mature one, only the devil can tell) in a white blouse, languid and beautiful. I look at her, she at me . . . I put on my pince-nez, she too . . . Oh, wondrous vision! I suffered catarrh of the heart and traveled further" (7 April 1887).[9]

Still, we have precious few such records that might indicate the mechanics of desire in Chekhov. For years the image of Chekhov as a sexual ascetic prevailed among biographers, particularly in the West, where interest in the question was higher in the first place, and where very few scholars had access to the archival materials that might have shown otherwise. Among Russian Chekhov scholars of the pre-*glasnost'* years, I believe, it was not only considerations of censorship that inhibited discussion of such matters, but also a charitable discretion and the lack of a theoretical interpretive framework—such as that offered by psycho-analytic theory—that would make the deployment of this material a valid act of scholarship rather than anachronistic and unprofessional gossip. All this has changed quite dramatically, in no small part owing to Donald Rayfield's 1997 biography of Chekhov. With guidance from Russian Chekhov scholars who knew the archive's holdings well and could provide unprecedented access to them, Rayfield utilized unpublished memoirs of and letters to Chekhov to re-place the sexual ascetic of critical tradition with a red-blooded, and at times Don Juanish, man of the flesh.[10]

To be sure, this material can serve to build only the sketchiest, most circum-stantial case regarding the psychodynamics of desire in Chekhov: as Chekhov rather defensively wrote to the love-struck Lidiia Avilova, "Another person's soul is a mystery" (30 August 1898), and it is certainly true that we lack the docu-mentation to speak of Chekhov's intimate life with anything approaching as-surance. The most pessimistic registration of this truth might dissuade us from attempting to "see" Chekhov altogether; such is the upshot of Janet Malcolm's caution: "Chekhov's privacy is safe from the biographer's attempt upon it—as, indeed, are all privacies, even those of the most apparently open and even exhi-bitionistic natures. The letters and journals we leave behind and the impressions we have made on our contemporaries are the mere husk of the kernel of our essential life. When we die, the kernel is buried with us. This is the horror and pity of death and the reason for the inescapable triviality of biography."[11] The truth in these words notwithstanding, there do exist facts with which we might proceed. Both psychoanalytic theory and common sense tell us that broadly replicated patterns of imagery in texts and behavior in life bespeak strong per-sonal inclinations in the author; there is no need, really, to make assertions re-garding their unconscious or conscious nature. What is more, among the husks there does remain the occasional kernel.

Consider, for instance, this episode from Chekhov's youth (though it comes to us at some remove from Chekhov himself, in the memoirs of Chekhov's brother Mikhail, who learned it not from Chekhov directly but from Aleksei Suvorin):

After the death of Anton Pavlovich, A. S. Suvorin told me, in his own words, the following: Somewhere in the steppe, on someone's estate, A. P., while still a high school student, was standing by a solitary well and looking at his reflection in the water. A girl of about fifteen came for water. She so captured the future writer that he embraced her right on the spot and began kissing her. Afterwards they both stood at the well for a long time and gazed silently into the water. He didn't want to leave, and she completely forgot about her water. Chekhov, already an impor-

tant writer, told Suvorin about this when they were discussing the theme of mutual attraction [*parallel'nost' tokov*] and love at first sight.[12]

This is material of truly privileged evidentiary status. If Suvorin can be trusted—
and there is no reason to think otherwise—Chekhov told this anecdote to illustrate something characteristic of the way desire was aroused in him. It was
Chekhov himself who advanced this little scene as exemplary; and what does it
show?

Quite remarkable here is the conflation of self-observation and observation
of the other. Chekhov's vignette depicts what might be called his narcissistic
capture: desire for the other emerges from the situation of visual self-contem-
plation; what is more, the erotic activity sparked by this exchange of gazes culminates in a return to viewing the self, in company with the other, in the
reflective surface of the well. Framed together with the observer (Chekhov), the
erotic object (peasant girl) becomes a self-object, an other that represents some
aspect of the self, and that also consequently blurs the distinction between self
and other: this girl is virtually taken into Chekhov's self. We can infer that there
is something about this loss of boundary that—under very particular conditions—arouses so intensively; we can infer, too, that the sudden and intense access of pleasure results from the embracing of a sexual object that fulfills a
missing self-object function and so completes the self. In short, bliss derives from
viewing a virtual image of the completed self.

A clinical psychologist might see in this the mechanism of sexual addiction.
If so, then we most likely are glimpsing another aspect of Chekhov's self that the
young man deliberately and with a great disciplining of soul and body squeezed
out of himself together with his tainted serf's blood. One might well read the
fundamental closedness and aloofness remarked even by those who were nearest Chekhov[13]—as well as his highly developed ethical code, and the ambivalence that marks the erotic in Chekhov—as defenses against or, more positively
put, residues of Chekhov's deliberate overcoming of the ruthless using of the
other that this scene represents. For in this little scene there is also a class difference in play: the girl is a peasant—nameless, ignorant, and laboring—who forgets what she came to the well for, which is to say, forgets who she is. The water
that was to serve for cooking or cleaning has become, rather, a semiotic medium,
as it had been for the young Chekhov from the start. She utterly loses her self
in Chekhov's need.

But there is also a literary side to Chekhov's anecdote about love at first sight.
Surely it must be read as a deliberate allusion to Ovid's Narcissus, gazing at his
own reflection in a pool of water. As is so often the case in Chekhov's writings,
the accidental and contiguous here becomes metaphoric: placing the acts of see-

ing beside those of touching suggests not only a causal connection but one of likeness as well. The erotic, in its most sudden and explosive variant, is about seeing; and what is seen—though it includes the figure of another human—is the self. Chekhov, whose vanity and self-love were remarked by so many who knew him and loved him, in effect characterizes himself as an epigone of Narcissus.

The one Chekhov story that can properly be called a positive and affirming love tale, "The Lady with the Lapdog" ("Dama s sobochkoi," 1899), ends with a scene very reminiscent of this one from Chekhov's youth. The adulterous couple whose vacation fling has grown into deep attachment meet in Moscow, where Gurov lives and Anna Sergeevna periodically travels on the pretext of consulting a physician. At the story's start the predatory Gurov seduced his object like an accomplished Don Juan and used her hedonistically: this is the meaning of his calm slicing and consumption of a melon after they first sleep together, and his irritation in the face of her moral suffering in this transgressive moment (S 10:132–33). Now, at the story's end, when Anna Sergeevna despairs at the shape her life has taken, he rises to comfort her with an embrace, "and at that moment caught sight of himself in the mirror."

> His head was beginning to turn gray. And it seemed strange to him that he had aged so much in those last years, had lost so much of his good looks. The shoulders on which his hands lay were warm and trembled. He felt compassion for this life, still so warm and beautiful, but probably already near the point where it would begin to fade and wither, like his own life. Why did she love him so? Women had always taken him to be other than he was, and they had loved in him, not himself, but a man their imagination had created, whom they had greedily sought all their lives; and then, when they had noticed their mistake, they had still loved him. And not one of them had been happy with him. Time passed, he met women, became intimate, parted, but not once did he love; there was anything else, but not love.
>
> And only now, when his head was gray, had he really fallen in love as one ought to—for the first time in his life. (S 10:142–43)[14]

This is of course something quite different from the explosive passion, unmediated by verbalization, that Chekhov recalled from his well-side encounter with a nameless peasant girl. And yet these two scenes share a peculiar and markedly narcissistic circumstance of seeing: both Chekhov and his character experience an access of emotion in a moment following, and arguably following from, viewing themselves in a reflective surface. So also in the Tula train station episode, the woman who momentarily excited Chekhov—in spite of being at such a distance that her age was not discernible—did so by playing a game of mirror, returning his gaze and the gesture of donning his pince-nez. In both "Lady with the Lapdog" and the well-side incident, too, it is all about the male character, from whose point of view the narrative emanates: "Why did she love him so?"

This passage from "Lady with the Lapdog" presents only the last of a whole series of images coordinating motifs of desire with those of seeing and being seen. The seaside promenade at Yalta is the proper setting for people-watching and self-display, and the story opens with Gurov observing a new face, that of a lone blonde woman, with the calculations of an experienced seducer: "'If she's here with no husband or friends,' Gurov reflected, 'it wouldn't be a bad idea to make her acquaintance'" (361; *S* 10:128). The two meet; they take walks; they observe other vacationers. On the evening before they first sleep together, "owing to the roughness of the sea, the steamer arrived late, when the sun had already gone down, and it was a long time turning before it tied up. Anna Sergeevna looked at the ship and the passengers through her lorgnette, as if searching for acquaintances, and when she turned to Gurov, her eyes shone. She talked a lot, and her questions were abrupt, and she immediately forgot what she had asked; then she lost her lorgnette in the crowd" (365; *S* 10:131). Anna Sergeevna's imminent acquiescence to her own and Gurov's desires is associated with a loss of vision: hence the misplaced lorgnette, and the eyes that shine rather than see. Later the two drive to Oreanda and sit on a bluff overlooking the sea. "Some man came up—it must have been a watchman—looked at them, and went away. And this detail seemed such a mysterious thing, and also beautiful" (367; *S* 10:134). After they part, Anna Sergeevna's image grows preternaturally sharp in Gurov's mind's eye: "Closing his eyes, he saw her as though live, and she seemed more beautiful, younger, more tender than she had been; and he himself seemed better than he had been then, in Yalta. In the evenings she gazed at him from the bookcase, from the fireplace, from the corner" (369; *S* 10:136). Months later Gurov travels to Anna Sergeevna's provincial town and reclaims her at the theater, where their affectionate meeting is observed by two smoking high school boys, peepers; "but Gurov did not care" (373; *S* 10:140).

Chekhov scholars have always understood "Lady with the Lapdog" as connected to Chekhov's relationship with Ol'ga Knipper. Although Chekhov's notebooks contain material that made its way into the story dating from before he met Knipper, and other prototypes for the lady with the dog have been proposed by memoirists and scholars, the bulk of Chekhov's work on the tale dates from the period of his increasing intimacy with her.[15] Indeed, Knipper herself appears to have read the story as having special significance for her: it "really set me to thinking seriously," she told him.[16]

To understand Chekhov's relationship with Knipper, it helps to consider the most important and long-lasting of his attachments preceding the one that resulted in marriage. This was with the friend of his sister, Lidiia (Lika) Mizinova.[17]

While much about this relationship remains unclear, the correspondence shows Chekhov seeking to establish a comfortable emotional (and at times geographical) distance from Mizinova while at the same time maintaining an intimate connection: sixty-seven letters from Chekhov to Mizinova are known, and ninety-eight sent by Mizinova to Chekhov.[18] In her commentary to their correspondence A. M. Dolotova writes, "The stylistics of Chekhov's letters to Mizinova played the role of a barrier erected by him between himself and Lika, a boundary established in relations with her."[19] At times, nevertheless, Chekhov clearly sought the close proximity of the high-spirited Lika; he instructed his sister to bring her to Melikhovo after the wounding fiasco of the *Seagull* premiere, for example, as though she might salve his soul. His letters to her abound with intimate material and professions of love, but only when masked by parodistic devices; thus as a joke he sends her a menacing letter, addressed to Lika's fictional lover Trofim, warning him to stay away from his woman, and signs the piece "Lika's lover."[20]

What Mizinova herself came to understand, and what scholars of Chekhov most often do not, is that, rather than a defense against or ascetic renunciation of erotic involvement, such joking may well be characteristic of peculiar conditions under which the erotic can in fact play out. Distance is the fundamental requirement for sexual pleasure through seeing. And this is how Mizinova expressed her frustration with the relationship in a letter to Chekhov: "I once stupidly acted as the cheese you refused to eat . . . You only like looking at it from afar, even when you're hungry, not eating it."[21]

In 1895 Chekhov wrote Suvorin, who had been exhorting him to take a wife: "If you please, I'll marry, if that's what you want. But my conditions: everything must be as it has been heretofore, that is, she should live in Moscow, and I in the country, and I'll visit her. I won't be able to stand the sort of happiness that continues day in and day out, morning to morning [. . .] I promise to be a splendid husband, but give me the sort of wife that, like the moon, would not appear in my sky every day. N.B.: marrying will not make me write better" (23 March 1895). While Chekhov's biographers often cite this letter as evidence that Chekhov abhorred the mundanity of conventional bourgeois marriage, to my knowledge none has drawn attention to the logic of seeing that underlies his metaphor: even when full, the moon nonetheless remains at a great distance, and one's contact with it can only be visual.[22] When Chekhov eventually married Knipper—a professional actress for whom he conceived a passionate attraction while observing her rehearse for the new Moscow Art Theater's premiere performance[23]—their conjugal life became organized very much along the lines he had laid out in the letter to Suvorin half a decade earlier. Chekhov lived in Yalta, while Knipper took an apartment in Moscow.

The correspondence shows how difficult this living arrangement was for them both, but particularly for Knipper. She expressed a willingness to give up the stage, but Chekhov would not hear of it. When she would question the life they were leading, Chekhov framed the situation in thoroughly practical terms: "If we're not together now, then it's not you or I who's at fault in that, but the demon who put a bacillus in me and the love of art in you."[24] Many years later, though, Ol'ga found the 1895 letter to Suvorin, and in it painful confirmation of her unspoken suspicion that the geographical distance separating them in marriage had been motivated more by Chekhov's deep psychological needs than by the exigencies of health and career.[25] Rather than putting a crimp in their married life, these factors may well have been the guarantee of an interspousal distance that made marriage conceivable.

Chekhov once told his brother that he would write "from a crack in the wall";[26] so too might be characterized his role of husband from afar. The correspondence between Chekhov and Knipper runs to over eight hundred letters and telegrams,[27] and not surprisingly, from the earliest times it frequently involved exchanges of photographs and avowals that one or the other is viewing or kissing the photograph. Knipper had keyed into something profound about Chekhov when, as their acquaintanceship first began to develop into intimacy, she asked for a picture of him "with your eyes open"; when she got one she wrote: "Hurrah, hurrah!!! Now I've got the Author Chekhov."[28] Chekhov had to threaten not to write again until he received a portrait of Knipper (10 February 1900). In March 1900 Knipper wrote Chekhov, "You know, not long ago I saw our meeting in a dream, and I'm sure nothing like it will occur in waking life."[29] For his part, Chekhov wrote from Nice at the end of 1900, "I often see you in my dreams, and when I close my eyes, I see you while awake" (21 December 1900). "How I'd like to look at my wife for a bit," he wrote in a fairly typical verbal caress a few years later (29 November 1903). Knipper knew which organ was Chekhov's most sensitive: "I kiss you, and I'm waiting. I kiss your eyes, so that nobody might love you."[30]

Above all, one wonders what the implications would have been for Chekhov's own visibility had he lived in Moscow with his actress-wife. Was there not the risk of becoming the character mocked in one of his notebook entries from the time of his marriage? "The husband of an actress sat beaming in a box seat during his wife's benefit performance, repeatedly rising to take bows" (S 17:80).

Savely Senderovich asserts, "There is no unambivalent, let alone positive, eroticism in Chekhov,"[31] and this verifiable observation complicates what we have discovered about the erotics of seeing in Chekhov. The image of Chekhov's youthful well-side encounter appears to have had a negative and quite threatening aspect as well. The prospect of merging with an other that was in some way powerful and overwhelming could raise acute anxiety; hence Chekhov's frequent epistolary recourse to the trope of being devoured or castrated. Such imagery abounds in Chekhov's letters to Knipper, as well as elsewhere in his relations with women and marriage, though, to be sure, always in joking accents. It appears too in the Saint George and descent thematic complex of Chekhov's fiction, through conflating the woman to be rescued with the beast of hell from which she might be saved. Thus "Ariadne" (1895) alludes ironically to the mythological Ariadne, the descent of Theseus, and his slaying of the Minotaur: here the sensuous and self-centered Ariadne, who summons the embedded narrator to rescue her, is herself a devourer of men.

Having married Knipper, a woman of German origin, Chekhov writes, "I am an entirely German husband in my conduct" (*P* 10:175), and he signs a whole series of letters to Ol'ga "The German Anton," "Your German Antoine," "Your A. Chekh the German," and so on. Rather than his wife becoming a part of his self, Chekhov jokes about the possibility of his self being absorbed into that of his wife, a possibility that, if realized, would both de-nationalize and unman him. Earlier in the courtship (26 September 1899) Knipper rebuked Chekhov for having called her a "serpentlet" (*zmeenysh*); he answered: "I did not call you a serpentlet at all, as you write. You're a serpent, not a serpentlet, a huge serpent. Isn't that flattering?"[32] When Chekhov thanks the actress for two photographs she has sent him, he writes that they are both fine, but in one of them "you look a bit like a Jewess, a very musical being, who goes to the conservatory and at the same time, just in case, is studying the art of dentistry and has a fiancé in [the very Jewish city of] Mogilev" (14 February 1900). At the end of December 1900 Chekhov writes Ol'ga from Nice: "I'm yours! Take me and eat me up with vinegar and Provence butter."[33] And toward the end of his life he writes in his notebook, "When I got married, I became a sissy" ("ia stal baboi," literally, I became a woman"; *S* 17:102).

This is but a representative sampling of what might be called Chekhov's peculiar "lover's discourse," a discourse that suggests—all joking aside—a concern about loss of self in union with the other. The language of classical psychoanalysis would have us speak of castration anxiety at this point, and though there is material suggestive of such injury—the image of Knipper as a frightful Jewess-dentist evokes the paradigm of the *vagina dentata*—the broader theoretical picture that pertains to castration in Freud's Oedipal model proves inadequate. More helpful are the characterizations of pre-Oedipal dynamics elaborated in variants of psychoanalytic theory known as object relations and self-psychology.[34]

Chekhov's likening of Knipper to a Jewess recalls his much earlier, brief and abortive engagement in 1886–87 to Evdokiia (Dun'ia) Efros, a Jewish friend of his sister. Elena Tolstaia has already noted an echo of Efros in the future wife of

Chekhov, but this association is far deeper and more personal than the "taste for exogamy Chekhov shared with many others of his generation."[35] The relationship between Chekhov and Efros appears to have been a quite tempestuous, almost physical battle. Thus Chekhov wrote to his then new friend Viktor Bilibin, the minor author and Petersburg employee of Leikin's *Oskolki:* "My *she* is a Jewess. If the rich little yid is brave enough to convert to Orthodoxy, with all its consequences, that's all right; if not, so be it . . . By the way, we have already had a falling out . . . Tomorrow we'll make it up, but in a week we'll break up again . . . She gets upset over her religion being in her way and breaks the pencils and photographs on my desk—that's typical . . . A malicious creature . . . There's no doubt I'll divorce her a year or two after the wedding" (1 February 1886). Scholars have found these remarks odd, since Chekhov had a number of close associates who were Jews and was by no means prone to the sort of overtly anti-Semitic remarks he permits himself here and elsewhere in regard to Efros. They are nevertheless echoed by frankly Judeophobic motifs in two significant works of this period, the story "Mire" ("Tina") and the play *Ivanov,* both of which may be linked to Chekhov's relations with Efros.[36]

Even odder was Chekhov's demand that Efros assume Russian Orthodoxy. Chekhov showed no particular concern when his older brothers were involved with Jewish women and, according to Rayfield, himself had a two-year affair with the Jewess who, years later, became his brother Aleksandr's second wife.[37] As a gymnasium student in Taganrog, Chekhov had organized a successful protest against the expulsion of a Jewish boy who had struck a fellow student who called him a "yid."[38] He cannot have been concerned about propriety, since he had already vigorously articulated a position of independence in such matters; in 1883 Chekhov had sharply criticized his brother Aleksander when the latter was troubled by the Chekhov family's opinion of his domestic affairs (he was involved in a common-law marriage at the time): "What do you care how this or some other *raskol'nik* [schismatic or old believer; Chekhov is referring to their father] views your cohabitation? [. . .] What is your cohabitation from your point of view? It's your nest, your source of warmth, your grief and delight [. . .] In your place, if I were a family man, I would not only not allow anyone to express their opinion, but even their wish to understand. It's my 'I,' my department, and no little sisters have the right (simply by virtue of the natural order of things) to stick their nose into it, wanting to understand and be touched" (20 February 1883). Chekhov's concern cannot have been religious, either, for he was by no means scrupulously Orthodox, if indeed he had faith at all. Most saliently, perhaps, when Chekhov did marry some fifteen years later, it was to a woman whom he called his "Lutheran." (It should be noted, however, that the fact that in Russia marriage had to be performed in either a church or a synagogue did provide a practical reason for conversion for those not content with a common-law arrangement.)

If Chekhov's demand that Efros convert was not motivated by religious conviction or adherence to the conventions of class and upbringing, then some other motivation must be sought. And here Chekhov's later jokes about becoming a German as the result of marrying Knipper provide a key.[39] Efros must convert—this wealthy and willful woman must lose a large part of her self in becoming Chekhov's wife—because otherwise Chekhov will become a part of *her* self. To marry a Jewess would make Chekhov the husband of a Jewess. Efros had already destroyed the pencils and photographs on Chekhov's desk, wrecking metonymic figures for his very self: the pencils he writes with, the photographs that, as objects for visual contemplation, tell Chekhov who he is, by whom he is loved. The logic of Chekhov's signing himself a "German" in letters to Knipper, if applied retroactively to his Jewish fiancée, suggests that if Efros had not become an Orthodox Russian, he would have become—willy-nilly, ceremonies notwithstanding—a Jew.

But what did it mean to be a Jew? For a male, first and foremost, it meant to be circumcised; and in much of the medical rhetoric of the day, it meant belonging to an evolutionarily degenerate race. Thus Sander Gilman has shown the deep connection between the ideas of castration and circumcision and the projection of pathology in the cultural construction of the Jewish body in central Europe of the nineteenth century.[40] There is in fact evidence that Chekhov contemplated precisely such consequences from marrying Efros; he even created a kind of deliberate hysterical symbolization of such an eventuality for bodily display. When Mariia Kiseleva remarked in a letter the "medal" or "decoration" (*orden*) he had been wearing at the time, Chekhov answered: "If you're alluding to that red lace, which I'm wearing around my neck out of respect for the taste and nose of the female Israelite known to you, then I hasten to assure you that there have been no services on my part, and therefore it is quite impossible to call that lace a medal. It's rather a noose—a symbol of love, of family happiness" (21 March 1887). I read this red—that is, bloody—ring around Chekhov's neck, insofar as it signifies something distinctively Jewish, as a far from innocent joke regarding the Jewish law of circumcision, and its relevance for him as the bridegroom of a Jewess. The mechanism of this symbol's formation is the very common displacement upwards, whereby the throat acquires phallic significance; we have seen Chekhov make use of this same figurative device in "At Sea" and "Work of Art" (see chapters 1 and 2). In this way Chekhov displayed his imminent "Jewification" and castration, or as he himself put it,

death by marriage to a Jewess.[41] The very best he might hope for is what marriage brings to Ivanov in the play *Ivanov*: the Russian hero has married a Jewess and, in consequence, become a neurotic.

But what frightened Chekhov about Efros somehow attracted him as well;
or so must be the upshot of her echo in the figure of Ol'ga Knipper, insofar as
Knipper did indeed remind Chekhov of a tooth-pulling Jewess. Chekhov remained friendly with both Efros and the man she soon married (Efim
Konovitser); in 1888 he sent her a lithographed copy of *Ivanov*, with this inscription: "To the (hissing) spectator, from the author."[42] And when Chekhov's
degenerate body had definitively betrayed him and sentenced him to exile in
Yalta, he repeatedly likened himself to the Jewish Alfred Dreyfus on Devil's Island.[43] It was Chekhov's destiny to lose the strong, autonomous selfhood he had
struggled so to achieve, if not to Efros or even to Knipper, then to consumption. Being devoured by that toothy other places the ill self in a category parallel to that of the slavish son of a serf, women, and Jews.

Chekhov's Wet Dreams: "Romance with a Contrabass" and "Fishy Love"

Chekhov's characteristic erotics of seeing define the structures and imagery in
two of his oddest and most dreamlike stories, "Romance with a Contrabass"
("Roman s kontrabasom," 1886) and "Fishy Love" ("Ryb'ia liubov'," 1892). Like
the anecdote of Chekhov's well-side encounter, these are tales of "love at first
sight," and though they have often baffled readers, they make new sense in the
present interpretive framework.

"Romance with a Contrabass" opens with the musician Smychkov carrying
his double bass to the dacha of Prince Bibulov, where he is to play for the engagement party of Bibulov's daughter. He pauses for a dip in the river and, having swum a bit to the side, catches sight of a "sleeping beauty" on the opposite
bank who has dozed off while fishing. Suddenly Smychkov "felt, against his will,
something in his chest rather similar to love. He stood before her for a long time,
devouring her with his eyes"; then he ties a bouquet of flowers to her hook so
as to leave her something "to remember me by" (*S* 5:179). When he emerges
from the river, however, he finds that his clothes have been stolen. He decides
to await darkness under a nearby bridge and then proceed to the nearest peasant hut. Meanwhile, the girl awakes and, finding her hook caught, strips to enter the river and free it. After her clothes are also stolen, she makes for the same
bridge as did Smychkov, spots him, screams, and faints. Regaining consciousness, she whispers: "Don't kill me! I'm the Princess Bibulova. I beg you! They'll

give you a lot of money." Smychkov explains that he too has been the victim of thieves, then makes a gallant proposal: "Mademoiselle! I see that my appearance upsets you. But, you will agree, it is impossible for me to leave here, for the same reasons it is for you. Here is what I have thought up: would you not care to lie in the case of my contrabass and cover yourself with its lid? This would hide me from you . . ." (S 5:1871–872). As darkness falls, Smychkov sets out for the dacha, savoring thoughts of reward from the girl's father, but when he spots two men he presumes to be the thieves, he drops the case and gives chase. Smychkov's fellow musicians, on their way to the engagement, then discover the case in the road and, bemoaning Smychkov's fate, carry it to the dacha. The bridegroom of the princess, who has been grandiosely and preposterously boasting of his ability to play Liszt on a double bass, opens the case to retrieve the instrument and exhibit his artistic pretensions, at which point his nude fiancée pops out and runs away. Meanwhile Smychkov, who believes himself guilty of having suffocated the princess by losing the case with her in it, goes mad, and lives to this day, the narrative tells us, under the bridge, still wearing only his top hat, and scraping out tunes on the double bass.

This story about seeing and being seen, hiding and showing—which, as is so often the case with the erotic in Chekhov's life and writings, is set near and in water—presents a fascinating series of the negations, inversions, and displacements characteristic of the figurative devices of dreams. It is a story that fails to make any sense at all if read as other than a transcribed dream; Tolstoy, while remarking Chekhov's great abilities as a humorist, expressed an inability to comprehend "Romance with a Contrabass."[44]

This pattern of distortion begins with the story's title. The "romance" of the title never occurs, but insofar as the story can be construed as a romance, then the "contrabass" of the title takes the place of the girl. Chekhov's plays on the quite conventional association between the shape of a double bass and that of the female body, too, in his early story "The Contrabass and the Flute" ("Kontrabas i fleita. [Stsenka]," 1885), though that piece reverses expected associations of gender and instrument. In "Romance with a Contrabass" Smychkov realizes the metaphor by literally placing the woman in the case. At the same time, however, encasing her is a means of covering her up, and so might be understood as a dramatization of the mechanism of repression; indeed, the whole story reads like an emblem of fractured repression or de-sublimation.

Love arises in Smychkov's breast "against his will." This allusion to the involuntary mechanism of male erection caps a passage cast in the elevated language of romantic love: Smychkov's "poetic soul," which had been so injured by his wife's betrayal of him with his friend Sobakin that "he had become a misanthrope," is resurrected by the sight of this "sleeping beauty" (S 5:179). The gallant bassist offers to enclose the girl in his case so that *she* won't see *him*—a curious and solipsistic inversion, since she is put into the case not in order to cover herself as clothing would, but to blind her. Were she fully clothed when she came upon Smychkov, he might have made the same proposal. Like the youthful Chekhov gazing into the well, or the character Gurov seeing himself and Anna Sergeevna in the mirror, Smychkov sees himself when he sees the naked princess; and, it might be added, he rather overvalues what it is of him that the girl might see: after all, she faints! The waterside setting of this tale inverts that of Chekhov's well-side episode, the most famous moment in the Narcissus myth, and, it should be noted, the overwhelming majority of scenes involving bathers in Western mythology and fine arts: Smychkov looks *out* of the water at his object. Instead of a male observer peeping at nude female bathers, a nude male bather peeps at a clothed female on the riverbank.

The exhibitionistic fiancé boasts to the prince about his mastery of an instrument, and the instrument he attempts to prove this on turns out to be the body of the prince's daughter. The contrabass, as the instrument of a professional musician, is a part of the musician's self, that part on which his professional pride is staked. The fiancé's claims of virtuosity on the double bass make him the double of Smychkov, and for both Smychkov and the fiancé, the girl takes the place of the male's instrument. As was the case with the candelabra in "Work of Art," then, the nude female body becomes a self-object for the male beholder, one on which pride and potency are staked. In a scenario of erotic potential, rather than putting his instrument into that body, Smychkov makes that body his instrument. And when she disappears, he is utterly abject—guilt ridden and, more to the point of the narcissistic dynamics I have been tracing, shamed.

Even stranger than "Romance with a Contrabass" is "Fishy Love," where similar thematics and setting take overtly allegorical and metaliterary turns. In the spring of 1892 Chekhov dusted off one of his early pseudonyms, "Man without a Spleen," to publish this trifle in Leikin's *Oskolki*. The only carp living in a pond near the dacha of General Mamochkin has fallen in love "up to his ears" with the dacha guest Sonia Momochkina. Every morning she comes to bathe, and the carp swims near and watches; he watches, too, as young men peep from behind the bushes. Overcome with passion, the carp "swam up to her and began greedily kissing her little feet, shoulders, neck . . . " (*S* 8:51). Despairing of reciprocal affection, he entertains thoughts of suicide, but he lacks the means. "And, thinking about death, the young pessimist dug himself into the mire and there wrote in his diary" (*S* 8:52). When the girl appears at the bank with a fishing pole, the carp decides to die by her hand: his erotic fantasy will culminate in being devoured by his love object (the self taken into the other). But it is not to be. Having hooked the carp, the girl jerks her pole too vigorously and tears off his lower lip; the irony of his fate drives the carp to laughter and madness. Here the narrator interjects: "But I am afraid that it might seem strange that I want to occupy the attention of the serious reader with the fate of such an inconsequential and uninteresting creature as a carp. However, what's strange in this? In thick journals women describe utterly useless gudgeon and ducks. And I am imitating these women. It might even be that I am myself a woman, and only hide under a masculine pseudonym" (*S* 8:52). This metaliterary escapade continues. A young poet is the nephew of an engineer employed at the nearby foundry. The carp sees him swimming in the pond and, having mistaken him for Sonia Mamochkina, kisses him on the spine, and so infects him with pessimism; when the poet returns to Petersburg, his visits to editorial offices there transmit this infection to others, "and since that time our poets began to write gloomy, despondent verse" (*S* 8:53).

The tale thus sets up an equivalence between the implied author and the diary-writing carp: the carp's loss of a part of his body is followed by the implied author's astonishing remark placing his own gender in question. These two moments reflect on each other, likening the implied author to the fish and the fish's injury to a loss of manhood. Writing—in particular, writing pessimistically, as Chekhov, the author of the collection of stories *Gloomy People* (*Khmurye liudi,* 1890), had been accused of doing—becomes associated with an unmanning narcissistic wound. This allegory was written long after Chekhov had ceased writing under pseudonyms and publishing in cheap comic venues. Suddenly he felt the need to write and place three stories, of which this was one, in his former vehicle *Oskolki;* and the tale appeared under an old pseudonym that, as though echoing the material of this story, evokes the lack of an organ: "Man without a Spleen."[45] Here the by now familiar explosive erotic impulses, sparked by seeing and being seen, set in water, and leading to misadventure, lead also to overt metapoetic commentary, though in the accents of humor. "Fishy Love" thus connects the theme of seeing and being seen, hiding and showing, with Chekhov's penchant for narrative self-reflexivity.

Seeing Hell, Transforming the Self: Land Diving in Chekhov

The explosive erotic potential of aquatic submersion—the instantaneous bliss or abjection that follows from waterside escapades in Chekhov's life and art— has its counterpart in a pervasive motif of the hero's descent to the underworld, the hard journey undertaken to transform the self.[46] Chekhov made repeated use of the archetypal motif of the hero's descent—katabasis—throughout his writing career; and what is this masterplot if not the most profound and culturally broad treatment of the theme of the heroic journey and the acquisition of privileged knowledge through seeing? As a mythopoetic principle structuring Chekhov's texts and investing them with latent meaning, the theme adds an oneiric dimension to Chekhov's oeuvre. But katabasis is also a leitmotif in the author's life, a deeply personal paradigm driving Chekhov's love of travel and penchant for observation, and investing these inclinations with meaning.

The most striking katabatic journey in both Chekhov's life and his writings was surely his epic project of visiting the prison colony of Sakhalin. "I was in hell, represented by Sakhalin, and in heaven, that is on the island of Ceylon," Chekhov wrote to Leont'ev-Shcheglov (10 December 1890) on returning from the east. The analogy with hell is predictable, if not a cliché; so too had the traveler and journalist George Kennan characterized a meeting with political convicts at Kara during his 1885 Siberian expedition: "There was not, in the whole environment, a single suggestion of the real, commonplace, outside world; and when the convicts, with hushed voices, began to tell me ghastly stories of cruelty, suffering, insanity, and suicide at the mines, I felt almost as if I had entered the gloomy gate over which Dante saw inscribed the dread warning, 'Leave hope behind.'"[47] But Chekhov could find precedent for weightier usage in Dostoevskii's treatment of the prison camp in *Notes from the House of the Dead* (*Zapiski iz mertvogo doma,* 1860), where descent is associated with rebirth on a higher plane of being. And Chekhov does follow Dostoevskii: the penal colony as hell is more than an apt metaphor charging social critique with effective imagery. In his pioneering cross-disciplinary work of sociology, medical geography, and travelogue, *Sakhalin Island* (*Ostrov Sakhalin*), as in the travel sketches Chekhov wrote en route (*From Siberia* [*Iz Sibiri*]) and in his letters, he conceived of this journey from the start along the lines found in paradigmatic katabatic journeys. He did not travel to a place that revealed itself to him as so horrible it could only be described as hell; he planned a trip to hell.

It follows that surfacings of the katabatic subtext in Chekhov's writings on Sakhalin acquire special interest to the reader less concerned with the social and natural history of Sakhalin than with Chekhov. The equation of this place with hell tends to shift the focus of Chekhov's narrative from the object of his pseudoscientific study to himself. When the hell metaphor is most apparent—when, for instance, it appears to him "as if all of Sakhalin is burning" and "everything is in smoke, as in hell" (*S* 14–15:54); or when he describes a spot where, "judging by sight, only toads and the souls of great sinners can live" (*S* 14–15:19); or when, during the visit of the area's governor-general, "people wandered the streets like shades, and they remain silent like shades" (*S* 14–15:65)—these moments are always characterized by the strange, uncanny effect the sights have on their reporter. He is witnessing a "dreadful picture" (*S* 14–15:54); it is oppressive (*skuchno*) on the streets; music arouses "deathly melancholy" (*smertnaia toska,* S 14–15:65).

These accesses of emotion occur repeatedly in conjunction with crossing a body of water. Such crossings, sometimes on ferries operated by hostile ferrymen, and always with great forebodings about what will be found on the other side, feature centrally in the travel sketches Chekhov wrote en route, that is, *before* he had experienced the Russian Devil's Island. When Chekhov departed for Sakhalin, he apparently had in mind as models for the feat he was about to accomplish not only the explorers and scientists whose works on the island he had studied but also Aeneas and Dante. The ten thousand census query cards Chekhov had printed once he arrived on Sakhalin testify to his intentions to gather empirical evidence as a social scientist; the katabatic imagery in his travel sketches suggests that the "hard journey" there and back was preconceived in mythopoetic terms. This would mean that Chekhov was somewhat disingenuous when he later wrote Suvorin, "While I was living on Sakhalin, I suffered only something of a sour stomach, as from rancid butter, but now, recollecting, Sakhalin appears to me a total hell" (9 December 1890).[48]

Of all the underworlds offered to Chekhov by the katabatic tradition, Dante's seems to have been most important for the Sakhalin book; this is no surprise, since the hell of Dante and of Christian mythology is, unlike the underworld of classical paradigms, tightly connected with notions of sin, crime, and punishment.[49] Nevertheless, a number of descent models from disparate arenas of discourse were available to Chekhov, and he was catholic in his borrowings. His descents echo those of Russian folklore, the myths of the ancients, canonical and apocryphal Orthodox Christianity, and contemporary popular culture, at times in disorienting conjunction.[50] In the de-sacralized modern world, myth making tends to be a rather idiosyncratic affair, and for the nonbelieving Chekhov,[51] descent meant something different from what it had meant for such Russian precursors as Gogol and Dostoevskii.

In certain works the demonic underworld of Slavic folklore appears key. This is signaled in the very title of Chekhov's ill-fated play of the year preceding his journey, *Wood Demon* (*Leshii,* 1889), for the wood demon is a Russian folkloric spirit who lives in the forest and is master of all other creatures living there.[52] The appellation "wood demon" belongs to the play's environmentalist hero, the physician Khrushchov. In the scene where he first appears on the stage, he declares his "hellish appetite" (*S* 12:137); later the mill Khrushchov owns is described by the character Diadin as "a secluded and poetic corner of the earth where you can hear water nymphs [*rusalki*] splashing at night . . . " (*S* 12:174). The play ends with allusions to the opera based on Pushkin's "Rusalka" (*S* 12:188, 394), and there is even a Gogolian black piglet poking around where it does not belong (*S* 12:184); both the water nymph and the piglet belong to the otherworldly and demonic of east Slavic folklore. This otherworld of woods and waters acquires a very positive value, and is set in opposition to the everyday social life of the play's characters. Nature and the spirit world are conceived as the center of their own values—they are *rodnoe*—while the world of human society is alien or other, *chuzhoe*. Remarks Khrushchov, "It's the earth itself that's crazy for still supporting us" (*S* 12:178).

What is more, this alien human world is in turn associated with the underworld of classical and canonical Christian mythologies, as reflected in "high" literature. The character Elena, married to a famous scholar but in love with Khrushchov, is its prisoner. "It's as if you all arranged to make my life hell," she complains (*S* 12:177). Meanwhile, a neighbor and would-be seducer obliquely offers to make Elena queen of his underworld through his repeated citation of Anton Rubenshtein's operatic version of Lermontov's "Demon": "And you will be queen of the world, my faithful mistress" (*S* 12:138, 143). This character owns two estates in the Caucasus—here the southern geographical location also represents the downward direction of the typical katabatic journey—to which he gallops back and forth "like one possessed" (*kak ugorelyi; S* 12:137). A life organized around the obsessive, useless scholarship of Elena's husband becomes associated with the hell of high culture and canonical literary tradition; life organized around ecology and ethical concerns, by contrast, is associated with the otherworld of Slavic folklore (in which demons are traditionally quite ambivalent, often harmful, but sometimes helpful). Elena's choices thus amount to two different types of underworlds. She eventually escapes to the mill, where she hides from both the wood demon (Khrushchov) and her husband. But when her husband and the others gather at the mill for a picnic, she reveals herself, declaring: "I'm ready. Well, take me, like the statue of the Commendatore [from *Don Giovanni*], and disappear with me down into your twenty-six gloomy rooms!" (*S* 12:197–98). This denouement is punctuated by an alarm indicating a huge forest fire in neighboring lands—hell bursting up to the surface of this world, as in stagings of Mozart's opera.

This hellish subtext was greatly attenuated when, seven years later, Chekhov reworked *Wood Demon* into *Uncle Vania* (*Diadia Vania*),[53] but hell burst into the foreground in Chekhov's major story of that same year, "Peasants" ("Muzhiki"). Previous readers noting the story's apocalyptic images have all viewed the descent imagery in this piece as indexical signs of chaos and poverty; these motifs are construed as illustrating "the hellish element in the peasants' lives"[54] rather than aspects of an overarching symbolic structure. Nevertheless, the whole of "Peasants" is structured as a descent to hell: it is an instance of psychopomps, escorting the soul of the dead (the dying Nikolai) to the underworld.[55] And the family returning from a reasonably successful life in Moscow to its native village really does go to hell, for the metaphoric association of the peasant village with hell becomes concretized during the catastrophic fire at the start of chapter 5. The previous chapter had presented the child Sasha's thoughts of God, church, and religious cosmology, especially hell and "the end of the world"; in the same chapter Fekla tells her dying brother-in-law that "the devil brought you here," and Granny curses Motka and Sasha. At the chapter's end Sasha is beaten by her grandmother and comforts herself with the thought that the old woman is surely bound for hell. She then dreams: "A huge stove, like a kiln, was burning, and the unclean spirit, with horns like a cow's, all black, was driving Granny into the fire with a long stick, like she herself had just been driving the geese" (S 9:294). Over the chapter break that follows, Sasha's dream materializes. The fire described in the next chapter erupts during the Feast of the Assumption, that is, on the festival marking the day when the Mother of God was bodily taken from this world to heaven. In Chekhov's text the figurative has also materialized: this peasant village is bodily carried down to hell.[56]

I have already mentioned the pattern of the hero's descent to rescue the beloved. In Chekhov's 1895 "Ariadne," the far-off southern lands to which the narrator travels substitute for the notion of lower lands, projecting the vertically organized space of katabatic myths onto the horizontal plane of geography. Like "Ariadne," the very early "Sinner from Toledo" ("Greshnik iz Toledo. [Perevod s ispanskogo]," 1881) treats the traditional descent pattern ironically. The story is set in Barcelona during the Inquisition, and the "sinner" has hidden his wife, who is accused of practicing witchcraft. Certain that his beautiful Mariia is no witch, he is nonetheless possessed by an insurmountable fear of hell, to which he expects to be condemned for studying the "black arts" of medicine and mathematics. The inquisitors' promise of absolution of all sins and an escape from hell in return for handing over his wife proves too great to resist: "He was ready to give up everything" (S 1:114). He poisons his wife and hands over her corpse to men he recognizes as "ravens," that is, black creatures of hell, so as to be cleansed of his own sins.[57] What began as a chivalric rescue of the beloved — one typical motivation for the hero's descent (as with Orpheus) — has ended in her betrayal to the pyre of Inquisition so as to avoid the katabatic journey altogether. The story turns on the contradictory co-presence in this young, skeptical man of science — an *intelligent* projected back in time — of contempt for the priests and what they are doing, and terror of the hell in whose name they act.

A simultaneous intellectual rejection of the devil and hell, and yet what can only be understood as a vision of them, appears in "A Doctor's Visit" ("Sluchai iz praktiki," 1898). This story features the journey there and back of an *intelligent* of Chekhov's time. A physician named Korolev — the name derives from *korol'* (king), a title appropriate for a hero summoned to do battle in the other world—is dispatched to attend to the daughter of a factory-owning family in the provinces in response to a "long, incoherently composed telegram" (*S* 10:75). This incoherence initiates a series of diabolic motifs that culminate in the doctor's vision of the factory as the devil itself. After examining the patient, Liza, and finding "nothing special" wrong with her (*S* 10:78), the doctor is persuaded to spend the night with her family. Unable to sleep, he wanders about the grounds of the factory complex, like a shaman roaming the underworld in search of the soul of his subject, and concludes that the whole factory is arranged to the advantage of one being only—the devil. This conclusion is repeated three times (the doctor's thoughts are reported via free indirect discourse), with the third and most emphatic as follows: "And he thought about the devil, in whom he did not believe, and looked back at the two windows in which lights were shining. It seemed to him that it was the devil himself watching him with those crimson eyes, that mysterious force which had established the relations between the strong and the weak, a gross blunder which is beyond correction by any means" (*S* 10:82). It subsequently emerges that the suffering girl makes sense of her situation through a similar mythopoetic operation: she tells him that "Lermontov's Tamara was alone and saw the devil" (*S* 10:84).[58] For the first time, Liza has found an interlocutor with whom she can speak the idiom of her soul. Their successful communication, a distinctive combination of socio-psycho-economic analysis and overt myth making, has a therapeutic effect on them both. The next day all are returned to the realm of the sun, that is, to "this" world. Church bells are ringing, the patient is dressed festively in white with a flower in her hair, and now the previously demonic "windows in the factory complex glistened gaily." Nevertheless, the doctor notices the same sadness in his patient, who "talked with an expression as if she wanted to tell him something special, something important, something for him alone" (*S* 10:85). However uplifting the rhetoric of the story's ending, the doctor's departure includes an ironic twist on the expected ending of a katabatic journey undertaken to rescue a beloved from the underworld: Korolev (married and a professional) abandons his patient, now adorned as a bride, to the sufferings that are sure to return as soon as the sun sets. An earlier story treating the same theme of a woman imprisoned by her patrimony of industrial wealth, "A Woman's Kingdom" ("Bab'e tsarstvo," 1894), makes similar use of the descent motif.[59]

The brief masterpiece "Student" ("Student," 1894), one of Chekhov's own favorite stories, is explicitly structured as a descent and ascent. Echoing Dante's *Inferno*, it opens with a seminarian suddenly finding himself in a dark wood; the hero moves in spirit and space from cheerfulness in a thick wood before the onset of darkness, to despondency with the coming of night and bitter cold in a low, marshy place, to euphoria with the crossing of a river and ascent. The cold winds are repeatedly associated with an untimely return of winter (S 8:306–7), in mythological terms the periodic descent of the underworld's female captive, Persephone. The Orthodox Christian mythological framework predominates here, however, since the story takes place at sunset on Good Friday, and the student's descent occurs during the same interval—between crucifixion and resurrection—when in the apocryphal tradition Christ made his own descent. This is known as the "harrowing of hell."

The story turns on the student's retelling of Peter's denial, one segment of the myth of Christ's death and resurrection, to two women working the village's kitchen gardens. As in "A Doctor's Visit," the central characters are transformed as the result of mythopoetic storytelling, with a male hero addressing females trapped in unhappy situations, captives in the underworld. Heartened by his ability to move them to tears, the student reasons: "If Vasilisa had cried, and her daughter got upset, then that which he had just told them, which had occurred nineteen centuries ago, relates to the present [. . .] The past, he thought, is connected with the present by an unbroken chain of events, one flowing from another. And it seemed to him that he had just seen both ends of that chain: he had managed to touch one end, and the other trembled" (S 8:309). Descent and ascent has enabled the hero to "see" two millennia of cultural continuity and provided him with new powers as a teller of the stories pertaining to that tradition. This journey to hell has been in part about poetics.

Such metaliterary implications are one traditional aspect of the descent motif. Their appearance in Chekhov anticipates the succeeding generation of poets, with the katabatic theme indicating an essentially symbolic and modernist dimension that Chekhov's writings had shown since the early stages of his career. For instance, in the overtly self-reflexive story "The Cynic" ("Tsinik," 1885), the vision of an animal menagerie as hell turns on the question of how the keeper narrates the lives of the beasts exhibited there;[60] though there may have been no direct influence, the story appears echoed in the 1905 lyric of Fedor Sologub, "We Are All Captured Beasts" ("My vse plennenye zveri"). In "Easter Eve" ("Sviataia noch'," 1886), crossing to the other world—in this case a monastery—is associated with artistic inspiration, indeed, becomes a lesson in writing. The genre is the acathist (*akafist*), church songs in praise of Christ, Mary, and certain saints; the artist is a monk who has died this Easter holiday. For the narrator, crossing becomes a lesson in the poetics of the acathist from the one monk who appreciated the song's artistry, the one monk who, because he must serve as the ferryman, will not be able to hear them performed. By contrast, the devout attending the Easter eve service are deaf to the music's beauty: for believers, of all people, the descent is meaningless, and they return from it exhausted, in lower form than in which they departed.

The descent into hell, always an ordeal, is something that a certain kind of hero does. For Lord Raglan, Joseph Campbell, and many others, it is in fact the paradigm of heroic activity; as Northrop Frye writes, the hero's descent "is not a good plot, but *the* good plot."[61] Among heroes who make the descent, it has become traditional to distinguish between the active hero and the passive, suffering hero. The former, who gets through his ordeal by martial feats or trickery, conquers the beast of hell and brings back a boon or his beloved, while the latter's initiatory journey—often of death and rebirth—provides him with esoteric knowledge and an elevated state of being.[62]

Both paradigms are always exploited in deeply ambiguous fashion in Chekhov's works. In the travel sketches *From Siberia* and in *Sakhalin Island,* the hell subtext emerges most notably when the narrative is focusing on the narrator, that is, on Chekhov. Indeed, it is one of the striking paradoxes of Chekhov's oeuvre that *Sakhalin Island*—a work of social science, which Chekhov wrote "to pay my debt to medicine"[63] and as a substitute for two doctoral theses begun and aborted earlier in his career—is also his most overtly subjective work. This study, with the travel sketches preceding it, is the only Chekhov narrative in which the author makes his genuine self manifestly visible.

If the hero's descent was a masterplot for the journey to Sakhalin, then it would appear that one purpose for the journey was to cast the traveling author as hero; Chekhov was setting himself a hero's task, a *podvig*.[64] In an uncharacteristic emotional outburst, just before leaving for Sakhalin, Chekhov played up this aspect of his impending voyage in a letter to V. M. Lavrov, who had published the criticism that Chekhov's writing was "unprincipled." Chekhov would not have responded to this charge, he wrote, except for the fact that "very soon I am departing Russia for a long time, perhaps never to return" (10 April 1890). Chekhov researched the explorers who preceded him, and their exploits were prominent in his consciousness before he departed; thus he wrote to Suvorin, "Not more than twenty-five or thirty years ago our own Russians, exploring Sakhalin, performed feats amazing enough to deify man" (9 March 1890). As Lord Raglan put it, "Heroes visit the underworld, the dwelling place of the dead . . . in order that they may return from the dead as gods."[65]

The active descent pattern involving the rescue of a beloved from the underworld and the conquering of hell—in its paradigmatic versions often requiring the slaying of a monster—imagines erotic pleasure only as the earned reward of the "hard journey" or *podvig*. Chekhov pretended not to understand why the love-struck Ol'ga Kundasova insisted on accompanying him, uninvited, on the beginning river stages of his 1890 voyage to Sakhalin; a sexual dalliance at such a journey's start was certainly counterindicated by the poetics of the journey to hell. But Chekhov rewarded himself after leaving Sakhalin with a dark-skinned woman under a palm tree in the "heaven" of Ceylon, and he crowed about it in his correspondence: "When I have children, I'll say to them, not without pride: 'Why, you sons of bitches, I've had relations in my day with a black-eyed Hindu girl, and guess where? In a coconut grove, on a moonlit night!'"[66]

This masterplot largely coincides with the mythologeme in Chekhov's writings, mentioned earlier, of Saint George the dragon slayer. One of Chekhov's ubiquitous allusions to the venerated saint occurs in "Peasants." There the young student who rides over to the village from the other side of the river dividing the peasant village from the gentry estate and extinguishes the fire, conquering hell, is named Zhorzh, or George; and it is to the point that, once finished with the fire, he turns his weapon (a hose) on the peasants themselves. But it is not only a matter of invoking a broadly understood pattern from the Russian religious culture. Savely Senderovich's excavation of a veritable cult of George in the Chekhov clan, in which the saint's name was also that of the grandfather who earned freedom for himself and his serf family,[67] signals a deeply personal aspect to the George motif, just as there is to that of the descent. How striking, in this context, that the most prized souvenirs Chekhov brought back from his trip to the Far East were mongooses—creatures whose serpent-killing abilities he touted on his return (see fig. 8).[68]

As the mongooses would suggest, Chekhov was apt to poke fun at his own deepest aspirations; thus, his letters anticipating the Sakhalin journey often joke about the risk of being eaten by bears or tigers, or murdered by escaped convicts: "I've bought myself a sheepskin coat, an officer's leather waterproof, big boots, and a big knife for cutting sausage and hunting tigers. I'm armed from head to foot."[69] Several years later, when Chekhov learned how G. I. Rossolimo's inquiries regarding the possibility of Chekhov's receiving a doctoral degree in medicine for his book on Sakhalin had been rebuffed by the dean, his response was to burst out laughing.[70]

Heroism of the active, triumphant sort is consistently travestied in Chekhov's poetic world, too; in this respect "Ariadne" and "Sinner from Toledo," in which the active heroic potentials associated with katabasis are invoked only to be treated ironically, are characteristic. The impossibility of heroic action in the present-day Russian milieu is also a prominent theme in *Wood Demon*. Shortly before the appearance of Elena at the picnic, Khrushchov declares to Professor Serebriakov: "The whole district—all the women—see a hero in me, a pro-

8. Chekhov (right) sailing home from Sakhalin with his mongooses, with naval lieutenant G. N. Glinka aboard the *Petersburg* (1890). Reprinted courtesy of The State Literary Museum (Gosudarstvennyi literaturnyi muzei), Moscow.

gressive man, and you are famous throughout Russia. And if they seriously consider people like me heroes, and if people like you are seriously famous, that means that when there's nobody else around even a dumb peasant is a nobleman, that there are no true heroes, no talents, no people who would lead us out of this dark forest, who would fix what we spoil, no real eagles who deserve the honor of fame" (S 12:194). The "dark forest" is Dante's, and the way out would involve a journey through hell. When Elena reveals herself in the play's denouement, the old man with whom she has been hiding, Diadin, echoes

Khrushchov's discourse on heroism and confesses to having "kidnapped" her, as Paris did Helen of Troy, but then immediately undermines his boast: "Although there are no pockmarked Parises, nevertheless my friend Horatio, there is much in this world of which our philosophers have not dreamt" (*S* 12:195). Habitually couching his speech in such allusions to classical literature, here Diadin underlines the non-heroical nature of his milieu by combining a reference to Homer's *Iliad* with a quotation from Prince Hamlet, whose very name evokes decades of Russian socio-literary criticism regarding the ineffective hero in Russian literature (dating from Ivan Turgenev's 1860 article "Hamlet and Don Quixote").[71] Indeed, one suspects that the name Diadin is derived from the *diadia* (old man) of Lermontov's poem "Borodino"; there the contrast between the elder, heroic generation that defeated Napoleon and a younger, non-heroic one received one of its paradigmatic articulations in Russian literature. So too in an 1895 letter to Bilibin, his former colleague from the "small press," Chekhov wrote, "I read a bit of you and I recall the past, and when I happen to encounter some young humorist I read [Lermontov's] 'Borodino' to him and say, 'You're no *bogatyrs!*'" (18 January 1895).[72]

In Chekhov, little separates such ironic treatments of the active descent pattern from the passive pattern. Chekhov departed for the Far East in a state of spiritual and physical exhaustion: he had lost his brother Nikolai a short time before taking the journey, and his blood-spitting and palpitations had already given him ample reason to contemplate, however quietly, his own mortality. If previous scholars have adduced the search for spiritual and creative rebirth as a reason for Chekhov's journey to Sakhalin, they have failed to see that Chekhov himself linked this search with the archetypal descent pattern.

Chekhov also appears to have understood, as Mircea Eliade has written, that in a world where traditional belief systems no longer underwrite the meaning of the descent masterplot, we can still find the pattern of descent and ordeals "in the spiritual crises, the solitude and despair through which every human being must pass in order to attain to a responsible, genuine, and creative life." According to Eliade, "If we look closely, we see that every human life is made up of a series of ordeals, of 'deaths,' and of 'resurrections.'"[73] Thus, although Chekhov often structured his works of fiction and drama as symbolic descents, the overt journeys of his neurotic heroes tend to be inward, and their most important confrontations (and failures) with the self. This is especially the case in stories with a rather explicit initiatory pattern—another typical descent motif[74]—the central events of which deserve to be called existential crises.[75] Here the epigraph to Freud's *Interpretation of Dreams* should be recalled: "Flectere si nequeo superos, Acheronta movebo." Chekhov's metaphoric association between the inner self or unconscious and the mythological underworld is one that Freud and psychoanalysts since have frequently employed.[76] To accomplish the journey means to see one's self profoundly, as well as to change that self.

There is a particular temporality that is characteristic of seeing the lower world, and this makes the descent motif relevant to Chekhov's very distinctive handling of time and memory. As was most clear in regard to "Ward 6" and "Black Monk," the ethical stance and faith in progress of a Chekhov character—how an individual sees the world and others—is apt to be coordinated with, if not conditioned by, how that individual conceives the temporality in which he or she lives.[77]

This theme is directly addressed in "Lights" ("Ogni," 1888). The story begins when three men—the railway engineer Anan'ev, his student assistant, and a doctor who is the story's frame narrator—are drawn out of the hut where they are spending the night by a barking dog. The dog, Azorka, appears to have barked at nothing, however; the doctor explains, "He can't stand being alone, sees horrible dreams all the time and suffers from nightmares, and when you yell at him, then he gets something like hysterics" (S 7:105). The nightmare of this anthropomorphized, angst-ridden hound becomes these three men's hellish vision of the steppe at night. What is visible reminds the narrator "of the times of chaos"; it is a picture "not of this world" (S 7:106). The dog's name, suggestive of the Azores islands, overlays this image of an existential void with that of the vast empty sea.

The engineer, a bit tipsy, relishes the scattered, dimly visible signs of the feat he is undertaking and the progress that will result from it: "Last year in this very place there was naked steppe, not a scent of the human spirit, and now take a look: life, civilization! And, God, how fine all this is! We're building a railway, and after us, perhaps in a hundred or two hundred years, good people will build factories, schools, and hospitals here" (S 7:106).[78] But the student sees with a far vaster temporal horizon: "At some time there lived in this world Philistines and Amalekites; they made war, played a certain role, and now there's no trace of them. And that's how it will be with us. Now we are building a railroad, we stand here and philosophize, but after two thousand or so years pass, there won't even be any dust left from this whole embankment and all these people now sleeping after their heavy labors. In essence, it's horrible!" (S 7:107). Such thoughts dismay Anan'ev; while they might be "fine and natural in old age," for a man of the student's age they are "anathema," an "illness" (S 8:108). As a younger man Anan'ev too suffered "thoughts of the aimlessness of life, the insignificance and transience of the visible world, Solomon's 'vanity of vanities,'" but he struggled to overcome them. After a long rant he tells the story of a despicable act he committed in that ungrounded period, "when all was deceit and illusion, and in essence and end results there was no difference between convict life on Sakhalin and life in Nice, and the difference between Kant's brain and that of a fly was fundamentally meaningless" (*S* 7:114): Anan′ev deceived, seduced, and betrayed a young married woman, Kisochka, who had known him as an idealistic and upright youth, and who trusted him thoroughly.[79] It took only two days for his conscience to drive him back to beg her forgiveness, however, and since then Anan′ev, who still blushes with shame as he tells his story, has seen both himself and Kisochka differently: "They say that every time, during the introductory lecture in a course on female illnesses, medical students are given the advice that before undressing and digitally examining a sick woman, they should recall that each of them has a mother, a sister, a bride . . . This advice would serve well not only for medical men, but for everyone who in one way or another encounters women in life. Now, when I have a wife and a daughter, oh how I understand that advice! My God, how I understand it!" (*S* 7:131). This story about time is thus also a story about seeing, and Anan′ev's reasonable temporal horizon and faith in progress go hand in hand with how he now sees himself, the world, and the future of his beloved family.

Nevertheless, the story ends on an ambiguous note. The student remains unconvinced, whereupon Anan′ev tells him that he expected nothing different: conviction "is achieved only by way of personal experience and suffering" (*S* 7:136), which is to say, the "hard journey" is not to be avoided. And the narrator departs, thinking, and repeating, "You can't figure out anything on this earth!" (*S* 7:140).[80]

Although Chekhov subsequently tended to avoid the direct philosophical meditation staged in "Lights"—or at the very least embedded his philosophizing more deeply in his narratives, as in "Ward 6"—characters in both his fiction and his drama often indulge in speculation about what will be in fifty, a hundred, or a thousand years, now with optimism, now with existential despair. Taken together, these remarks create a highly ambiguous picture. Thus the indifference of nature to man that appalls the student in "Lights" becomes a "pledge of our eternal salvation" in the lyrical passage describing Gurov's reflections on a bench overlooking the sea in "Lady with the Lapdog" (*S* 10:133). Both the low and high points of "Student" involve reflections on how the present is connected with the past. And the physician in "A Doctor's Visit" promises his patient a bright future—perhaps beyond their lifetimes—when the social ills entrapping them will have been overcome, while the medical man in *Wood Demon* declares, "If in a thousand years man is happy, then to some small extent I shall be guilty of it" (*S* 10:141).

The theme of time and memory is no less vexed when elaborated within the bounds of an individual life. In "Grisha" (1886) and "Steppe" ("Step′," 1888), both in large part ventures into child psychology, the retention of impressions surpassing the child's ability to assimilate them causes illness. In "Rothschild's Fiddle," the undertaker Iakov, a sullen and cruel man obsessed with financial losses, becomes human when he recalls a loss suppressed from consciousness, that of his child who died fifty years ago.[81] The first-person narrator of "My Life: The Story of a Provincial" ("Moia zhizn' [Rasskaz provintsiala]," 1896), one of Chekhov's gloomiest works, opens the final chapter of the story by saying that if he had a ring, he would etch inside it the words "Nothing passes," because "each of our tiniest steps has meaning for present and future life" (*S* 9:279). As in "Student," however, this linkage of temporalities holds as much anguish for the narrator as it does hope: he is oppressed by painful memories that recede only in the oblivion of menial labor. It appears that he and others of his generation might free themselves from the social and psychological legacies of their fathers only at the cost of self-destruction. This motif of absolute memory arises in contrast to that of amnesia, since the ring is proposed in response to the one his wayward wife has inscribed in the (then) dead language of King Solomon's Hebrew: "Everything passes."[82] But her notion that all is forgotten, that all links eventually rupture, is no less ambiguous than its antithesis. "When I'm sad," she writes, "then these words cheer me up, and when I'm cheerful, they sadden me" (*S* 9:272). In "My Life" the opposing attitudes toward time expressed by the two mottos come to stand for opposing character types and ethical codes. In "Lights" and "Student," characters literally *see* time, and the works turn on the question of how they see it.

In name the underworld presents itself as a spatial dimension, but the very special temporal values it embodies are central to Chekhov's art. Forgetting and remembering have traditionally been central events in katabatic journeys. Although the poles of memory and forgetting are not uniformly located, respectively, in the other world or in this world, they nonetheless operate as a structuring semantic opposition. So it is in Plato's Myth of Er, where pasts are contemplated for a thousand years, futures are then chosen, and all of it is forgotten (because of a drink from the River of Heedlessness on the Plane of Forgetting) before reemergence in the upper world; so it is in the underworlds of Virgil and Dante, where nothing has been forgotten, and where even the future can be glimpsed;[83] and so it is in Freud's underworld of the unconscious, where, indeed, "nothing passes."[84]

It is precisely this sharp opposition between the position where "nothing passes" and the one where "everything passes" that is underlined in Chekhov's works. One of the most succinct expressions of this is found in "Kashtanka," a story about a dog that is really about time and memory. Kashtanka's descent into the hellish circus ring and her ascent to her former masters in the audience at the story's end constitute "a restoration of ruptured time."[85] But this happy ending to a children's tale also represents an atavistic throwback, a dark negation of progress; for the animal trainer whom Kashtanka abandons is another version of the scientist presented in "Three Years" and Chekhov's notebook (see chapter 3) as emblematic of human advancement: having "managed to train a cat, a mouse, a pigeon hawk, and a sparrow to eat from one dish," he allows us to "hope that education will accomplish the same with people" (*S* 9:56). The tradesman to whom Kashtanka flees from the circus ring, whose call is more archaic and therefore more powerful than that of her benevolent current master, fed her poorly and used to beat her.

Ice and Eros at the End of Time

The descent motif echoes from afar in Chekhov's last play, *Cherry Orchard*. The twice-occurring, uncanny twang is one of the most overtly symbolic moments in his oeuvre, and the sound's effect on the characters creates deep but obscure implications. The character Lopakhin's explanation of its source—that a cable has snapped in a nearby mine shaft—evokes an image of unseen plutonic depths, an underworld of wealth-producing mines. In the most literal sense, his mention of mines adds a subterranean dimension to the play's setting; and this opens up the space necessary for a descent into the earth, a descent into hell.

Chekhov's last, unrealized playwriting project also exploited the descent motif; but it promised, too, to stage dreaming itself, as well as the conjunction of seeing and the erotic—indeed, the whole complex of imagery I have been tracing in this chapter. Both Stanislavskii and Knipper discuss the new work Chekhov was conceiving in the last year of his life. Stanislavskii reports: "He was dreaming of a new play, along completely new lines for him. To be sure, the plot of the play he had thought up was not Chekhovian. Judge for yourself: two friends, both young, love the same woman. This shared love and jealousy create complicated interrelations between them. It ends with them both departing on an expedition to the North Pole. The set for the last act depicts a huge ship, icebound. In the play's finale both friends see a white specter gliding across the snow. It's obviously the shade or soul of the beloved woman, who has died in the far distant homeland."[86] Knipper's account of Chekhov's idea differs slightly from Stanislavskii's: there is no mention of the friend and rival; rather, the dreamer, who is a scientist (*uchenyi*), has either been unloved or betrayed by the object of his affection.[87] The staging device with which the projected play was to end—so reminiscent of Symbolist drama, and of the budding playwright Konstantin Treplev's dictum that the future of the theater lies in the depiction not of reality but of dreams—certainly departs from the naturalistic Chekhov Stanislavskii had been staging. But by now we are in a position to see (*pace* Stanislavskii) this plot summary as quintessentially Chekhovian; indeed, it represents a highly condensed emblem of what we have been observing over the course of this study, though not without modifications attributable to an awareness of approaching death.

This vision at sea very much recalls the two such visions of an erotic object framing Chekhov's early story "At Sea" (discussed at length in chapter 1), which Chekhov had revised only a few years before. That story's original version comprised two acts of seeing: first the dreamy, solipsistic narrator gazes out to sea and apprehends the image of his imaginary beloved; at the end of the story, the narrator is observing the bridal chamber through a peephole together with his father, who is also his Oedipal rival. These two configurations correspond to those in the two variants of Chekhov's last idea for a play, as reported by Knipper and Stanislavskii: in one the male observer is alone, in the other he is oddly accompanied by his adversary, to whom he is also attached by affective relations. Also striking in Stanislavskii's version is that the friends and rivals both see the beloved's specter; such a shared hallucination, observed simultaneously by two people, is no longer a hallucination. Chekhov in essence reverses the dramatic convention by which delusive visions are staged, as in Shakespeare's *Macbeth*: specters, which are of course played by embodied actors and are visible to the audience, are not "seen" by characters other than the deluded one. The culmination of Chekhov's play would have gone beyond revealing the subjective seeing of his hero; it would have made his dreams real and objective.

The heroic expedition to the polar north enacts another of Chekhov's archetypal journeys to hell. What little we know of Chekhov's conception suggests that the betrayed lover and scientist (*uchenyi*) undertakes this journey to heal the narcissistic injury of a failed passion. He will exercise his professional scientific gaze while accomplishing a heroic feat or *podvig,* and in Stanislavskii's variant, he will overcome his ambivalence toward his loved rival—in a sense, take him back into his self—by taking him along (recall the sailor in "At Sea" helping his father up the stairs at the story's end). The mission fails, however; his ship becomes icebound, his seeing degenerates to an unscientific extreme (he sees a specter), and the love object he glimpses can only be a sign of his abject failure, precisely the opposite of the black monk who validates Kovrin's grandiose fantasy of the self in "Black Monk." What is more, the fantasy of rescuing the erotic object that lies at the core of the katabatic masterplot also collapses: the beloved has perished. The lover is frozen in place, unable to complete the voyage from which he might have returned reborn, whole.

The frozen seascape of the play's last scene recalls the frozen landscape dramatized in Treplev's play within the play in *Seagull*. Here, as in Treplev's play, the setting "is dramatizing in mythopoetic language a physical world that is delicately poised between death and life, between sterility and creation [. . .] We have here, essentially, a dramatization of unliberated life and creation; and, it is further apparent, this is also a crucial self-dramatization."[88] The world and everything in it has frozen and died, leaving only the observing self alive; but this is of course an inverted vision of the death of that self.

A setting that in earlier times and warmer climes provided the conditions for explosive erotic potential in Chekhov's life and writings has been shock-cooled. This scene represents both a fantasy of control over eros—its deliberate suppression—and anticipation of the emptiness and literal death such an absence of eros represents.

Conclusion: Seeing Chekhov's Things

I feel as if I've dried out, like an old bookcase (*shkaf*).
— Chekhov, letter to A. I. Smagin (16 December 1891)

We have been viewing Chekhov's person, and apprehending the meaning of that visibility, through his letters, through memoirs about him, and, most
important, through the fiction and drama he created. There is yet another body
of material that might be assembled and analyzed to the same end, however. I
have in mind aspects of the mundane, material organization of his life: the things
he kept around him, the objects that he arrayed in the threshold space between
himself and the outside world.

Many photographs have been published of Chekhov alone and with intimates
and acquaintances.[1] But a century after Chekhov's death, there is no better way
for biographers, critics, and highly interested readers—today's *antonovki,* as the
female "groupies" who shadowed Chekhov in his last years in Yalta were
called[2]—to feel that they know Chekhov than for them to visit the home-museums devoted to him in Moscow, Melikhovo, Yalta, and Gurzuf. There one can
see Chekhov's personal possessions and private spaces. This is most true of the
so called White Dacha (*belaia dacha*) in Yalta, which Chekhov himself built and
still occupied at the time of his death in Badenweiler; it houses the largest collection by far of genuine artifacts from the author's life, and in 1922 became the
first Chekhov museum.[3] (By contrast, Chekhov's house at the estate of Melikhovo, where he lived for most of the 1890s, is a facsimile—the original was
burned after the Civil War—and items in it are for the most part duplicates of
Chekhov's original possessions; so too are the materials on display in the Gurzuf
cottage and in the home-museum in Moscow.)

We are in a sense authorized to approach Chekhov's personal (and poetic) world through his things by the avowed materialism that makes Chekhov a descendant of Chernyshevskii and his doctor-heroes. Chekhov's most famous remarks on the topic were made in a polemical letter (of 7 May 1889) to Alexei Suvorin. Materialism, he says,

> is something indispensable and inevitable and beyond human power. Everything that lives on earth is necessarily materialistic [. . .] Creatures of a higher order, thinking humans, are [. . .] necessarily materialists. They search for truth in matter because there is nowhere else for them to search: all they can see, hear and feel is matter. They can necessarily seek out truth only where their microscopes, probes and knives are effective. Prohibiting materialist doctrine is tantamount to preventing man from seeking out the truth. Outside of matter there is no experience or knowledge, and consequently no truth [. . .] It seems to me that, when a corpse is being dissected, even the most inveterate spiritualist must *necessarily* come up against the question of where the soul is.[4]

What stronger argument could be made for understanding Chekhov through the material objects he kept close at hand and his organization of the space surrounding him? Note, too, how Chekhov clinches his case: his authority in addressing this question ultimately rests on his professional identity as a physician, trained to cope with the thingness of human beings; he has performed autopsies.[5]

The White Dacha

In early fall 1898 Chekhov bought a piece of property on a hillside that was then outside and above Yalta, overlooking the town and its lovely bay. By the end of August 1899 he had moved into his new home, though it was not quite complete. According to the architect Chekhov engaged to build the house, L. N. Shapovalov, Chekhov and his sister Mariia Pavlovna were extremely involved in the architectural design process, and Chekhov visited the site daily to supervise construction. This house deserves to be read and interpreted no less than the last few literary masterpieces he wrote there. As a gesture toward the wealth of meaning represented by this object, let us begin with one small example of how the physical space of the home can also encompass a symbolic dimension, underwritten by the idiosyncratic cultural history of one family.

There was a Chekhov family legend surrounding the birth of the eldest Chekhov sibling, Aleksandr Pavlovich. Aleksandr came into the world during an inauspicious moment of the Crimean War, while Pavel Egorovich and

9. Chekhov and his architect L. N. Shapovalov during the building of the White Dacha. From
Zinovii Papernyi, *Taina siia . . . Liubov' u Chekhova* (Moscow: B.S.G.-Press, 2002), 272–73.

Evgeniia Iakovlevna were fleeing their home in Taganrog to escape the shelling
of the port city by Russia's enemies. The house in the hills that Chekhov built
forty-five years later included, naturally enough, generous southern windows
from which town and bay could be viewed; this was especially true of Mariia
Pavlovna's room, which is set apart from and on a floor above the others. Even
today this room—though maintained as it was when Mariia Pavlovna died—
remains a private part of the museum, off-limits to the public. According to the
curators, this is due to the poor condition of the second floor, where plaster is
cracking in the ceiling, and because the stairway and hallway cannot withstand
the wear and tear of parading visitors. And yet the way this private home, transformed into a public institution, has been subsequently subdivided into private
and public spaces reflects something that was true in the time when Chekhov
still lived there.

A standing joke among the Chekhov family in the Yalta period held that, from
Mariia's windows a cannon could defend the city against any attack that might

10. The White Dacha, Yalta, from "About Chekhov," pamphlet of the Chekhov Museum (Dom-muzei A. P. Chekhova), Yalta.

come by sea. No doubt the legend of the first Chekhov family flight from Taganrog served as a backdrop to this joke about repulsing an invasion from the heights of the newly reconstituted Chekhov home. Such an association between the two homes was apparent in the symbolizing function of artifacts that, for the family (minus the late Pavel Egorovich), recalled those Taganrog days: the most valued icon in the Yalta home was the one with which Chekhov's parents were blessed when they married, to which Pavel Egorovich prayed before fleeing Taganrog in 1854, and which he credited with saving the house while those all around were hit by shells.

If the joke about Mariia's windows had special resonance because of the family-historical memory of fleeing Taganrog in the face of the English attack, then that memory could not help but be associated also with the family's next escape from Taganrog—to Moscow two decades later—as a result of financial collapse. This catastrophe resulted in part from Pavel Egorovich's expenditures in building a new house for his family. The young Chekhov was left behind in Taganrog for three years (July 1876 to August 1879), for a time with his younger brother Ivan and then alone. He sold off the family's remaining possessions, paid debts, and forwarded what remained to Moscow; he completed his secondary school education while supporting himself by tutoring; and Chekhov even managed to send some of his earnings to his desperate family during this period. Biographers of Chekhov invariably understand this traumatic episode, from which Chekhov emerged as a remarkably mature and determined young man, as crucially formative. Chekhov hinted at this himself in his famous letter to Suvorin about squeezing the slave's blood out of his veins, discussed in chapter 3.

The home Chekhov built more than thirty years later in Yalta thus also recalls the home Chekhov's father built and lost. Chekhov's impressive drive for professional success and financial security was always a struggle for something beyond personal status: he sought to "make good" for his family. One could argue that building the White Dacha as a home for his mother and his sister as well as himself, as the culminating step in this heroic struggle, in some sense made right the psychic damage or loss that attached in legend to the family's origins and subsequent history; and this is reflected in the collective military fantasy—for that joke does involve a fantasy—centered, ironically enough, on the bedroom of the one female Chekhov sibling. I would not wish to make more of this set of associations than the unsound second floor of Chekhov's home-museum could withstand; suffice it for the moment to have indicated one potential arena of personal meanings encoded into this thing that Chekhov built.

It will not do to reduce the dynamic and multilateral symbolizing potential of the Yalta home to a static projection of Chekhov's unconscious. As the social psychologists Mihaly Csikszentmihalyi and Eugene Rochberg-Halton put it in their pioneering study of domestic symbols and the self:

> Like some strange race of cultural gastropods, people build homes out of their own essence, shells to shelter their personality. But, then, these symbolic projections react on their creators, in turn shaping the selves they are. The envelope thus constructed is not just a metaphor. The home is an empirical and normative entity, constituted through time by the objective patterns of psychic activity that people invest in different areas of the house, in different objects, and in different activities. Thus the home is a goal or intention that becomes realized through the attention the inhabitants give to it. In their words, the home is a craft cultivated by all its members [. . .] But the home, as already stated, is also an objective entity with its own "personality," which exerts a reciprocal influence on the individual family members. It represents the *gestalt* of the family and forms an essential part of the *social self* of the individual.[6]

One hundred years after its construction the White Dacha also greatly influences the way we view Chekhov. Those who have seen this home firsthand, inside and out, and sat on the bench in his garden where, they are sure to be told by their guide, he chatted with Maksim Gorkii, feel a deeper connection with Chekhov; they know him personally. Visiting Chekhov's home-museum means partaking in Chekhov's legendary hospitality, even if one falls short in the prominence required to rate signing the guest book. A veritable subgenre of Chekhov studies could be established on the basis of the common device whereby the author opens his or her essay, and thus frames his or her under-standing of Chekhov, with a visit to this house, whether in Chekhov's lifetime or decades later; it is particularly favored in less scholarly approaches. The great American short story writer John Cheever adopted this tactic, writing of his tour of the home, "The sense that Chekhov was with me was, of course, very keen";[7] so too, more recently, has Janet Malcolm.[8] The same is of course true of Melikhovo and the home-museum in Moscow, though to a lesser extent: be-cause these sites and/or their contents are less genuine, they do not contain the aura of Chekhov in the same way the Yalta house does.

These homes in which Chekhov lived, these visible and tangible components of the author's self, tend also to affect the way we periodize Chekhov's life. Thus Chekhov's sister later wrote, in the first lines of her little book about the house, "In the life of my brother, the writer Anton Pavlovich Chekhov, there were four periods: the Taganrog, the Moscow, the Melikhovo, and the Yalta periods."[9] Al-though she speaks of "the *writer*" Chekhov, it is where he lived that defines his career.

Touring the White Dacha is about "seeing Chekhov" in other senses as well. If the material laid out in the preceding chapters does make the case for pro-found and wide-ranging implications deriving from issues of seeing and being seen in Chekhov the person and his writings, then this interpretive framework also ought to help make sense of the house. Consider, for example, its situation. The piece of land on which it was built, like the other two properties Chekhov purchased near Yalta, is distinguished by two key features: a degree of elevation, from which the view is impressive, and a peripheral location (or such was the case when Chekhov bought the site). The house is also not particularly notice-able from the street (though this would have been far less true at first, when no greenery obstructed the view of passersby and the road had not yet been ele-vated). In addition to the quite obvious practical reasons for buying property outside the center of a fast-developing town—favorable price chief among them—a wish to position oneself in a particular way in regard to one's own gaze and that of others seems quite probable as well.

But let us turn to the house itself, inside which the rooms of greatest inter-est are, naturally, Chekhov's own: his study and his bedroom.

Chekhov's study comprised a space with both private and public dimensions that appear to have been structured with some care. In design, decoration, and use, it reflects Chekhov's concerns about seeing and being seen, showing and hiding; and a number of key items in it are arrayed so as to create a series of highly polarized symbolic fields in other respects as well.

To be sure, Chekhov worked in his study (when bad health did not force him to make use of the small table beside his bed); but it was also the room in which visitors were seen, that is, where visitors could view the living, breathing (often with difficulty) Chekhov. Although he was a very private man, and clearly one who detested public attention, Chekhov's accessibility to others—particularly in this period of his life—was astonishing. Not only invited intimates and acquaintances but also many strangers who had the impudence to appear at his door easily gained entry.

The study's most prominent architectural feature is the huge picture window that faces south and sports a sill broad and low enough to provide seating. When the house is viewed from the south, this window draws a great deal of attention. According to the curators, the stained glass panes that further distinguish this window were incorporated so as to soothe Chekhov's troublesome, astigmatic eyes. Indeed, Chekhov's eyes gave him a great deal of grief, as evidenced by the many complaints in his letters. One wonders, though, why the window must be justified on the basis of Chekhov's illness. Might curators have found it an excessive, immodest, and attention-drawing decorative detail in a house that, like its owner, is very often lauded as modest?[10] There had been colored glass windows at Melikhovo, too.

According to the late chief curator of the home, Iurii Skobolev, Chekhov particularly enjoyed peering out this window—often with binoculars—and the sill was there so that, in his weakened state, he would have a place to sit while he lingered, watching.[11] In previous domiciles Chekhov had often written while positioned so as to view others or a landscape, or to eavesdrop. Thus in the Moscow apartment he occupied for a short time in the fall of 1885, before moving to the house where the Moscow Chekhov Museum is located, Chekhov wrote while listening to the weddings, funerals, and other goings on in the rental hall on the floor above him.[12] At Bogimovo, Chekhov "always wrote not at his table, but on the window sill, now and then glancing at the grounds."[13] In such instances Chekhov again realizes his metaphor of "writing from a crack in the wall," as discussed in chapter 1. The window in the study of his Yalta home appears to have been designed to accommodate just such inclinations.

Chekhov made particular use of the window when *antonovki* or other uninvited guests would call: while he or a family member was conversing with the visitors, he would turn his back to them, proceed to the window, and listen while observing the bay through binoculars. This is how one memoirist describes Chekhov's defensive use of these binoculars:

11. Chekhov's Yalta study, featuring picture window, from Tat'ana N. Barskaia, *Anton Chekhov. Pis'ma iz Ialty* (Yalta: El'ga, 1997).

Being in Yalta, I stopped by to see Anton Pavlovich. He was sitting on the balcony, and by him on a cord lay large maritime binoculars.

"These are my savior," he laughed, pointing toward the binoculars.

"Just how your savior?"

"Here's how. When folks come and start intelligent conversations, I pick up the binoculars and look through them. If it's day, toward the sea; at night, at the stars. Then these guests get the impression that I'm thinking about something important, profound, they're afraid to disturb me and they too fall silent."

A bit later we descended to the garden and sat on the bench there . . . A certain lady came and started talking about his writings. For a long time he looked to one side, then to the other, and then he stood and gave the request:

"Masha! Bring me the binoculars!"[14]

As both a physician and a patient, Chekhov knew well what it meant to be subjected to the objectivizing gaze of others, which is very likely why, from the time he first began spitting blood in 1884 until a massive hemorrhage made him an invalid in 1897, he refused to allow himself to be examined by another physician. When doting fans arrived to see him in the flesh, he defended himself by himself seeing: he turned his back to them and assumed the active position of observer, even as gawkers made him into a celebrity "thing." Perhaps here it would not be amiss to recall, from chapter 1, my treatment of Chekhov's voyage to Sakhalin as just such a defensive gesture, and of his behavior while Nemirovich-Danchenko read the manuscript of *The Seagull.*

We know how distasteful it was for Chekhov to be a public figure, how he avoided attending ceremonies and giving speeches, how he walked out of restaurants when attention was drawn to him, and how upsetting it could be for him to see his name in print. He was a private man. It is hard to imagine a more uncomfortable moment for Chekhov than the hour he stood on the stage of the Moscow Art Theater to be celebrated during the premiere of *Cherry Orchard,* discussed in chapter 1. And yet Chekhov's Yalta study has a quality to it that is very much like the stage he was compelled to take during his jubilee evening, for here are exhibited the gifts and souvenirs collected over twenty-five years of literary activity, as well as photographs of Chekhov's literary patriarchs and his coevals. Even during his own lifetime, Chekhov's study showed visitors—and *himself*—who he was, where he had been, what he had done. In this arena his self was very much on display.

Bunin wrote that Chekhov's desk and study were so crammed with trifles and souvenirs that he, Bunin, "couldn't have written a single line among them."[15] In addition to the sheer quantity and variety of distracting objects, Bunin had to contend with the absence of a clear code underwriting their meanings, or perhaps rather a baffling multiplicity of such codes. Take, for example, the objects representing Chekhov's parents on display in the room. Are the walking sticks of Pavel Egorovich that stand against the protruding brickwork of the fireplace mere mementos of the father, unburdened by deeper meaning, and their placement an accidental result of the design of the fireplace, which created an angle where they could be stood? And how are we to read the semiotic differences between how his parents are represented in the room? Whereas Chekhov's mother (who outlived Chekhov) is portrayed iconically, by a blown-up photograph, his father's presence is metonymic: the sticks are things that the man *used,* and manly things besides. Chekhov's possession and display of those sticks symbolized his inheritance of the patriarchal role in the family, a transition of power that took place long before Pavel Egorovich died. Did they also recall the generous beatings Chekhov and his older siblings received from their father as children? And perhaps the sticks' pose by the hearth is no accident, but alludes to folk beliefs regarding the fireplace as the domicile of house spirits, themselves linked to ancestors. The very clutter of the room may itself have some kinship with the general store of Pavel Egorovich, in which Chekhov grew up working, and which his brother Aleksandr described thus: "In a word, this was a mixture of the most varying sorts of goods, not submitting to any sort of classification."[16] In certain respects, however, Chekhov's study proves to be highly ordered.

12. In Chekhov's Yalta study, the fireplace and his father's walking sticks. Personal photograph, published by permission of the Chekhov Museum (Dom-muzei A. P. Chekhova), Yalta.

One object of particular interest in the study is the long, narrow landscape by Isaak Levitan, mounted in a niche above the fireplace. The painting, *Stogi sena v lunnuiu noch'* (Haystacks on a moonlit night), was dashed off by the visiting artist so that Chekhov would always be able to see the central Russian landscape for which he declared himself to be pining. This iconic sign is also a metonymic sign of Levitan himself, however, and has always been of great value as such— to Chekhov, to his sister (who relished it for the next fifty-five years), and to the museum's curators today. This multiple encoding can be felt in the way museum guides talk about the object: it signifies Chekhov's love for the homeland, his Russianness; it indicates how Chekhov was loved by Levitan; and it is a proud sign of the cultural and financial value of the museum's holdings (which fact was sadly confirmed by a burglary in the late 1990s that cost the museum several treasures, including an icon that had been painted by Pavel Egorovich and was presumably taken for its silver frame).[17]

The painting above the fireplace faces another landscape by Levitan, *Reka Istra* (The river Istra), hung on the opposite wall at the back of the alcove behind Chekhov's desk. One might view these two works as creating an axis along which the open space of Levitanish Russian countryside projects across the center of Chekhov's study and right through his desk. It turns out that establishing

13. In Chekhov's Yalta study, the alcove behind his desk. Personal
photograph, published by permission of the Chekhov Museum
(Dom-muzei A. P. Chekhova), Yalta.

such axes or semantic fields, stretching between related objects deployed on opposite sides of the study, appears to have been a fundamental compositional principle in the arrangement of Chekhov's most important and eye-catching
possessions. Although in this case the association between the two objects so
connected is based on the sameness of author, theme, and style—they are both
landscapes by Levitan—the other correlations I have noted feature sharp po-
larizations; that is, objects are related as opposites or inversions of one another.

On the north wall of that alcove hangs the portrait of Chekhov's mother; a line between it and the walking stick of his father would, once again, cross the center of the study. Against the east wall, between the alcove and the picture window, is propped a large photograph of Turgenev; catty-corner from it, on the north end of the west wall, the most prominent item is a photograph of Tolstoy, while below it stands a statue of him as well. Tolstoy dominates a collection of photographs of literary and theatrical friends and associates of Chekhov (including the famous picture of Chekhov reading *Seagull* to the actors of the Moscow Art Theater); Turgenev, with whom Chekhov had no personal connection, but with whose art Chekhov's has been most often compared, hangs by himself in the diagonally opposite corner. On the north side of Chekhov's study are grouped his books (including those he published); to their left (from the point of view of one seated behind Chekhov's desk), and on the adjoining wall to the right of the fireplace, hang and stand photographs and other objects that show what he accomplished in life: one can look here to see mementos of Chekhov as a cultural figure. And indeed, in what is by far the most frequently encountered photograph of Chekhov in his study,[18] Chekhov stands pressed into the

14. Chekhov in his Yalta study beside his bookcase and under a photograph of himself and collaborators on *Russian Thought* (1900). From the collections of Peter Urban, copyright © Diogenes Verlag AG Zürich.

corner among these objects, as though this were the appropriate spot for making his bodily self visible to posterity. The opposing wall, by contrast, is taken up almost entirely by the large picture window, from which Chekhov could look out onto the world; between the right side of the window and the doorway to Chekhov's bedroom is also located the telephone, and yet another small Levitan painting, *Dub i berezka* (Oak and birch), a gift of the late 1880s.

In sum, the predominant objects in Chekhov's study appear to organize its space according to the opposition of seeing and being seen. Seated behind his desk, Chekhov places himself on a west-east axis that features objects representing family life and intimates; this collection of signs of the personal self continues along the wall to his right, toward the door, with displays of photographs of his siblings and wife, and below them his most intimate friends and profes-

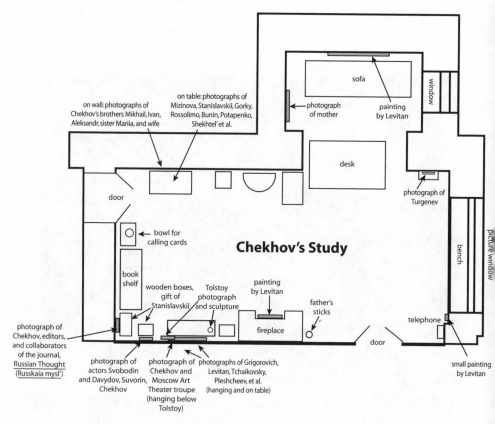

15. Diagram of Chekhov's study, Yalta.

sional associates (Komissarzhevskaia, Shekhtel', Bunin, Leont'ev-Shcheglov, Nemirovich-Danchenko, Gorkii, Mizinova, et al.). Glancing to the right from behind that desk, Chekhov sees himself, signs of his own visibility to others,
mementos of his public career as an author; glancing to the left, he is in a position to observe the outside world through his picture window (and his telephone). I have made an attempt to diagram this spatial configuration.

One odd feature of Chekhov's study is its relative lack of books. What is more,
of the 203 items on his single bookshelf's five tiers (multivolume collections are
listed as one item) I count at least seventy-five works by Chekhov published
during his lifetime in Russian and other languages. While Chekhov was clearly
quite attached to his memorabilia, he donated the lion's share of his books to
the Taganrog library, of which he was a devoted (but, at his insistence, anonymous) patron. Some two thousand books came from Chekhov's own collection—the largest shipment taking place when he moved from Melikhovo to
the new house at Yalta—while many more were bought for the library or ca-
joled as donations from authors and publishers.[19] He was particularly apt to give
away volumes that he might have been expected to keep as valuable mementos, such as those autographed by authors and presented to him as gifts. He did
hold on to useful reference books, works by particularly close friends, and the
classics most often alluded to in his own writings: volumes of Garshin, Korolenko, Nekrasov, Uspenskii, Giliarovskii; collected works of Tolstoy, Turgenev,
Pushkin, Gogol; and Shakespeare in translation (including three versions of
Hamlet).[20]

Chekhov also held on to his medical books, though his days of medical practice had definitively ended;[21] there were close to thirty medical books on the
fourth and fifth shelves of his bookcase. In the last years of his life they presumably served the same function as the three medical instruments that always
lay on his desk: his stethoscope pipe, his plessor or hammer, and his plessimeter
(an oblong plate of hard rubber, ivory, or other flexible substance, placed against
the surface and struck with the hammer in mediate percussion). Mariia
Chekhova and many other memoirists and biographers have read these objects,
which no longer served as professional tools ready for use, as symbolizing an
identity that remained important to Chekhov; so too at the other end of his career, on his first vacation from the university (July 1880), he had carried to the
south a human skull in his bag.[22] At the apex of his literary success, Chekhov
himself was still apt to make remarks like, "Listen, I'm not a playwright, I'm a
doctor."[23] As Mikhail Gromov put it, "Chekhov would never have said: 'I'm a
good writer.' But he said many times: 'I'm a good doctor.'"[24] In his memoirs,
Dmitrii Likhachev recalls a conversation he had (while imprisoned on Solovki)
about the idiosyncratic dress of all significant turn-of-the-century writers; only

Chekhov eschewed such a unique and statement-making appearance. His interlocutor "considered this and said:'Yes, but Chekhov dressed like a typical doctor.' I thought back to my childhood, when I'd often been ill and children's
doctors had treated me, and I'd been taken from doctor to doctor. No doubt
Chekhov had had a 'doctorly self-awareness' in his dress."[25]

A number of items in Chekhov's study serve the purpose of maintaining that
"doctorly self-awareness," and of showing his doctor's self to others. But there
is more that can be said about those instruments. We have before us a *selection*
from Chekhov's bag, and it is worth noting that the instruments Chekhov chose
to display to others and himself were *diagnostic* rather than *therapeutic*. This assemblage of artifacts thus signifies a physician's identity insofar as the physician
is *he who examines;* it is an identity founded on an empowered, penetrating, professional gaze. Interestingly enough, however, these are also instruments for
sounding and listening—precisely those that would be of greatest service in diagnosing Chekhov's own illness, tuberculosis. As such, the instruments Chekhov
kept on his desk constitute an extremely ambivalent dual sign: Chekhov as doctor, Chekhov as patient; Chekhov seeing, Chekhov seen.

Now let us turn to Chekhov's bedroom. Bunin wrote that an extraordinary
cleanliness prevailed in all his rooms, and that the bedroom "was like a girl's."[26]
This was truly private space, and its compact, spare, and tidy nature contrasts
markedly with the study's. The objects in it appear above all functional and de-
void of meaningful associations, though biographers do often remark the narrow, monkish iron bed that was brought from Melikhovo, as well as an heirloom
cabinet brought all the way from Taganrog, and which, according to Mariia
Pavlovna,[27] inspired the hundred-year-old book cabinet Gaev eulogizes in the
first act of *Cherry Orchard:* "Dear, most esteemed cabinet! I hail your existence,
which for more than one hundred years now was directed to the bright ideals
of the good and of justice; your silent summons to fruitful work did not weaken
over the course of one hundred years, supporting *(through tears),* in generations
of our clan, courage and faith in a better future, and cultivating in us the ideals
of good and social consciousness" (*S* 13:206–8).

During the jubilee celebration of his twenty-five years of literary activity,
Chekhov transformed the *shkaf* of his play into a metaphor for his self: while
standing before a packed theater audience and listening to similar speeches about
himself, he drolly interjected the remark "Shkaf," likening himself to the object
of Gaev's absurd encomium. In the play the *shkaf* is a kind of realized synecdoche, twice removed: the value associated with contents—literature, contained
in books—attaches instead to the container for books, a bookcase. And praise
of the exterior empties the interior of meaning. Chekhov the celebrant mim-

16. Chekhov's bedroom, Yalta. Personal photograph published by permission of the Chekhov Museum (Dom-muzei A. P. Chekhova), Yalta.

icked the situation of his character Nikolai Stepanych of "Boring Story," who becomes inwardly emptier as his famous name resounds throughout Russia. There is something vacant, in precisely this sense, about Chekhov's bedroom: it is not just truly private; it is lonely, closed, *inscrutable,* a space where there is nothing to see, or in psychoanalytic parlance, an emblem of diffused identity.[28] No knickknacks, not a single decorative item—just two calendars, and above the head of his bed, hanging on the wall, his leather traveling bag. It is as if embedded in the most deeply hidden space of the self were nothing beyond a mortally ill man's anxiety about passing time (*two* calendars!)[29] and a wish to be else-where, on the road. Such a view matches some of Chekhov's unhappier self-characterizations, as well as those of friends, like Bunin, who, while boasting of his own closeness to Chekhov, claimed that Chekhov never had a "close friend" or "deep love."[30]

Chekhov as a Cultural Object

But Chekhov was loved: after all, he was showered with gifts during and after the jubilee. The great obligation of selecting a meaningful object to be presented on behalf of the Moscow Art Theater fell to Stanislavskii. He searched antique shops, and in the end decided on an ancient piece of embroidered cloth. It was used to decorate a wreath, to which was attached a photograph of the theater troupe; he thought this would at least be "an artistic thing." Chekhov was not a gracious recipient. He told Stanislavskii that the valuable material belonged in a museum; what he really needed, he said, was a mousetrap, and the best gifts he had received were fishing poles.[31] Back in Yalta, Chekhov complained to Dr. I. N. Al'tshuller that someone had disseminated the notion that he was a lover of antiques, and now he found himself inundated with them.[32]

Only months away from death and barely able to stand through the presen-tation ceremony, Chekhov is showered with antique items of artistic value: these objects are synecdochic figures for culture itself, and for the long-livedness of art. They affirm the good taste and cultural refinement of both donor and re-ceiver, but that is not all: their aesthetic value and their ancientness convey a promise that Chekhov and his art will also live on. Most important, unlike fish-ing poles and mousetraps, these are items that will be arrayed on the walls and the furniture of Chekhov's home to be contemplated rather than used as action objects. Here I borrow a distinction—useful too for thinking about Pavel Egorovich's walking stick and the doctor's instruments on Chekhov's Yalta desk, as well as the objects Dun'ia Efros wrecked on Chekhov's desk in Moscow years before—elaborated by Csikszentmihalyi and Rochberg-Halton. Whereas "action objects" "are instruments for *doing*" that "require some physical ma-nipulation to release their meaning" and develop "a self's sense of mastery," "contemplation objects" allow "an achievement of selfhood based on conscious reflection."[33] The Chekhov who contemplates the wreath and other antiques presented as tokens of his life's accomplishment, and for whom these objects will tell him what he is, is to be assured that he too belongs to that antique realm himself: prized, immortal.

But Chekhov did not care to think of himself this way. It made him feel like the empty *shkaf*. For all his complaints of isolation, bad health, and bad humor when he was writing from distant Yalta, now, having found himself very much front and center, he says that the objects he craves are mousetraps and fishing poles—both tokens of a domestic Chekhov, and objects for solitary and active use (though not too active: as a pastime, fishing in a sense denies the notion of vigorous activity, while mousetrapping is a diminutive, and in Chekhov's practice famously non-lethal, variant of hunting).[34]

But Chekhov *was* capable of enjoying praise from admiring readers, and the conditions under which he could obtain such pleasure are quite revealing. These could not be more different from standing on the stage of the Moscow Art Theater as a cultic object to be viewed by others, and in reference to which these others might signal their own cultural refinement; for the telegrams that flowed in from all corners of Russia had been sent not only to praise Chekhov but also—and perhaps most important—to identify their authors as "cultured." So it goes in one of Chekhov's notebook entries: "They were celebrating the jubilee of a humble man. They seized upon the chance to show themselves, praise one another. And only toward the end of the dinner did they notice: the celebrant hadn't been invited, they forgot" (S 17:70). The happy variant of this scene would have had the celebrant observing the festivities through a keyhole. Recall (from chapter 1) the artist Aleksandra Khotiaintseva's depiction, both in her memoir and in a caricature, of a delighted Chekhov listening through the wall of his pension in Nice as a husband and wife read one of his stories aloud; or Mariia Pavlovna's account of the train trip during which Chekhov, remaining incognito, discussed the works of the brilliant author Chekhov with a passenger sharing his compartment. What made these encounters with admirers pleasurable for Chekhov, we can by now speculate with some assurance, is that in them he was more an observer than the observed. And though Chekhov in one sense pretends to be other than himself in these instances, the presence by his side of a trusted intimate who knows him well simultaneously anchors his identity. Even as others make him the object of discussion, he assumes an active self outside the range of their seeing: a voyeuristic perspective on the event allows his seeing to supersede that of those who think they are looking at him.

So too in virtually all photographs of him, Chekhov gazes directly and penetratingly at the camera and, by extension, the viewer of his photograph: it is as though his seeing is stronger than ours. Although in photographic portraits of Chekhov alone he very occasionally looks to one side or the other, in pictures in which he appears with others, Chekhov always stares directly at the camera, at times to odd effect. The famous photograph of Chekhov in the company of the actors of the Moscow Art Theater is a case in point: he alone meets the eyes of the photograph's beholders. Two other pictures included here (Chekhov with

17. Chekhov and the actors of the Moscow Art Theater (May 1899). Reprinted courtesy of The State Literary Museum (Gosudarstvennyi literaturnyi muzei), Moscow.

Gorkii and Chekhov with Tat′iana Shchepkina-Kupernik and the actress Lidiia Iavorskaia) exemplify a behavioral characteristic of Chekhov that will be evident to anyone who leafs through a biography or collection of photographs pertaining to the author. (See figures 17–19.)

One very notable exception to this pattern seems to prove the rule: in a strangely posed photograph of Chekhov sitting together with the academician (an archaeologist and Byzantine art historian) N. P. Kondakov and his son, taken in 1900 (and included in the display to the right of Chekhov's desk), both Chekhov and Kondakov avert their eyes toward the ground, while the youth asserts himself with a bold gaze at the camera's lens. Having observed how consistently Chekhov reserved this position of seer of the seeing for himself, one can only presume that his ceding of that position to the boy for the purpose of this photograph was deliberately staged; the effect is to heighten the vitality and potential of the son at the expense of his elders. Chekhov always struck a pose when he was photographed, and that pose generally called attention to and resisted the inevitably objectifying function of his transformation into a photographic image at the ocular disposal of others. "*I* see *you!*" his photographs seem to say; at the very least, if he is to be seen, then he will appear to see himself being seen, and the pleasures and powers of seeing will be his. In this photograph, however, Chekhov arranged for something quite different to occur; we can only guess why, but the quite apparent artificiality of this tableau vivant certainly sharpens the contours of the pattern I have been fleshing out.[35] (See fig. 20.)

The anxiety about becoming an object that was so evident as Chekhov stood on the stage to be celebrated during the intermission of *Cherry Orchard* found full realization, of course, the moment Chekhov died (though one might argue that this happened shortly before his death, when he was compelled to change

18. Chekhov and Maksim Gorkii, from N. I. Gitovich, *Letopis' zhizni i tvorchestva A. P. Chekhova* (Moscow: Gosudarstvennoe izdatel'stvo khudozhestvennoi literatury, 1955), 623.

19. Chekhov with Tat'iana Shchepkina-Kupernik and the actress Lidiia Iavorskaia in an 1893 photograph jokingly referred to as "The Temptations
of St. Antony." Reprinted courtesy of The State Literary Museum (Gosudarstvennyi literaturnyi muzei), Moscow.

hotels so as not to disturb guests with the easily anticipated unpleasant company
of his corpse). The coda of virtually every Chekhov biography echoes the bitter, bereft remarks of Maksim Gorkii, first in a letter to his wife and then somewhat toned down in his memoirs, on how Chekhov's corpse was conveyed to
Moscow in a freight car designated "wagon for oysters" (*vagon dlia ustrits*).[36]
Gorkii's upset reflects his understanding of the final step in Chekhov's transformation to "thingness," utterly accessible to the crowds following his coffin. As
for Chekhov, one of the last items in his notebook reads, "I would like it if in
the other world I could think about this life thus: those were wonderful visions . . ." (*S* 17:102).

20. Chekhov with Professor Kondakov and Kondakov's son (1900). From the collections of Peter Urban, copyright © Diogenes Verlag AG Zürich.

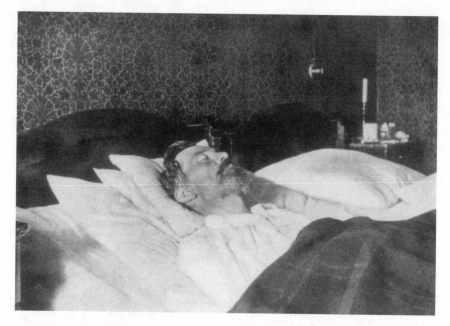

21. Chekhov in his deathbed in Badenweiler (1904). Reprinted courtesy of the Chekhov Museum (Dom-muzei A. P. Chekhova), Yalta.

Reading Chekhov's Body

Chekhov always dressed meticulously; in this he followed his father, who had maintained sartorial dignity even during the worst years of the family's financial crisis.[37] After an 1889 visit to Petersburg left Chekhov appalled at his brother Aleksandr's domestic comportment, he sent a letter in which he railed particularly against Aleksandr's habit of walking about his flat without trousers, in front of his wife and housekeeper. Educated and respectful husbands, he says, "rush to put on their neckties in the morning, so as not to offend their wives with their improper appearance, that is to say, the carelessness of their dress" (2 December 1889). It is therefore quite tempting, and perhaps a little disturbing, to imagine Chekhov's reaction to the deathbed photograph printed here. In it, too, the metaphoric association of Chekhov with *shkaf* becomes utterly concrete, and beholders of this empty object can be expected to gush a Gaev-like sentimentality.

I have argued that Chekhov's thirteen-year disavowal of his ill bodily self sought to ward off the implications that, as a physician, he knew would follow his identification as a tubercular. Careful attention to clothing, and rigid adher-

ence to a semiotics of dress whose signification was clear and unchanging—
"Chekhov dressed like a typical doctor"—might well be construed as a strategy for rendering the body otherwise unreadable, for obscuring telltale signs of
the degenerate patient masquerading as a physician. But there were certainly
more pragmatic (and less speculative) motivations to deny the reality of his illness as well; for Chekhov did deny its reality in his remarks to others, and most
likely in his own thinking, too, at least at times.

Chekhov clearly sought to shield his family—in particular his mother and
his sister—from anxieties about his health and their own future without him.
When his brother Mikhail once chanced to see the blood in Chekhov's phlegm
at Melikhovo, he was told: "This is only a trifle. You must not say anything to
Masha or Mother."[38] Indeed, the only reasonable chance of prolonging his life
would have required moving to a presumptively therapeutic climate and adopting a softer lifestyle, measures rendered unthinkable by his familial responsibilities.[39] Thus as early as 1888 he responded sardonically to the urgings of his
friend the physician E. M. Lintvareva that he "take measures" to safeguard his im-
periled health: "I don't understand my health. I was spitting blood for four days,
but now, aside from an insignificant cough, there's nothing . . . You advise me to
take measures, but you don't name these measures. Should I take Dovorov powder? Anise drops? Go to Nice? Not work? Let's agree, doctor: we won't speak
ever again of either measures or of [the defunct journal] *Epoch* . . ." (27 October 1888). Chekhov knew the impotence of medical science at the time to help
him and courageously chose to conduct his life as though he had no mortal illness, avoiding at all costs an exhibitionistic and sympathy-arousing stance.

Chekhov was not entirely above making pragmatic use of his illness, however. In 1894 he wrote Lika Mizinova, whom he managed to avoid seeing on a
trip to western Europe during her moment of desperate need: "I'm not entirely
healthy. I cough almost without stopping. Obviously, I've let my health go [*i
zdorov'e prozeval*], just as I missed out on you" (18 September). In this short letter Chekhov adopts an elegiac tone that might flatter Mizinova while simultaneously relying on ill health to distance himself from her. In 1884, when
Chekhov was beset by the first overt symptoms of his illness, he did receive medical attention, and he spoke about his condition in communication with his publisher Nikolai Leikin. His letter to Leikin of 10 December opens rather
dramatically: "Three days have already gone by with blood coming from my
throat, like out of the blue. This bleeding keeps me from writing, and it will keep
me from going to Piter [St. Petersburg] . . . Well, thanks a lot, I wasn't expect-
ing this! I haven't seen white sputum for three days, and I can't say when the
medications that my colleagues are stuffing me with will help." Here Chekhov
offers no assurance of the insignificance of his illness, as he will, by contrast, in

a letter to P. A. Sergeenko one week later (17 December 1884). And the letter to Leikin, like most of his missives to his first important publisher, emphasizes Chekhov's dire financial straits: the body of the letter ends with the complaint that he is unable to visit his patients but does not want to give up the earnings they would bring by passing them on to other doctors. A year and a half later Chekhov again bemoans his health to Leikin: "I'm sick. Blood-spitting and weak . . . I'm not writing . . . If I don't sit down to write tomorrow, then excuse me: I won't manage to send a story for Easter . . . I ought to go to the south, but there's no money. Regarding a trip to Piter, it's worth thinking over. I'll probably come if not held back by lack of money or illness . . . " (6 April 1886). This communication occurs during a period when Chekhov is distancing himself from his first patron. New, more profitable, and artistically more gratifying publishing venues have opened up in the past year, and Chekhov now views Leikin less as the facilitator of his career than as a factor inhibiting further growth; indeed, in other letters he characterizes Leikin as a dishonest and manipulative publisher who has stooped to deceit to maintain control over his protégé. In a letter to his brother Aleksandr written not long after the watershed visit to Petersburg in December 1885, he calls Leikin the "lame devil." A year later he wrote Aleksandr, "If the demon is named in holy scripture as the father of the lie, then our editor can be called at least its uncle" (3 February 1886).[40] In writing to Leikin, then, Chekhov invokes his illness not to arouse sympathy, nor to excuse himself from working, but to hold at bay a demanding and rather low-paying publisher who, as the self-proclaimed discoverer of Chekhov, tends to overstate his rights. Chekhov's confession of illness is less an act of intimacy than a manipulative ploy toward a man who deserves no better. In any case, he will soon exchange his relationship with Leikin for a closer one with the far more powerful Aleksei Suvorin.

Chekhov's tactics with Leikin could backfire, however. Some years later, in 1893, he became quite annoyed on hearing that Leikin was spreading the word that, in the report of Aleksandr, "You, my friend, are dangerously ill with consumption and will die soon." Moreover, Leikin was boasting that Chekhov "had entrusted only him, Leikin, the only person in the world, with the sad tale of his all too early demise from an incurable ailment."[41] Chekhov responded a few days later: "Thank Leikin for his sympathy. When he succumbs to apoplexy, I'll send him a telegram. The whole family is healthy. I too. I do cough a bit, but it's still a long way from consumption. Hemorrhoids. Catarrh of the intestine. I get migraines, sometimes for two days. Laziness and negligence" (29 October 1893).

There were indeed times when it seemed that Chekhov, for all the diagnostic talents touted by himself and, in memoirs, by others, was in "massive denial"[42] about his illness and had in fact managed to convince himself what he told others: that his blood-spitting had sources other than pulmonary tubercular infec-tion. We are likely confronting a kind of double consciousness or self-deception here, a simultaneous—or at times serial—knowing and not knowing. The unanswerable question is to what extent this mode of coping was deliberate on Chekhov's part. Most often, letters that overtly dismiss symptoms as insignifi-cant also hint at darker implications. Thus an 1888 letter to Pleshcheev remarks: "I'm in a bad mood: I've been spitting blood. It's probably a trifle, but it's still unpleasant"; but this is followed immediately by a motif of sudden and cata-strophic death: "Today on Kuznetskii while my sister was there a high brick wall fell across the street and crushed a lot of people" (10 October). As is so often the case in Chekhov's verbal art, accidental contiguity here suggests an inner connection.

Boris Shubin points to an instance when Chekhov discussed the physician's need to lie, which was standard protocol in the case of cancer and tuberculosis. Chekhov also portrayed the deliberate self-deception of a physician in "Boring Story," in which the narrator is an eminent professor of medicine who has di-agnosed his own fatal condition but maintains the hope that he might be mis-taken.[43] Chekhov did inform certain intimates about the history and frequency of his blood-spitting, but he also made light of these symptoms. In an 1888 let-ter to Suvorin he claimed not to have the totality of symptoms that indicate consumption; besides, if that first hemorrhage in 1884 "had been a symptom of consumption, then I would long ago have been in the other world—there's my logic" (14 October 1888). This last phrase—"there's my logic"—undercuts what Chekhov has just asserted, however: rather than referring to an authorita-tive body of medical knowledge, he relies on a peculiar "logic" of his own, and this is tantamount to admitting his deception of himself and others and re-questing that Suvorin collude. In a later letter, also to Suvorin, Chekhov simi-larly reasons away the significance of his illness with a deliberately twisted logic. He complains of having been kept awake the preceding night by "fierce palpi-tations" and difficulty in breathing. "But I did not become afraid," he boasts. Be-sides, he explains, it's the maladies you don't suspect that will kill you: "What's really terrifying is what you're not afraid of; that which arouses apprehensions is not terrifying. All healing nature, which is killing us, is at the same time clev-erly deceiving us, like a nanny deceives the little child she is carrying out of the living room to sleep. I know that I'll die from an illness I won't be afraid of. Hence: if I am afraid, that means I won't die" (24 August 1893). But Chekhov had begun by asserting he was not afraid!

These two letters overtly dismiss his symptoms as insignificant while imply-ing otherwise between the lines. Even where Chekhov confronts the serious-ness of his condition directly, however, the end result is the same: an argument for turning a blind eye to the matter. Thus an 1891 letter to Suvorin lists his troubling symptoms and declares:"I've begun thinking that my health will never return to its former condition. However, it's all as God wills. Medical attention and worries about my physical existence arouse something close to repulsion in me. I won't seek medical attention. I'll take the waters and quinine, but I won't allow myself to be sounded" (18 November). And this was only one month after Chekhov's aunt Feodosiia Dolzhenko died of tuberculosis.[44]

Such tactics for disavowing one's illness and the fears it arouses are at once a disavowal of a significant portion of one's very self. But what, let us ask, were the costs to the self of denying a part of the self? Might not such self-deception have contributed to the feelings of emptiness alluded to in Chekhov's descriptions of himself as an old bookcase (*shkaf*)?[45]

In March 1897, while Chekhov was dining with Suvorin in a Moscow restaurant, his condition loudly declared itself with a hemorrhage that nearly killed him. Chekhov brought up the subject of the therapeutic lie while recuperating in Suvorin's suite (before a second hemorrhage sent him to a clinic). According to Suvorin:"He lay at my place for two days. He was frightened by this attack and told me that this was a very grave condition.'To calm patients we tell them when they're coughing that it's gastric, and when they're hemorrhaging that it's hemorrhoidal. But there's no such thing as a gastric cough, and the hemorrhage is always from the lungs."[46] On the larger issue, deception was no longer possible. Henceforth Chekhov would put himself under the care of physicians and organize his life in greater accord with their (at times contradictory) therapeutic principles. In 1901 he told his close friend, the exiled sociologist M. M. Kovalevskii:"It's hard for me to make up my mind on any sort of lengthy project. As a physician I know that my life will be short."[47] It still outraged him, nevertheless, to be seen by others as ill: when, in October 1898, newspapers reported in front-page stories that his condition had worsened, he became furious and rushed to inform intimates that he was fine.[48] There would be many such incidents. Chekhov's ill body was now quite visible to the public, in whose mind the train ride in the car marked "for oysters" had already begun.

It is in this context that we might understand Chekhov's notorious dissatisfaction with the portrait of him that was commissioned by Pavel Tretiakov. The artist I. E. Braz destroyed his first attempt, for which Chekhov had posed in July 1897 at Melikhovo; Braz blamed his failure on the overly prominent features of illness still deforming his subject a few months after his first serious hemorrhage.[49] Chekhov sat for a second painting while in Nice the following March. This painting was hung in Tretiakov's gallery, but Chekhov remained far from happy with the result. Four years later, in a letter to the physician M. A. Chlenov, he complained of the time he had spent sitting for both efforts and wrote, "If I've become a pessimist and write gloomy stories, then my portrait is responsible for that" (13 February 1902). Here Chekhov jokes about the possibility of one's inner self suffering alteration or damage as a result of being seen by others; but by now we are in a position to appreciate that joke's serious side. Julie de Sherbinin has argued that Chekhov's distaste for this portrait had to do with how much of him it showed and how unhealthy he looked in it. And she advances the brilliant hunch that Chekhov, in describing its portrayal of his pallid face and red nose ("as if I've sniffed some horseradish," he wrote Aleksandra Khotiaintseva), was unpleasantly reminded of the famous portrait by I. E. Repin of a red-nosed Modest Mussorgsky, made March 1881 in the hospital where Mussorgsky would die only a few days later, which also hung in Tretiakov's gallery.[50]

Khotiaintseva, who executed several caricatures of Chekhov either eavesdropping on others or himself being peeped at in addition to the one previously mentioned, dashed off two caricatures of Chekhov viewing his own portrait in the Tretiakov Gallery. Khotiaintseva was evidently attuned to the excitements and discomforts seeing and being seen could provoke in Chekhov. In the watercolor reproduced in figure 22, Chekhov stands in line with other patrons viewing his portrait. Only one other painting in the gallery is identifiable: this is Repin's portrait of Mussorgsky, distorted so that instead of looking up and to the right as in the original, Mussorgsky looks down and to his left—at Chekhov.

Chekhov, studying his portrait among the others, must have asked himself: how will that body be read? Indeed, how do we read it a hundred years after Chekhov's death? The sociologists of medicine Claudine Herzlich and Janine Pierret lump Chekhov together with the tubercular writers Franz Kafka, Katherine Mansfield, and Marie Bashkirtseff as figures all "steeped in the Romantic myth" of their illness.[51] A student who, inspired by Susan Sontag's *Illness as Metaphor,* wrote in an essay "Chekhov is a romantic personality, a sickly and incredibly talented artist, whose illness is eating away at his body, alienating him and making him intriguing," is in fine company: even scholars of the social construction of medicine have proved unable to see beyond such stereotypical images of the romantic tubercular in Chekhov's case.

To be sure, Chekhov was embedded in a culture in which a variety of discourses assigned meaning to his ill body; the most prominent of these discourses pertained to Chekhov's own professions of medicine and literature. But Chekhov, if he can be compared to Kafka, was Kafka's inverse. For Kafka, as Sander Gilman has shown, illness quite literally becomes a metaphor realized, the manifestation of his culturally constructed marginal identity as a Jew: "It is not tu-

22. Chekhov viewing his portrait in the Tretiakov Gallery. Watercolor by A. A. Khotiaintseva (1898). Courtesy of The State Literary Museum (Gosudarstvennyi literaturnyi muzei), Moscow.

berculosis but rather his psychic state mirrored in the tuberculosis."[52] Chekhov, by contrast, struggled hard to deny the metaphoricity of his disease, and his self was defined not by the disease but by this struggle.

One of Chekhov's notebook entries reads: "A husband and wife followed idea X rigorously their whole lives, and built their life around it as according to a formula. And only with impending death did they ask themselves: perhaps the proverb *Mens sana in corpore sano* tells an untruth" (S 17:68). I would be tempted to say that not talking about his illness for those many years, not naming it, was at least in part a defense against the untruth of metaphor; if, as the poet Fedor Tiutchev famously put it, "The thought uttered is a lie,"[53] then Chekhov's disease was to be articulated only in the body and not in falsifying language about it. But there is a tremendous loss associated with such silence, for in the end illness is made meaningful precisely by how we talk about it.

The metaphor of an empty bookcase may be seen as emblematic not only of the ill body, but also of the impossible wish to expunge language from that body and its illness, and of the voided self that would be the consequence of realizing that wish.

Seeing Chekhov means witnessing Chekhov's lifelong struggle to determine how he would be seen, and how he would define his self through his seeing.

Notes

Introduction

1. A. B. Derman, *Tvorcheskii portret Chekhova* (Moscow: Mir, 1929), 12.

2. One might well consider this wealth of information to blame. A. P. Kuzicheva discusses the special problems posed by the sheer mass and variety of primary biographical materials and their contradictory nature, and she outlines a number of pitfalls threatening the necessarily selective biographer of Chekhov, in "Chekhov o sebe i sovremenniki o Chekhove (Legko li byt' biografom Chekhova?)," *Chekhoviana. Chekhov i ego okruzhenie,* ed. A. M. Turkov et al. (Moscow: Nauka, 1996), 15–31.

3. Most notably in his 1847 *Selected Passages from Correspondence with Friends* (*Vybrannye mesta s perepiski s druz'iami*), where one can find such statements as: "I have already got rid of many of my abominations by transmitting them to my heroes, I have turned them to ridicule in them and compelled others to laugh at them as well." Nikolai Gogol, *Selected Passages from Correspondence with Friends,* trans. Jesse Zeldin (Nashville: Vanderbilt University Press, 1969), 107–8.

4. Thus when certain students marching in his funeral procession were asked by onlookers who was being buried, they answered, "a *katorzhnik* [convict]." See Joseph Frank, *Dostoevsky: The Mantle of the Prophet, 1871–1881* (Princeton: Princeton University Press, 2002), 755.

5. A point that Ilya Ehrenburg made, though to a different end, in "On Re-reading Chekhov," in *Chekhov, Stendhal, and Other Essays,* trans. Anna Bostock et al. (New York: Alfred A. Knopf, 1963), 70.

6. See the editors' commentary in I. S. Turgenev, *Polnoe sobranie sochinenii i pisem v dvadtsati vos'mi tomakh,* vol. 9, ed. E. I. Pokusaev (Moscow: Nauka, 1965), 459–60.

7. Maksim Gorkii (1868–1936), *Childhood* (*Detstvo,* 1913), *My Apprenticeship* (*V liudiakh,* 1916), *My Universities* (*Moi universitety,* 1922); Vladimir Korolenko (1853–1921), *The History of My Contemporary* (*Istoriia moego sovremennika,* pub. 1922); Ivan Bunin (1870–1953), *The Life of Arsen'ev* (*Zhizn' Arsen'eva,* completed 1952).

8. Ernest J. Simmons, *Chekhov: A Biography* (Boston: Little, Brown and Co., 1962), 488.

9. Zinovii Papernyi, *Zapisnye knizhki Chekhova* (Moscow: Sovetskii pisatel', 1976), 9–10.

10. Two exceptions to this rule are books that attempted to make sense of Chekhov's relations with women:Virginia L. Smith, *Anton Chekhov and "The Lady with the Dog"* (London: Oxford University Press, 1973); Carolina De Maegd-Soëp, *Chekhov and Women: Women in the Life and Work of Chekhov* (Columbus: Slavica, 1987).

11. The term *intelligentnost'* is impossible to translate into English. It indicates a high level of education and cultural refinement, good manners, a responsible and professional attitude in one's occupation, and attention to ethics.

12. Emphasis added. Cited from Gennadii Shaliugin, "Chekhov v krugu kolleg," in *Brega Tavridy,* no. 5–6 (1999): 276.

13. James McConkey, *To a Distant Island* (Philadelphia: Paul Dry Books, 2000), 19.

14. Aleksandr Kuprin, "Pamiati Chekhova," in *A. P. Chekhov v vospominaniiakh sovremennikov,* ed. N. I. Gitovich (Moscow: Khudozhestvennaia literatura, 1986), 514.

15. I. L. Leont'ev-Shcheglov, "Iz vospominanii ob Antone Chekhove," ibid., 55.

16. Cited from *Anton Chekhov's Life and Thought: Selected Letters and Commentary,* trans. Michael Henry Heim and Simon Karlinsky, selection, commentary, and intro. Simon Karlinsky (Berkeley: University of California Press, 1973), 367.

17. Vsevolod Meyerhold, "Naturalistic Theater and Theater of Mood," trans. Joyce C. Vining, in *Chekhov: A Collection of Critical Essays,* ed. Robert Louis Jackson (Englewood Cliffs, N.J.: Prentice-Hall, 1967), 66.

18. For an exploration of the epistemological implications of this problem in Chekhov — the degree to which problems in seeing and being seen were problems of disciplinary knowledge for him — see the excellent work of Cathy Popkin, including "Chekhov as Ethnographer: Epistemological Crisis on Sakhalin Island," *Slavic Review* 51, no. 1 (1988): 36–51; "Chekhov's Corpus: Bodies of Knowledge," in *Essays in Poetics* 18 (September 1993): 44–72; "*Historiia Morbi* and the 'Holy of Holies': Scientific and Religious Discourse and Čechov's Epistemology," in *Anton P. Čechov, philosophische und religiöse Dimensionen im Leben und im Werk: Vorträge des Zweiten Internationalen Čechov-Symposiums, Badenweiler, 20.–24. Oktober 1994,* ed. Vladimir B. Kataev, Rolf-Dieter Kluge, and Regine Nohejl (Munich: Otto Sagner, 1997), 365–77; and, with Louise McReynolds, "The Objective Eye and the Common Good," in *Constructing Russian Culture in the Age of Revolution: 1881–1940* (Oxford: Oxford University Press, 1998), 57–76.

19. This citation from Chekhov's letter to Suvorin serves as the epigraph to Savely Senderovich's pathbreaking study of the Saint George complex in Chekhov, *Chekhov — s glazu na glaz: istoriia odnoi oderzhimosti A. P. Chekhova. Opyt fenomenologii tvorchestva* (St. Petersburg: Dmitrii Bulanin, 1994); there it becomes a metaphor for both how Chekhov sees and how his verbal art ought to be read.

20. Participant in the Petrashevskii Circle, arrested together with Dostoevskii and others in 1849.

21. See the exchange in *Perepiska A. P. Chekhova v trekh tomakh,* ed. V. Vatsuro et al., vol. 1, ed. M. P. Gromov (Moscow: Nasledie, 1996), 1: 486–91.

22. I. N. Potapenko, "Neskol'ko let s A. P. Chekhovym (k 10-letiiu so dnia ego konchiny)," in Gitovich, *A. P. Chekhov v vospominaniiakh sovremennikov,* 296.

23. Letter to Suvorin, 7 January 1889. It should be noted that, although Chekhov most

definitely has himself in mind here—and such has been the correct understanding of all the biographers and critics who invariably refer to this statement—he nonetheless puts it in the third person. After speaking of his own literary career to that point, and the lengthy process of acquiring "virility" and a "feeling of personal freedom," he encourages Suvorin to "write a story about [. . .] a young man, son of a serf, former shop-boy, choir-boy, gymnasium and university student." In other words, this confessional moment evolves into a handy subject for a short story, a micro-narrative whose form distances him from his own life experiences.

24. Exemplary in this regard is Ehrenburg's "On Re-reading Chekhov," in which Chekhov's "humility" is a central theme.

25. For a broader frame of reference that helps make sense of Chekhov's strongly gendered scientific vision, see Ludmilla Jordanova, *Sexual Visions: Images of Gender in Science and Medicine between the Eighteenth and Twentieth Centuries* (Madison: University of Wisconsin Press, 1989).

26. See G. I. Rossolimo, "Vospominaniia o Chekhove," in Gitovich, *A. P. Chekhov v vospominaniiakh sovremennikov*, 436.

27. See Michael Finke, "Chekhov's 'The Steppe': A Metapoetic Journey," in *Metapoesis: The Russian Tradition from Pushkin to Chekhov* (Durham: Duke University Press, 1995), 134–66.

28. Vladimir Nemirovitch-Dantchenko, *My Life in the Russian Theatre*, trans. John Cournos (1936; rpt. New York: Theatre Arts, 1968), 154, 188.

29. T. L. Shchepkina-Kupernik, "O Chekhove," in Gitovich, *A. P. Chekhov v vospominaniiakh sovremennikov*, 247.

30. See Meyerhold, "Naturalistic Theater and Theater of Mood," 62–68. So too Harvey Pitcher argues that the fundamental characteristic of the mature Chekhov play is its foregrounding of feelings and emotions (*The Chekhov Play: A New Interpretation* [Berkeley: University of California Press, 1985], 1–34).

31. S. D. Balukhatyi, "*Chaika* v Moskovskom Khudozhestvennom teatre," in *Voprosy poetiki* (Leningrad: Izdatel'stvo Leningradskogo universiteta, 1990), 198; translated as S. D. Balukhaty, "*The Seagull* at the Moscow Art Theatre," in *The Seagull Produced by Stanislavsky*, ed. and intro. S. D. Balukhaty, trans. D. Magarshack (New York: Theatre Arts, 1952), 76–77. On the reception of Chekhov in theater criticism, see A. P. Kuzicheva, *A. P. Chekhov v russkoi teatral'noi kritike. Kommentirovannaia antologiia* (Moscow: Chekhovskii poligraficheskii kombinat, 1999).

32. For a summary and critique of this point of comparison between theater and cinema, see Barbara Freedman, *Staging the Gaze: Postmodernism, Psychoanalysis, and Shakespearean Comedy* (Ithaca: Cornell University Press, 1991), esp. chap. 2, "A Fractured Gaze: Theater, Cinema, Psychoanalysis," 47–77.

33. Pitcher, *The Chekhov Play*, 19, 21.

34. See, for instance, Leonid Andreyev, "Tchekhov and the Theatre," in *Anton Tchekhov: Literary and Theatrical Reminiscences*, trans. and ed. S. S. Koteliansky (1927; rpt. New York: Benjamin Blom, 1965), 174–75.

35. Iurii Sobolev, *Chekhov. Stat'i. Materialy. Bibliografiia* (Moscow: Federatsiia, 1930), 94.

36. See exemplary discussions of this aspect of *Seagull* in Leonid Grossman, "Roman Niny Zarechnoi," *Prometei* 2 (1967): 218–89 (esp. 252–69); Balukhatyi, "*Chaika*," 166–67; and Pitcher, *The Chekhov Play*.

37. See Pitcher's remarks regarding the infantile aspect of Treplev's relations with his

mother and the "lack of identity" at the core of characters in *Seagull* (*The Chekhov Play*, 53, 66–67).

38. See A. P. Evgen'eva, ed., *Slovar' russkogo iazyka v chetyrekh tomakh*, 2d ed. (Moscow: Russkii iazyk, 1982).

39. The minor author Lidiia Avilova had given Chekhov a book-shaped charm engraved with title, page, and line numbers referring to a volume of stories Chekhov had presented to her; the message thus encoded read, "If sometime you have need of my life, come and take it." When Chekhov and Avilova next met—at a masquerade at Suvorin's theater in St. Petersburg—Chekhov promised the masked Avilova that he would respond to her in his new play, *Seagull*. Avilova, who attended *Seagull's* premiere, eventually figured out that the page and line numbers on the medallion Nina gives Trigorin referred to her, Avilova's, published volume. Chekhov's response: "Young maidens should not be attending masquerades." The episode is recounted in Avilova's unreliable *Chekhov in My Life* ("A. P. Chekhov v moei zhizni," in Gitovich, *A. P. Chekhov v vospominaniiakh sovremennikov*, esp. 153, 158, 164, 167). See the discussion in Harai Golomb, "Referential Reflections around a Medallion: Reciprocal Art/Life Embeddings in Chekhov's *The Seagull*," *Poetics Today* 21, no. 4 (winter 2000): 681–709.

40. See Grossman, "Roman Niny Zarechnoi."

41. Leont'ev-Shcheglov, "Iz vospominanii ob Antone Chekhove," 67–68.

42. A. P. Chudakov, *Chekhov's Poetics*, trans. Edwina Cruise and Donald Dragt (Ann Arbor: Ardis, 1983); see also A. P. Chudakov, *Mir Chekhova. Vozniknovenie i utverzhdenie* (Moscow: Sovetskii pisatel', 1986), 318.

43. A position somewhat at odds with most, but very much in consonance with my own in this book, is argued by Iurii Sobolev, according to whom the "personal element" that Chekhov felt one "had to fear" was present in his stories to such a degree that it "put the certainty of his 'ideal objectivity' into doubt" (see his *Chekhov. Stat'i. Materialy. Bibliografiia*, 71; for further discussion of authorial subjectivity, *nabliudatel'nost'* [powers of observation], and the effect that medical training had on Chekhov's writing, see also 68–69).

44. Mikhail Gromov, *Chekhov* (Moscow: Molodaia gvardiia, 1993), 336.

45. I. A. Bunin, *O Chekhove (Nezakonchennaia rukopis')* (New York: Izdatel'stvo imeni Chekhova, 1955), 58.

46. V. G. Korolenko, "Anton Pavlovich Chekhov," in Gitovich, *A. P. Chekhov v vospominaniiakh sovremennikov*, 37–38.

47. Potapenko, "Neskol'ko let s A. P. Chekhovym," 297.

48. Harvey Pitcher, *Chekhov's Leading Lady: A Portrait of the Actress Olga Knipper* (New York: Franklin Watts, 1980), 10.

49. Potapenko, "Neskol'ko let s A. P. Chekhovym," 303–5.

50. Mariia P. Chekhova, *Iz dalekogo proshlogo* (Moscow: Gosudarstvennoe izdatel'stvo khudozhestvennoi literatury, 1960), 89.

51. Bunin, *O Chekhove*, 108. Bunin notes, however, that Chekhov also expressed quite the opposite notion: "A writer should be destitute, he should be in a situation where he knows that he'll die of hunger if he doesn't write, if he gives in to his laziness. Writers ought to be put on chain gangs and forced to write by punishment cells, whippings, beatings . . . Oh, how I thank fate that I was so poor in my youth!" (107).

52. Potapenko, "Neskol'ko let s A. P. Chekhovym," 298, 317.

53. Chekhova, *Iz dalekogo proshlogo,* 171.

54. I follow a pattern established by two monographs on Chekhov that discover recurring patterns of symbolism in his writings and demonstrate their deep psychobiographical significance: Senderovich, *Chekhov—s glazu na glaz;* and Julie de Sherbinin, *Chekhov and Russian Religious Culture: The Poetics of the Marian Paradigm* (Evanston: Northwestern University Press, 1997).

55. I provide a short account of Chekhov's life and works in "Anton Pavlovich Chekhov (17 January 1860—2 July 1904)," in *Russian Literature in the Age of Realism,* vol. 277 of *Dictionary of Literary Biography,* ed. Alyssa Dinega Gillespie (Detroit: Gale, 2003), 54–79.

56. Thus Cathy Popkin argues "against the overblown mythology of the 'two Chekhovs'" in her study of "Chekhov's preoccupation with significance, insignificance, and tellability." "If anything," she concludes, "I am left with a renewed sense of continuity" (*The Pragmatics of Insignificance: Chekhov, Zoshchenko, Gogol* [Stanford: Stanford University Press, 1993], 27). And Zinovii Papernyi reaffirms the obvious in his insistence that "Antosha Chekhonte and Chekhov—they're different names, but one artist" (*Zapisnye knizhki Chekhova,* 63).

1. To Be Seen or Not to Be Seen

1. T. L. Shchepkina-Kupernik, "On Chekhov," in *Anton Chekhov and His Times,* ed. Andrei Turkov, trans. Cynthia Carlile and Sharon McKee (Fayetteville: University of Arkansas Press, 1995), 46. See also N. I. Gitovich, *Letopis' zhizni i tvorchestva A. P. Chekhova* (Moscow: Khudozhestvennaia literatura, 1955), 400–401.

2. Cited with alterations from Vladimir Nemirovitch-Dantchenko, *My Life in the Russian Theatre,* trans. John Cournos (1936; rpt. New York: Theatre Arts, 1968), 57.

3. Mariia P. Chekhova, *Iz dalekogo proshlogo* (Moscow: Khudozhestvennaia literatura, 1960), 164.

4. This one made in the note to Suvorin explaining Chekhov's departure (18 October 1896).

5. Ronald Hingley, *A Life of Anton Chekhov* (Oxford: Oxford University Press, 1989), 224; see also 220–24; Donald Rayfield, *Anton Chekhov: A Life* (London: HarperCollins, 1997), 390–401; Gitovich, *Letopis',* 431–35; and among Chekhov's many letters describing how he felt at this time, his letter of 11 November 1896 to A. F. Koni.

6. Chekhova, *Iz dalekogo proshlogo,* 164; Mikhail P. Chekhov, *Anton Chekhov i ego siuzhety* (Moscow, 1923), 126.

7. Thus in a letter of 22 October 1896 disputing Suvorin's accusation of cowardice in the *Seagull* affair, Chekhov acknowledges that his "vanity was wounded," but claims to have recovered quickly. In 1900, when neither had long to live, Isaak Levitan congratulated Chekhov, who had been selected as a member of the Russian Imperial Academy of Sciences (Division of Russian Language and Literature), and asked him if he was still suffering from the fever he had complained of in his last letter: "I'm inclined to think that this fever of yours is the fever of the self-enamored—your chronic illness! [. . .] That's your Achilles' heel—you exposer of other people's Achilles' heels!" (*Perepiska A. P. Chekhova v trekh tomakh,* ed. V. E. Vatsuro et al. vol. 1, ed. M. P. Gromov [Moscow: Nasledie, 1996], 215). For a rather ill-natured and, on balance, unfair memoir of Chekhov that foregrounds this aspect of his personality, see N. M.

Ezhov, "Anton Pavlovich Chekhov (Opyt kharakteristiki)," *Istoricheskii vestnik: istoriko-literaturnyi zhurnal,* no. 8 (August 1909): 489–519.

8. A third defensive tactic is the general "contempt" that Chekhov often, and in a variety of ways, expressed toward the theater, and which accompanied and rendered less vulnerable the love he had shown for it since his Taganrog days. See the sharp observations in Aleksandr Roskin, "Istoriia odnogo provala i odnogo triumpha," in his *A. P. Chekhov. Stat'i i ocherki* (Moscow: Khudozhestvennaia literatura, 1959), esp. 124.

9. Nemirovitch-Dantchenko, *My Life,* 142. This letter of refusal has been lost; see editors' commentary in *Perepiska A. P. Chekhova,* vol. 3, ed. V. B. Kataev, 68.

10. Ol'ga Knipper-Chekhova, "O A. P. Chekhove," in *A. P. Chekhov v vospominaniiakh sovremennikov,* ed. N. I. Gitovich (Moscow: Khudozhestvennaia literatura, 1986), 615–16; see also K. S. Stanislavsky, "A. P. Chekhov at the Arts Theater," in Turkov, *Anton Chekhov and His Times,* 91–92; S. D. Balukhaty, "*The Seagull* at the Moscow Art Theatre," in *The Seagull Produced by Stanislavsky,* ed. S. D. Balukhaty, trans. David Magarshack (New York: Theatre Arts, 1952), 62. Mariia Chekhova later challenged this version of events; see Chekhova, *Iz dalekogo proshlogo,* 187; and Harvey Pitcher, *Chekhov's Leading Lady: A Portrait of the Actress Olga Knipper* (New York: Franklin Watts, 1980), 39.

11. *Perepiska A. P. Chekhova* 3:67. According to M. O. Goriacheva, *Seagull* was staged in twenty-one cities in Russia between November 1896 and December 1898; see her discussion of its career between the Aleksandrinskii and the Moscow Art Theaters in "*Chaika* mezhdu Aleksandrinskoi i Khudozhestvennym," in *Chekhoviana. Polet Chaiki,* ed. V. V. Gul'chenko et al. (Moscow: Nauka, 2001), 52–65.

12. Letter to Leikin, 15 November 1887.

13. See also Leont'ev-Shcheglov's recollections of Chekhov's intense discomfort at receiving praise during a banquet celebrating the success of *Ivanov* (I. L. Leont'ev-Shcheglov, "Iz vospominanii ob Antone Chekhove," in Gitovich, *A. P. Chekhov v vospominaniiakh sovremennikov,* 64); referred to also in the commentary to Chekhov's letter (*P* 3:382).

14. Christine Mitchell Havelock, *The Aphrodite of Knidos and Her Successors: A Historical Review of the Female Nude in Greek Art* (Ann Arbor: University of Michigan Press, 1995), 43 and passim. See also "Frina," in *Entsiklopedicheskii slovar',* vol. 36a (St. Petersburg: Brokgauz-Efron, 1902), 801–2.

15. From Lidiia Avilova, *Chekhov in My Life,* cited from Vladimir Rynkevich, *Puteshestvie k domu s mezaninom* (Moscow: Khudozhestvennaia literatura, 1990), 13.

16. Chekhova, *Iz dalekogo proshlogo,* 211.

17. I. N. Potapenko, "Neskol'ko let s A. P. Chekhovym (K10-letiiu so dnia ego konchiny)," in Gitovich, *A. P. Chekhov v vospominaniiakh sovremennikov,* 345–46.

18. Stanislavsky, "A. P. Chekhov at the Arts Theater," 109, 125–26; 114–15.

19. Rayfield, *Chekhov: A Life.*

20. Cited from Iurii Sobolev, *Chekhov. Stat'i. Materialy. Bibliografiia* (Moscow: Federatsiia, 1930), 89. See also the memoir of Leont'ev-Shcheglov for a number of similar remarks by Chekhov ("Iz vospominanii ob Antone Chekhove," 59–70, esp. 59).

21. I. N. Potapenko, "Neskol'ko let s A. P. Chekhovym," 331.

22. Ibid., 332.

23. Nemirovitch-Dantchenko, *My Life,* 210.

24. One month later Chekhov used the same metaphor in a letter to Leont'ev-Shcheglov (18 February 1889).

25. Janet Malcolm discusses the pragmatic distinctions between writing a play ("the play-wright feels a crowd of actors, directors, scenery designers, costumers, lighting specialists, and sometimes even an audience at his back") and the "private" act of writing a story or a novel, and concludes, "The theater drew and repelled Chekhov in equal measure" (*Reading Chekhov: A Critical Journey* [New York: Random House, 2001], 171).

26. Marena Senderovich, "Chekhov's Name Drama," in *Reading Chekhov's Text,* ed. R. L. Jackson (Evanston, Ill.: Northwestern University Press, 1993), 31–33.

27. See the editors' commentary, *S* 2:554.

28. Among 1883 stories see also "The Deputy, or the Tale of How Desdemonov Lost 25 Rubles" ("Deputat, ili povest' o tom, kak u Dezdemonova 25 rublei propalo"), "The Wicked Boy" ("Zloi mal'chik"), "The Daughter of Albion" ("Doch' Al'biona"), and "Patronage" ("Protektsiia").

29. As pointed out in the editors' commentary to the story (*S* 4:474). In Pushkin's origi-nal, however—"Chto slava?—iarkaia zaplata / na vetkhom rubishche pevtsa"—"tatters" are those of a bard (*pevets*) rather than a "Blind man," and the remark is made by the bookseller rather than the poet.

30. For two of the many occasions on which Chekhov used this witticism, see his letters to Aleksandr P. Chekhov, 17 January 1887, and to Aleksei Suvorin, 11 September 1888.

31. For this reason the biographer Ronald Hingley justly considers May 1885 as opening a new era in Chekhov's literary career (*A Life of Chekhov,* 57–60).

32. *Perepiska A. P. Chekhova,* 1:289–90.

33. See discussion in Senderovich, "Chekhov's Name Drama," 35.

34. Among the stories in the first half of 1886, see "The Night before My Trial" ("Noch' pered sudom"; first written 1884), "The Commotion" ("Perepolokh"), "Requiem" ("Panikhida"), "Aniuta," "A Person" ("Persona"), "The Witch" ("Ved'ma"), "A Little Joke" ("Shutochka"), "Agaf'ia," "In the Spring" ("Vesnoi"), "The Nightmare" ("Koshmar"), "Love" ("Liubov'"), "A Male Acquaintance" ("Znakomaia muzhchina"), "At the Boarding School" ("V pansione"), "Because There Was Nothing to Do" ("Ot nechego delat'"), "Romance with a Contrabass" ("Roman s kontrbasom"), and "The Pharmacist's Wife" ("Aptekarsha").

35. Literally, "Awl in the Bag," from the saying, "You can't hide an awl in a bag" ("Shilo v meshke ne utaish'").

36. Ernest Simmons, *Chekhov: A Biography* (Boston: Little, Brown and Company, 1962), 67.

37. See *S* 18:319–20, and Mikhail Gromov, *Chekhov* (Moscow: Molodaia gvardiia, 1993), 123.

38. Ieronim Iasinskii, *Roman moei zhizni. Kniga vospominanii* (Moscow: Gosudarstvennoe izdatel'stvo, 1926), 265.

39. Senderovich, "Chekhov's Name Drama," 33.

40. Jean Starobinski, "Pseudonymous Stendhal," in *The Living Eye,* trans. Arthur Gold-hammer (Cambridge: Harvard University Press, 1989), 78–111.

41. Ibid., 82.

42. E. A. Dinershtein, *A. P. Chekhov i ego izdateli* (Moscow: Kniga, 1990), 58.

43. See Senderovich, "Chekhov's Name Drama," 36–46.

44. *Perepiska A. P. Chekhova,* 1:307.

45. For another angle on the personal aspect of this story, which reads it as a reaction to *The Disciple* by Paul Bourget, see Katherine Tiernan O'Connor, "Čechov the Materialist ver-sus Suvorin the Anti-materialist or the Unboring Story of Chekhov, Suvorin, and Paul Bour-

get," in *Anton P. Čechov, philosophische und religiöse Dimensionen im Leben und im Werk: Vorträge des Zweiten Internationalen Čechov-Symposiums, Badenweiler, 20.–24. Oktober 1994,* ed. Vladimir B. Kataev, Rolf-Dieter Kluge, and Regine Nohejl (Munich: Otto Sagner, 1997), 379–83. O'Connor reads the epithet "boring" as connoting "death" in this story and elsewhere in Chekhov; see Katherine Tiernan O'Connor, "Chekhov's Death: His Textual Past Recaptured," in *Studies in Poetics: Commemorative Volume, Krystyna Pomorska (1928–1986),* ed. Elena Semeka-Pankratov (Columbus: Slavica, 1995), 45.

46. M. O. Goriacheva, "O lichnosti i literaturnoi reputatsii Chekhova v maloi presse kontsa 1880-kh–nachala 1900-kh godov (Po materialam gazety 'Novosti dnia')," in *Chekhoviana. Chekhov i ego okruzhenie* (Moscow: Nauka, 1996), 118.

47. See ibid., 118, 129; and Chekhov's letter to E. B. Konovitser of 6 August 1896.

48. Senderovich, "Chekhov's Name Drama," 45.

49. See, for instance, his 1890 letters of 5 March to I. M. Lintvareva, 9 March to Suvorin, and 22 March to Leont'ev-Shcheglov.

50. On Chekhov's desire to build a house for himself apart from his family at Melikhovo, see his letter to Suvorin of 24 August 1893.

51. See V. A. Feider, *A. P. Chekhov: Literaturnyi byt i tvorchestvo po memuarnym materialam* (Leningrad: Academia, 1928), 356–57. This practice of Chekhov's is discussed further in my conclusion.

52. Khotiaintseva drew a caricature of this incident. See A. A. Khotiaintseva, "Vstrechi s Chekhovym," in Gitovich, *A. P. Chekhov v vospominaniiakh sovremennikov,* 367.

53. Chekhova, *Iz dalekogo proshlogo,* 248–49.

54. See editors' commentary, *S* 4:517.

55. The Russian title, "V more," was accompanied by the subtitle "Rasskaz matrosa" (A sailor's story) in the version published in the second Marks edition of Chekhov's collected works in 1903 (*S* 2:530).

56. *Moskovskii listok* had just replaced a pseudonym used by Chekhov's brother Aleksandr with "A. Chekhov," misleading Chekhov's Moscow readership into taking the attached story as Chekhov's, while *Novosti dnia* had published under Chekhov's real name a story submitted under a pseudonym—a story, wrote Chekhov, that "I would have been ashamed to send to *Oskolki* [Leikin's paper]."

57. See the editors' commentary in *P* 9:532. On the story's reception, see Iurii Sobolev, *Chekhov. Stat'i. Materialy. Bibliografiia* (Moscow: Federatsiia, 1930), 153–57.

58. Subsequent references are to R. G. Nazirov, "Chekhov i Giugo: Polemicheskoe prodolzhenie," *Filologicheskie nauki* 6, no. 4 (1983): 21–25. The references to Hugo's novel rely on Victor Hugo, *Toilers of the Sea,* trans. Isabel Hapgood (New York, 1881).

59. M. Smolkin, "Shekspir v zhizni i tvorchestve Chekhov," in *Shekspirovskii sbornik,* ed. A. Anikst (Moscow: Vserossiiskoe teatral'noe obshchestvo, 1967), 80. See also Eleanor Rowe, *Hamlet: A Window on Russia* (New York: New York University Press, 1976), 107–13.

60. *Hamlet* 1.1.147–49, in *The Riverside Shakespeare* (Boston: Houghton Mifflin, 1974), 1143. All subsequent citations of *Hamlet* are from this edition.

61. See the discussion of the "mousetrap" in Chekhov's *Seagull* in Thomas G. Winner, "Chekhov's *Seagull* and Shakespeare's *Hamlet:* A Study of a Dramatic Device," *American Slavic and East European Review* 15, no. 1 (February 1956): 105–11.

62. See the discussion in Smolkin, "Shekspir," 80–84.

63. Sigmund Freud, *The Interpretation of Dreams,* trans. and ed. James Strachey (New York: Avon Books, 1965), 294–300.

64. Sophocles, *Oedipus the King,* trans. Bernard Knox (New York: Washington Square Press, 1994), 62, 98.

65. See the editors' commentary in *S* 1:530, 532.

66. Defined in psychoanalytic literature as a "scene of sexual intercourse between the parents which the child observes, or infers on the basis of certain indications, and phantasies. It is generally interpreted by the child as an act of violence on the part of the father." Jean Laplanche and J. B. Pontalis, *The Language of Psycho-Analysis,* trans. Donald Nicholson-Smith (New York: Norton, 1973), 335.

67. This is in accordance with Freud's observations regarding the inability of the unconscious to operate according to either/or logic or to express it in dreams (*Interpretation of Dreams,* 351–52).

68. See Sigmund Freud, "Instincts and Their Vicissitudes," trans. Cecil M. Baines, in *General Psychological Theory: Papers on Metapsychology,* ed. Phillip Rieff (New York: Collier Books, 1963), 93–96.

69. For a concise discussion of the Oedipus complex, which includes key references, see Laplanche and Pontalis, *Language of Psycho-Analysis,* 282–87.

70. Gitovich, *Letopis',* 74.

71. The phrase belongs to Peter Rudnytsky, *Freud and Oedipus* (New York: Columbia University Press, 1987), 49.

72. Shchepkina-Kupernik, "O Chekhove," 235–36.

73. See editors' commentary in *S* 1:586. For a study of Chekhov and women, see Carolina De Maegd-Soëp, *Chekhov and Women: Women in the Life and Work of Chekhov* (Columbus, Ohio: Slavica Publishers, 1987); see also the penetrating remarks in Savely Senderovich, "Anton Chekhov and St. George the Dragonslayer: An Introduction to the Theme," in *Anton Chekhov Rediscovered: A Collection of New Studies with a Comprehensive Bibliography,* ed. Savely Senderovich and Munir Sendich (East Lansing, Mich.: Russian Language Journal, 1987), 167–87. Rayfield, *Chekhov: A Life,* provides the richest account of Chekhov's relations with women, though some of his interpretations of the documentary evidence—previously closely held, if not censored—have been disputed; see, for instance, V. B. Kataev's review of the book in *Chekhovskii vestnik,* no. 2 (1997): 6–12.

74. See, for example, Freud's treatment of the issue in "The Passing of the Oedipus-Complex," trans. Joan Riviere, in Sigmund Freud, *Sexuality and the Psychology of Love,* ed. Philip Rieff (New York: Collier Books, 1963), 176–82.

75. This story, which will be addressed in the next chapter, was included in the Marks edition of Chekhov's collected works and therefore would have been recently revisited by the author.

76. See editors' commentary in *P* 10:300–301.

77. Chekhova, *Iz dalekogo proshlogo,* 34–35, 43, 77.

78. In the words of Harold Bloom, these are "as cases akin to what Freud called the family romance" (*The Anxiety of Influence: A Theory of Poetry* [New York: Oxford University Press, 1973], 7).

79. Thus in his mean-spirited memoir N. M. Ezhov wrote of the story that famously attracted D. M. Grigorovich's attention, "Eger'" ("The Huntsman"): "Chekhov borrowed

everything in it from Turgenev's "Svidanie" ("The Tryst"), indeed, he subsequently also took a lot from Turgenev" ("Anton Pavlovich Chekhov [Opyt kharakteristiki]," *Istoricheskii vestnik*, 1909, no. 8 [August]: 504).

80. See the treatment of the "anxiety of influence" in *Seagull* in James M. Curtis, "Ephebes and Precursors in Chekhov's *The Seagull,*" *Slavic Review* 44, no. 3 (fall 1985): 415–37.

81. See also "First Debut" ("Pervyi debiut," 1886), in which a young lawyer suffers through his first case as a defense attorney. His more experienced adversaries trounce him, but they say that he did a fine job and shows promise, "only he wrongfully implicated Hamlet in his speech."

2. Looking the Part

1. I should note Bruno Bettelheim's inclusion of the term "scopophilia" among those he finds mistranslated in the standard edition of Freud's work in English, part of a pattern, in Bettelheim's view, of obscuring the ordinary German linguistic register and humanistic orientation of Freud's vocabulary and rendering it more "scientific" through recourse to Greek roots. See *Freud and Man's Soul* (New York:Vintage Books, 1984), esp. 90–91.

2. It will become clear, therefore, that I use the term "professional" in its dictionary definition, not as a category of sociological or historical understanding of the formation of corporate and class identities, interest groups, or loci of power. Key terms of Foucauldean discourse appear here largely as homonyms.

3. The memoir was first published serially in the journal *Mir bozhii*, went through nine editions before the Revolution, and was widely translated (G. A. Brovman, *V. V. Veresaev: zhizn' i tvorchestvo* [Moscow: Sovetskii pisatel', 1959], 89). Chekhov liked the work, though the edition on his bookshelf has uncut pages (E. A. Dinershtein, *A. P. Chekhov i ego izdateli* [Moscow: Kniga, 1990], 15).

4. V. V. Veresaev, *Sobranie sochinenii v piati tomakh*, vol. 1, ed. Iu. U. Babushkin (Moscow: Ogonek, 1961), 256–57. Translations from this source are my own, though I have consulted (and used in the classroom) V. Veresaeff [V. Smidovich], *The Confessions of a Physician,* trans. Simeon Linden (London: Grant Richards, 1904).

5. Ibid., 257.

6. Ibid., 258.

7. Ibid., 262–63.

8. Ibid., 263.

9. Ibid., 267–68.

10. Ibid., 381–88 (chap. 16).

11. Ibid., 271–73.

12. Ibid., 288.

13. Ibid., 275–78; emphasis added.

14. Ibid., 360.

15. Ibid., 410.

16. On a very relevant theatrical metaphor pervading the cycle, see Natalia Pervukhina, "*Notes of aYoung Country Doctor:* A Haven in the Limelight," *Slavic and East European Journal* 40, no. 4 (winter 1996): 685–99.

17. Mikhail Bulgakov, *A Country Doctor's Notebook,* trans. Michael Glenny (London: Harvill Press, 1990), 13. All translations of the Bulgakov cycle are taken from this source.

18. Ibid., 15.

19. Ibid., 17.

20. Ibid., 20.

21. Ibid., 24.

22. Ibid., 24–25.

23. Ibid., 97.

24. Ibid., 99.

25. Ibid., 107.

26. Ibid., 107–9.

27. Sigmund Freud, "Instincts and Their Vicissitudes," trans. Cecil M. Baines, in *General Psychological Theory: Papers on Metapsychology,* ed. Philip Rieff (New York: Collier Books, 1963), 83–103.

28. See Robert Louis Jackson, "'If I forget thee, O Jerusalem': An Essay on Chekhov's 'Rothschild's Fiddle,'" in *Anton Chekhov Rediscovered: A Collection of New Studies with a Comprehensive Bibliography,* ed. Savely Senderovich and Munir Sendich (East Lansing, Mich.: Russian Language Journal, 1987), 35–49.

29. The story was apparently written in autumn 1884 but rejected for publication because of its length by *Strekoza.* A year later it was published in *Oskolki;* see editors' commentary, *S* 3:562–63.

30. Aleksandr Kuprin, "Pamiati Chekhova," in *A. P. Chekhov v vospominaniiakh sovremennikov,* ed. N. I. Gitovich (Moscow: Khudozhestvennaia literatura, 1986), 520–21.

31. For a fascinating reading of this story with a similar focus, see Cathy Popkin, "Chekhov's Corpus: Bodies of Knowledge," in *Essays in Poetics* 18 (September 1993): 44–72.

32. Theodor Reik, *Masochism in Modern Man,* trans. Margaret H. Hegel and Gertrud M. Kurth (New York: Grove Press, 1957), 48.

33. In fact, the story had a very long period of gestation and by some accounts goes back to 1887 (see editors' commentary, *S* 8:466), a period when such narratives were more characteristic.

34. See the overview of critical reception in *S* 8:478–83.

35. *S* 8:467–71.

36. This notebook entry relates to a 1901 incident in which Chekhov received severe treatment while going through customs at Odessa; see *S* 17:76, 307.

37. See also the unused incident appearing twice in Chekhov's notebooks, dating from the late 1890s: "An officer with his wife went to the *banya* together, and both were washed by a soldier-servant, whom they obviously did not consider a human being" (*S* 17:44, 156–57, 284).

38. See editors' commentary, *S* 8:475.

39. Savely Senderovich, *Chekhov—s glazu na glaz: istoriia odnoi oderzhimosti A. P. Chekhova. Opyt fenomenologii tvorchestva* (St. Petersburg: Dmitrii Bulanin, 1994), 233–34.

40. Letter of 3 August 1892, cited from *Perepiska A. P. Chekhova v trekh tomakh,* vol. 2, ed. and commentary A. M. Dolotova (Moscow: Nasledie, 1996), 298. Similar reproaches were directed at Chekhov by his wife, Ol'ga Knipper: "You live your own special life, and look at everyday life rather indifferently. How horrible, Anton, if all that I write will arouse a smile

in you and nothing beyond that" (28 August 1902; cited from Zinovii Papernyi, *Taina siia* . . . *Liubov' u Chekhova* [Moscow: B.S.G Press, 2002], 236).

41. Janet Malcolm, *Reading Chekhov: A Critical Journey* (New York: Random House, 2001), 193.

42. N. I. Gitovich, *Letopis' zhizni i tvorchestva A. P. Chekhova* (Moscow: Khudozhestvennaia literatura, 1955), 86–92.

43. Ibid., 120.

44. Mikhail P. Chekhov, *Vokrug Chekhova: vstrechi i vpechatleniia* (Moscow: Moskovskii rabochii, 1960), 137.

45. On the lasting importance to Chekhov of his professional (and official) identity as a physician, see, for instance, Iurii Sobolev, *Chekhov. Stat'i. Materialy. Bibliografiia* (Moscow: Federatsiia, 1930), 194–96.

46. See editors' commentary, *S* 6:647.

47. *Perepiska A. P. Chekhova,* 1:252.

48. Many insightful remarks on this topic were offered in the papers of Radislav Lapushin, "The Dark Side of the Mirror: The Mystery of Reflection in Early Chekhov," and Galina S. Rylkova, "The Death of Ivan Dmitrich: Sick to Death of/in Chekhov's Stories," both presented at the 2002 national convention of the American Association for the Advancement of Slavic Studies in Pittsburgh, Penn.

49. In the original version of the story, and until the twelfth edition of *Pestrye rasskazy,* the phrase was "still as a statue" ("nepodvizhna, kak statuia," *S* 4:433). Certainly a statue is more readily associated with immobility than a mirror; one can speculate that Chekhov changed the simile in order to accentuate the motif of reflection, and thereby also the association between Nelli and the reader.

50. Lucien Dällenbach, *The Mirror in the Text,* trans. Jeremy Whiteley and Emma Hughes (Chicago: University of Chicago Press, 1989).

51. Charles Isenberg, *Telling Silence: Russian Frame Narratives of Renunciation* (Evanston: Northwestern University Press, 1993).

52. Lapushin, "The Dark Side."

53. The story is found in *S* 5:447–50. In view of the story's brevity, page references are omitted.

54. Donald Rayfield, *Anton Chekhov: A Life* (London: HarperCollins, 1997), 145.

55. See Chekhov, *Vokrug Chekhova,* 137. The album is in the collection of the Chekhov Museum in Yalta and is stored upstairs in Mariia Pavlovna's desk. The album is approximately six by eight inches and two and a half inches thick, with slots for two photographs per page. Photos of the surviving Ianov sisters occupy the album's first page, pictures of the artist and his friend Isaak Levitan and a portrait of Chekhov's father, the second. I am most grateful to Gennadii Shaliugin and the curators of the Chekhov Museum for allowing me to see Mariia Pavlovna's room and examine this artifact.

56. There had been an earlier instance of a handmade gift from a female patient (and family friend, and one of a trio of sisters, no less) made into an object of art: the pillow that Elizaveta Markova sewed in order to thank Chekhov became, in February 1884, the butt of an unpublished parodistic series of testimonials signed by Chekhov's friends Aleksandr Ianov (Mariia's brother), the artist Iakov Turlygin, the poet Liodor Pal'min, Chekhov's brother Nikolai, and Chekhov in the guise of A. Chekhonte; see "Attestat"(*S* 18:12–13 and 223–24).

According to Donald Rayfield, Chekhov had an affair with Elizaveta Markova, and his brother Nikolai with one of her sisters (*Chekhov: A Life*, 107).

57. So, too, Chekhov spoke of his own reaction to observing Ol'ga Knipper rehearsing with the Moscow Art Theater when he first met her; in a letter to Suvorin he wrote: "Irina [played by Knipper] was in my opinion delightful. Her voice, nobility, sincerity—so fine that it itches even in the throat" (8 October 1898). In his notebook there is an entry similarly displacing sexual arousal to the throat: "While at dinner I saw a beauty [*uvidel khoroshen'kuiu*] and choked; then I saw another beauty, and choked again. I never ate; there were a lot of beauties" (*S* 17:79). Last, as evidence that one of Chekhov's contemporaries understood "tears come up to your throat" in like fashion, I cite V. A. Gol'tsev, who, in an article on Chekhov that included a reading of "Work of Art," followed a citation of this line with the remark "*Avis* to our decadents," a clear signal that he had apprehended the line's sexual content ("A. P. Chekhov [Opyt literaturnoi kharakteristikoi]," in *A. P. Chekhov: pro et contra. Tvorchestvo A. P. Chekhova v russkoi mysli kontsa XX–nachala XX v. (1887–1914). Antologiia*, ed. I. N. Sukhikh, commentary A. D. Stepanov [St. Petersburg: Izdatel'stvo Russkogo Khristianskogo gumanitarnogo instituta, 2002], 244; rpt. from *Russkaia mysl'* [1894]).

58. For example, in discussions at the Second International Chekhov Symposium at Badenweiler in 1994.

59. While this moment of narcissistic infantile grandiosity could be situated in a number of psychoanalytic developmental schemes for ego formation—the Lacanian "mirror stage" is probably the most popular in literary studies—I sense the closest clinical and theoretical equivalent in Mahler's "practicing period"; see Margaret Mahler, Fred Pine, and Anni Bergman, *The Psychological Birth of the Human Infant: Symbiosis and Individuation* (New York: Basic Books, 1975). For a brief critique of Mahler's study on personal and methodological grounds, see John E. Gedo, *Spleen and Nostalgia: A Life and Work in Psychoanalysis* (Northvale, N.J.: Jason Aronson, 1997), 94–97, 227–28.

60. Helen Block Lewis, *Sex and the Superego: Psychic War in Men and Women*, rev. ed. (Hillsdale, N.J.: Lawrence Erlbaum Associates, 1987), 192; also stated repeatedly in her *Shame and Guilt in Neurosis* (New York: International Universities Press, 1971). I am grateful to Deborah Martinsen for pointing me in this direction.

61. On the narcissistic aspect of exhibitionism, see Otto Fenichel, *The Psychoanalytic Theory of Neurosis* (New York: W. W. Norton & Co, 1945), 72. For an interesting treatment of narcissism as the process of regulating the sense of self, see Robert D. Stolorow and Frank M. Lachmann, *Psychoanalysis of Developmental Arrests: Theory and Treatment* (New York: International Universities Press, 1980). Freud discussed shame as an inhibitor of exhibitionism and scopophilia in "Three Essays on Sexuality," in *The Standard Edition of the Complete Psychological Works of Sigmund Freud*, 24 vols., ed. James Strachey (London: Hogarth Press, 1953–74), 7:135–243, discussed by Lewis, *Shame and Guilt*, 24–25, and in Fenichel, *Psychoanalytic Theory of Neurosis*, 139. Lewis writes: "Since shame and triumph experiences are the very stuff with which so many adult and childhood sexual fantasies are concerned, the focus on shame experiences facilitates the recovery of childhood fantasy life, both oedipal and preoedipal. . . . The 'high,' 'giddy' feelings which are part of triumphant pleasure can also generate excitement which the person feels incongruous with his adulthood and would prefer to bypass. They can thus also be the occasion for the start of an ideational sequence leading to obsessive doubt and a sense of guilt" (*Shame and Guilt*, 59).

62. Senderovich, *Chekhov—s glazu na glaz,* 131–32.

63. Personal examination of artifact, Chekhov Museum, Yalta.

64. In a letter to his architect friend Shekhtel, he wrote: "I could devour a whorelet like Nadia [Ianova] . . . In Babkino there's still nobody to screw" (cited from Rayfield, *Chekhov: A Life,* 157).

65. From a letter to Mariia Kiseleva, 21 September 1886.

66. The *Domostroi* was a sixteenth-century didactic text that told how the home ought to be organized in Orthodox Muscovy. As such, it is a striking document of the patriarchal social order of the day. See *The Domostroi: Rules for Russian Households in the Time of Ivan the Terrible,* ed. and trans. Carolyn Johnston Pouncy (Ithaca: Cornell University Press, 1994).

67. Fenichel, *Psychoanalytic Theory of Neurosis,* 345, 347–48.

68. Freud, *Standard Edition,* 17:217–56.

69. In Sigmund Freud, *Sexuality and the Psychology of Love,* ed. Philip Rieff (New York: Collier Books, 1963), 212–13. See also Freud's codification of symbols in *The Interpretation of Dreams* (New York: Avon Books, 1965), 392, 447; and Otto Fenichel, "The Symbolic Equation: Girl = Phallus," in *The Collected Papers of Otto Fenichel,* 2d ser. (New York: W. W. Norton & Co., 1954), 3–18.

70. Luce Irigaray, "Another 'Cause'—Castration," in *Feminisms: An Anthology of Literary Theory and Criticism,* ed. Robyn R. Warhol and Diane Price Herndl (New Brunswick, N.J.: Rutgers University Press, 1991), 405, 408–9.

71. In fact, this daily paper's range was much wider than its original format and name imply.

72. This point has apparently been missed by scholars, perhaps because the novel's title was translated quite freely in the *Stock Exchange Gazette* as *In the World of Artists: A Novel from the Parisian Life of Émile Zola* (*V mire khudozhnikov—roman iz parizhskoi zhizni Emilia Zolia*); see editors' commentary, *S* 5:672.

73. Émile Zola, *The Masterpiece,* trans. Thomas Walton (New York: Oxford University Press, 1993), 47.

74. Ibid., 49.

75. Ibid., 163.

76. Ibid., 278.

77. See the introduction by Roger Person, ibid., xii–xxvi, and the treatment in Frederick Brown, *Zola: A Life* (New York: Farrar Straus Giroux, 1995), esp. 552–63. The novel was the final blow to Zola's relationship with Cézanne.

78. Zola, *The Masterpiece,* 307–9.

79. I am very grateful to the Slavic Reference Librarians at the University of Illinois (Champaign-Urbana) for finding and making available to me the relevant pages from this edition of *Birzhevye vedemosti.*

3. Self and Other through the Lens of Science

1. For a study highlighting the ambiguities and change over time in Chekhov's attitude toward the positivistic ideologies in which he was steeped, and which includes many insightful readings of individual Chekhov works, see Petr Dolzhenkov, *Chekhov i pozitivizm* (Moscow: Dialog-MGU, 1998).

2. See the editors' commentary to "Panikhida" (*S* 4:516).

3. According to Chekhov's next letter to Aleksandr, "v khmel'nom vide" (13 May 1883).

4. For studies of the scientific bases of Chekhov's worldview, see John Tulloch, *Chekhov: A Structuralist Study* (New York, Barnes & Noble, 1980), and Dolzhenkov, *Chekhov i pozitivizm*. On Darwin in Russia, see James Allen Rogers, "Darwinism, Scientism, and Nihilism," *Russian Review* 19, no. 1 (January 1960): 10–23, and "Charles Darwin and Russian Scientists," *Russian Review* 19, no. 4 (October 1960): 371–83; Alexander Vucinich, *Darwin in Russian Thought* (Berkeley: University of California Press, 1988); Daniel P. Todes, *Darwin without Malthus: The Struggle for Existence in Russian Evolutionary Thought* (New York: Oxford University Press, 1989). On Buckle, see Giles St. Aubyn, *A Victorian Eminence: The Life and Works of Henry Thomas Buckle* (London: Barrie Books, 1958), 31–32; Vucinich, *Darwin in Russian Thought*, 9–10; and Alexander Vucinich, *Social Thought in Tsarist Russia: The Quest for a General Science of Society, 1861–1917* (Chicago: University of Chicago Press, 1976), esp. 8–9. Buckle's influence on Chekhov is discussed in Dolzhenkov, *Chekhov i Pozitivizm*, 15, 113–15. On Spencer and Chekhov, see Shoshana Knapp, "Herbert Spencer in Čexov's 'Skučnaja istorija' and 'Duel'": The Love of Science and the Science of Love," *Slavic and East European Journal* 29, no. 3 (1985): 279–96.

5. N.V. Shelgunov, "Progressivnaia reaktsiia," *Delo* 4 (1879): 148; cited from Todes, *Darwin without Malthus*, 35.

6. *Anton Chekhov's Life and Thought: Selected Letters and Commentary*, trans. Michael Henry Heim and Simon Karlinsky, selection, commentary, and intro. Simon Karlinsky (Berkeley: University of California Press, 1973), 176; cited widely, including in Tulloch, *Chekhov*, 59; Nancy Frieden, *Russian Physicians in an Era of Reform and Revolution, 1856–1905* (Princeton: Princeton University Press, 1981), 130.

7. This is studied in Todes, *Darwin without Malthus;* see also Vucinich, *Darwin in Russian Thought*, and Stephen Jay Gould, "Kropotkin Was No Crackpot," in *Bully for Brontosaurus: Reflections in Natural History* (New York: W. W. Norton & Company, 1991), 325–39.

8. Henry Thomas Buckle, *Essays* (New York: D. Appleton and Co., 1863), 203. The editors of Chekhov's collected works indicated that Buckle's lecture "The Influence of Women" was the source of Chekhov's reference (*P* 1:345).

9. Buckle, *Essays*, 206.

10. Vucinich, *Social Thought*, vii.

11. Nikolai Chernyshevsky, *What Is to Be Done?*, trans. Michael Katz (Ithaca: Cornell University Press, 1989), 301–2.

12. See Herbert Spencer, *Education: Intellectual, Moral, and Physical* (New York: A. L. Burt Co., n.d.).

13. In, for instance, Carolina De Maegd Soëp, *Chekhov and Women: Women in the Life and Work of Chekhov* (Columbus, Ohio: Slavica, 1987), 84ff.; Tulloch, *Chekhov*, 149–52; and Barbara Heldt, *Terrible Perfection: Women and Russian Literature* (Bloomington: Indiana University Press, 1987), 48.

14. See, for example, the remarks of M. P. Chekhov in *Vokrug Chekhova* (Moscow: Moskovskii rabochii, 1960), 83, and Chekhov's didactic missives to his youngest brother, Mikhail, from April 1879 (*P* 1:29–30) and to his older brother Nikolai (March 1886; *P* 1:221–25).

15. See, for example, the treatment of "Duel" in Vladimir Kataev, *If Only We Could Know! An Interpretation of Chekhov*, trans. Harvey Pitcher (Chicago: Ivan R. Dee, 2002), 112–19.

16. The impact of heredity on illness was central to Chekhov's foray into historical forensic medicine. In an 1890 letter to Suvorin, Chekhov asserted with great confidence that Dmitrii of Uglich could indeed have killed himself with a knife during an epileptic fit, and that the False Dmitrii was without doubt an impostor, since he did not show signs of the inherited disease that had afflicted the genuine Dmitrii and would still have been with him in adulthood: "When you happen to write about this, say that this America was discovered by the physician Chekhov" (17 March 1890). The discovery had been made when Chekhov was gathering materials for another unrealized dissertation project (but one that was pursued to some length), a history of doctoring in Russia.

17. For treatments of this topic in Chekhov and in Russia, see Knapp, "Herbert Spencer"; Tulloch, *Chekhov;* and Laura Engelstein, *The Keys to Happiness: Sex and the Search for Modernity in Fin-de-Siècle Russia* (Ithaca: Cornell University Press, 1992), esp. chapt. 4 (128–64). On degeneration in European science and culture (focused on France, England, and Italy), see Daniel Pick, *Faces of Degeneration: A European Disorder, c. 1848–c. 1918* (Cambridge: Cambridge University Press, 1989). For a treatment of Nordau's impact on the Russian Symbolists, and much useful bibliographic material on Nordau in Russia, see Ronald Vroon, "Max Nordau and the Origins of Russian Decadence: Some Preliminary Observations" (*http://pbunjak .narod.ru/zbornik/tekstovi/09_Vroon.htm*). A particularly interesting treatment of this topic is to be found in Laura Goering, "'Russian Nervousness': Neurasthenia and National Identity in Nineteenth-Century Russia," *Medical History* 47 (2003): 23–46. Chekhov's editors point out that Nordau's *Degeneration* was widely discussed in the Russian press in the spring and summer of 1893 (*S* 8:492).

18. Sander L. Gilman, "Hugh W. Diamond and Psychiatric Photography," in *The Face of Madness: Hugh W. Diamond and the Origin of Psychiatric Photography,* ed. Sander L. Gilman (New York: Brunner/Mazel, 1976), 13.

19. Ibid., 5. See the comprehensive discussion of this point in Pick, *Faces of Degeneration.* On Charcot's visual poetics of psyche (and Freud's new focus on the narrative rather than the pictorial), see Stephanie Kiceluk, "The Patient as Sign and Story: Disease Pictures, Life Histories, and the First Psychoanalytic Case History," *Journal of Clinical Psychoanalysis* 1, no. 3 (1992): 333–68; and Sander L. Gilman, "History and Images in Medicine," in *History and . . . Histories within the Human Sciences,* ed. Ralph Cohen and Michael S. Roth (Charlottesville: University Press of Virginia, 1995), esp. 98–101.

20. See R. B. Kaganovich, *Iz istorii bor'by s tuberkulezom v dorevoliutsionnoi Rossii* (Moscow: Akademiia meditsinskikh nauk, 1952), 9–14.

21. Vladimir A. Giliarovskii, *Moskva i moskvichi: ocherki* (Minsk: Narodnaia asveta, 1981), 258–59.

22. Chekhov, *Vokrug Chekhova,* 250.

23. Ibid., 272.

24. There can be no doubt that Chekhov was aware of his illness long before he was forced to acknowledge it openly by a hemorrhage in March 1897. See, for instance, comments about blood-spitting in letters to Leikin (10 December 1884), his cousin Nikolai (March 1886), and E. A. Lintvareva (27 October 1888); and his brother Mikhail's remarks that Chekhov's first hemorrhage was in 1884, and that he would never allow himself to be sounded by other physicians, which would have disclosed the state of his lungs (*Vokrug Chekhova,* 194–95). Bunin tells how Chekhov asked him what he, Bunin, would write about him in his memoirs. Bunin responded, "You're the one who will write about me. You'll outlive me."

"Sure—you could be one of my children."

"No matter. You have the blood of common folk."

"And you have gentry blood. Peasants and merchants degenerate horribly quickly. Read my story 'Three Years.'" I. A. Bunin, "Chekhov," in *A. P. Chekhov v vospominaniiakh sovremennikov,* ed. N. I. Gitovich (Moscow: Khudozhestvennaia literatura, 1986), 492.

25. See Rufus W. Mathewson, Jr., "Intimations of Mortality in Four Čexov Stories," *American Contributions to the Sixth International Congress of Slavists, Prague, 1968, August 7–13,* vol. 2, *Literary Contributions,* ed. William E. Harkins (The Hague: Mouton, 1968), 261–83.

26. Chekhov, *Vokrug Chekhova,* 231.

27. The work was inspired by the eminent Darwinian botanist A. K. Timiriazev's brochure "A Parody of Science" ("Parodiia nauki"), which denounced a botanical laboratory at the zoo (see the editors' commentary in *S* 16:507–11).

28. See the more extensive treatment of "Duel" and Chekhov's engagement with theories of evolution and degeneration in Tulloch, *Chekhov,* 117–31.

29. The phrase is from Cathy Popkin and Louise McReynolds, "The Objective Eye and the Common Good," in *Constructing Russian Culture in the Age of Revolution: 1881–1940,* ed. Catriona Kelly and David Shepherd (Oxford: Oxford University Press, 1998), 75.

30. Anton Chekhov, "Duel," in *Ward Six and Other Stories,* trans. Ann Dunnigan (New York: Signet, 1965), 61–161, quotation at 100. Citations follow (with occasional modifications) this translation. Further references to this source will be cited in the text, with the page number from the Signet edition preceding reference to Chekhov's collected works (*S*).

31. The critical tradition of identifying this position as Vagner's appears unjust. Vagner was not prone to the simplistic sociobiological and biopsychological extrapolations from the animal world to humans characteristic of von Koren, and in fact argued against such methodologies while attempting to put social psychology on scientific grounds; see the discussion of his work in A. B. Brushlinskii et al., "Ocherk zhizni i nauchnoi deiatel'nosti V. A. Vagner," in V. A. Vagner, *Izbrannye trudy po zoopsikhologii,* ed. A. B. Brushlinskii et al. (Moscow: Nauka, 2002), 272–83. Vagner was also a talented pianist and a personality with more facets than the character von Koren. In his application of the discourse of science to the sphere of the moral and ethical, von Koren does, however, recall Turgenev's Bazarov of *Fathers and Sons* (1862); this aspect of the novel is treated in Michael Holquist, "Bazarov and Sečenov: The Role of Scientific Metaphor in *Fathers and Sons,*" *Russian Literature* 16, no. 4 (November 1984): 359–74.

32. See, for example, Dmitrii Pisarev's 1862 (published 1868) pseudoscientific political essay "Bees," trans. R. Dixon, in Dmitry Pisarev, *Selected Philosophical, Social, and Political Essays* (Moscow: Foreign Language Publishing House, 1958), as well as the extended beehive metaphor for Moscow in Tolstoy's *War and Peace.*

33. The commentators to the story in Chekhov's collected works point out that the phenomenon of the duel had again become quite current in Russian society and the topic of much debate in the press. Chekhov's treatment of the theme here (as well as in *Three Sisters*) is thus far from anachronistic. As always, his characters respond to the realities of the day. See also Aleksandr Kuprin's long tale "Duel" ("Poedinok," 1905).

34. A point made in Tulloch, *Chekhov,* 124–25.

35. A. P. Chudakov, *Chekhov's Poetics,* trans. Edwina Cruise and Donald Dragt (Ann Arbor: Ardis, 1983), 204.

36. See, for instance, the treatment in Thomas Winner, *Chekhov and His Prose* (New York:

Holt, Rinehart & Winston, 1968), 106–12; the brief summary of scholarship in A. S. Skafty-mov, "O povestiakh Chekhova 'Palata No. 6' i 'Moia zhizn'," in *Nravstvennye iskaniia russkikh pisatelei* (Moscow: Khudozhestvennaia literatura, 1972), 381; N. M. Fortunatov, *Puti iskanii: O masterstve pisatelia* (Moscow: Sovetskii pisatel', 1974), 158–78; and, more recently, Liza Knapp, "Fear and Pity in 'Ward Six': Chekhovian Catharsis," in *Reading Chekhov's Text,* ed. R. L. Jackson (Evanston: Northwestern University Press, 1993), 145–54.

37. On associations between Ragin's views and those of Marcus Aurelius, Schopenhauer, and Tolstoy, see the editors' commentary to "Ward 6" in *S* 8:447–50. Skaftymov ("O poves-tiakh Chekhova") argues against interpreting the story as a polemic with Tolstoy, against iden-tifying Ragin's position with that of Marcus Aurelius, and for viewing the story as a serious engagement with the thought of Schopenhauer; Karl Kramer also argues against reading the story as a polemic with Tolstoy (*The Chameleon and the Dream: The Image of Reality in Čexov's Stories* [The Hague: Mouton, 1970], 132–33). See also Andrew Durkin's treatment of the story as a response to Dostoevskii, in particular *The Brothers Karamazov,* in "Chekhov's Response to Dostoevskii: The Case of 'Ward Six,'" *Slavic Review* 40, no. 1 (spring 1981): 49–59.

38. See the discussion of this and other oddities of the story in the context of Chekhov's oeuvre in the commentary to Chekhov's collected works (*S* 8:450–51).

39. Anton Chekhov, "Ward 6," in *Ward Six and Other Stories,* trans. Ann Dunnigan (New York: Signet, 1965), 7–59, quotation at 9. Translations of "Ward 6" are taken, with occasional minor modifications, from this source. References are given in the text to both this Signet edition and the scholarly edition of Chekhov's collected works; if the Signet reference is ab-sent, the translation is mine.

40. Thus, the four paragraphs covered by this summary begin, "If you are not afraid of be-ing stung by the nettles, come with me along the narrow path leading to the annex, and let us see what is going on inside"; they end: "The beds in the room are screwed to the floor. Sitting or lying on them are men in blue hospital gowns and old-fashioned nightcaps. These are the lunatics" (72–73).

41. See editors' commentary, *S* 8:463.

42. G. I. Rossolimo, "Vospominaniia o Chekhove," in Gitovich, *A. P. Chekhov v vospomi-naniiakh sovremennikov,* 436.

43. Kramer relates Ragin's *futliarnost'* (encasedness) to the theme of despotism in the story (*Chameleon,* 129–32).

44. Thus the critic and theorist of literature A. L. Volynskii (pseudonym for Khaim Lei-bovich Flekser) wrote, "Ragin is a madman who is free only because the proper moment has not arisen; he's free, so to speak, out of misunderstanding." A. L. Volynskii, "Literaturnye za-metki," in *A. P. Chekhov: Pro et Contra. Tvorchestvo A. P. Chekhova v russkoi mysli kontsa XIX—nachala XX v. (1887–1914),* ed. I. N. Sukhikh (St. Petersburg: Izdatel'stvo Russkogo Khristian-skogo gumanitarnogo instituta, 2002), 222.

45. V. V. Veresaeff [V. Smidovich], *The Confessions of a Physician,* trans. Simeon Linden (Lon-don: Grant Richards, 1904), 196–97; original in V. V. Veresaev, *Sobranie sochinenii v piati tomakh,* vol. 1, ed. Iu. U. Babushkin (Moscow: Pravda, 1961), 367–68.

46. Nancy Frieden points out that this section of the journal "provided a forum for physi-cians to air grievances and answer critics," a fact that creates additional interpretive possibil-ities (*Russian Physicians,* 116).

47. See, for instance, Chekhov's letter to Suvorin of 7 May 1889.

48. Engelstein, *Keys to Happiness,* 152.

49. Ibid., 144; see also Karlinsky's discussion in *Anton Chekhov's Life and Thought,* 311.

50. See the discussion of this point, and the summarizing typology of critical positions, in I. N. Sukhikh, "Zagadochnyi 'Chernyi monakh' (Problemy interpretatsii povesti Chekhova)," *Voprosy literatury,* no. 6 (June 1983): 109–24.

51. See Chekhov, *Vokrug Chekhova,* 248–51. See also the editors' commentary to "The Black Monk" in *S* 8:488–96. For a penetrating article that suggests a whole series of personal dimensions to the story, see S. V. Tikhomirov, "'Chernyi monakh.' Opyt samopoznaniia melikhovskogo otshel'nika," in *Chekhoviana. Melikhovskie trudy i dni,* ed. V. Ia. Lakshin et al. (Mosow: Nauka, 1995), 35–52.

52. On the story as a late manifestation of literary romanticism, see Joseph L. Conrad, "Vestiges of Romantic Gardens and Folklore Devils in Chekhov's 'Verochka,' 'The Kiss,' and 'The Black Monk,'" in *Critical Essays on Anton Chekhov,* ed. Thomas A. Eekman (Boston: G. K. Hall & Co., 1989), 78–91; see also David Matual, "Chekhov's 'Black Monk' and Byron's 'Black Friar,'" *International Fiction Review* 5 (1978): 46–51. Associations with Russian Symbolism have been drawn in Sukhikh, "Zagadochnyi 'Chernyi monakh,'" 117; V. I. Kuleshov, "Realizm A. P. Chekhova i naturalizm i simvolizm v russkoi literature ego vremeni," in *Etiudy o russkikh pisateliakh (issledovaniia i kharakteristiki)* (Moscow: M.G.U., 1982), 245–61; and Paul Debreczeny, "'The Black Monk': Chekhov's Version of Symbolism," in Jackson, *Reading Chekhov's Text,* 179–88. Chekhov's editors also suggest reading the story in the context of fin-de-siècle pseudoscientific theories of degeneration (Nordau, Minskii, etc.; *S* 8:492).

53. For a very informative treatment of this point, see Rosalind Williams, *Notes on the Underground: An Essay on Technology, Society, and the Imagination* (Cambridge: MIT Press, 1990), esp. chap. 7, "The Underground and the Quest for Security."

54. On echoes of the New Testament Book of Revelations in "The Black Monk," see Sukhikh, "Zagadochnyi 'Chernyi monakh,'" 117–18. The motif of historical time also runs counter to the Persephone-Demeter mythological framework that Donald Rayfield has identified in the story ("Orchards and Gardens in Chekhov," *Slavonic and East European Review* 67, no. 4 [1989]: 537).

55. Charles Darwin, *The Origin of Species by Means of Natural Selection, or the Preservation of Favored Races in the Struggle for Life, and The Descent of Man and Selection in Relation to Sex* (New York: Modern Library, 1936), 16, 20, 38–39; David L. Hull, *Darwin and His Critics: The Reception of Darwin's Theory of Evolution by the Scientific Community* (Cambridge: Harvard University Press, 1973), 39–40.

56. Darwin, *Origin of Species,* 373–74.

57. Buckle, *Essays,* 203. Buckle was remarkably close to his own mother, whose early death devastated him.

58. Ibid., 170–71.

59. Ibid., 206.

60. Ibid., 203. In spite of the obvious semantic parallelism, it is unlikely that these names derive directly from the Buckle text. One Russian translation of Buckle that Chekhov might have read does render "veils" as *pokryvalo,* associable with *kovër;* but "dust" is translated as *prakh.* G. T. Bokl', *Vliianie zhenshchin na uspekhi znaniia* (St. Petersburg: A. Buinitskii, 1864), 51, 47.

61. See, for instance, the discussion by Nikolai Strakhov, *Bor'ba s zapadom v nashei literature: istoricheskie i kriticheskie ocherki,* book 2 (The Hague: Mouton, 1969; rep. Kiev, 1897), 296,

314, 333–34. In an article first published in *Russkii vestnik* in 1887, Strakhov is reviewing the anti-Darwinian book of N. Ia. Danilevskii, *Darvinism*.

62. Chekhov was referring to Professor Zakhar'in (*P* 3:295).

63. Among fictional works it is surpassed in length only by the early *Shooting Party* (*Drama na oxote*, 1884); see E. A. Polotskaia, "'Tri goda'. Ot romana k povesti," in *V tvorcheskoi laboratorii Chekhova*, ed. L. D. Opul'skaia, Z. S. Papernyi, and S. E. Shatalov (Moscow: Nauka, 1974), 13. Not surprisingly, this is the story toward which there are the most remarks in Chekhov's creative notebook (*S* 9:451).

64. Polotskaia, "'Tri goda,'" 28.

65. Ibid., 25.

66. Chekhov had planned to have the narrative follow Kostia to America, but did not because his own trip to the world's fair did not come off (see Polotskaia, "'Tri goda,'" 21).

67. See note 24.

68. Chekhov's notebooks are notoriously slippery terrain, and it is dangerous to assume that entries directly express the author's own opinions. They are often unattributed citations of projected fictional characters, pithy verbal indications of a particular position on the world that Chekhov notes as such, and not because they express his own point of view. Here one would want to analyze authorial stance in regard to the character Iartsev, a man who, interestingly, like Chekhov's brother Aleksandr, has studied both philology and chemistry at the university, and whose perspective on the phenomena he studies crosses disciplinary boundaries: "When he talked about something from botany or zoology, he resembled a historian; when he was discussing some sort of historical question, he resembled a natural scientist" (*S* 9:54).

69. For a discussion of Chekhov's view of the visual arts that introduces qualifications into this analogy, see Andrew Durkin, "Čechov's Art in Čechov's Art," in *Anton P. Čechov, philosophische und religiöse Dimensionen im Leben und im Werk: Vorträge des Zweiten Internationalen Čechov-Symposiums, Badenweiler, 20.–24. Oktober 1994*, ed. Vladimir B. Kataev, Rolf-Dieter Kluge, and Regine Nohejl (Munich: Otto Sagner, 1997), 575–79.

70. As pointed out in Iurii Bychkov, *Tainy liubvi, ili "Kukuruza dushi moei". Perepiska A. P. Chekhova s sovremennitsami* (Moscow: Druzhba narodov, 2001), 132–33; and in Donald Rayfield, *Understanding Chekhov: A Critical Study of Chekhov's Prose and Drama* (London: Bristol Classical Press, 1999), 125–26, where this formula is offered: "The line between Shamokhin and Chekhov is fuzzy: we can say that Shamokhin is never a Chekhov, but that Chekhov is sometimes a Shamokhin" (126).

71. See discussion in E. J. Simmons, *Chekhov: A Biography* (Boston: Little, Brown and Company, 1962), 333–34; Donald Rayfield, *Anton Chekhov: A Life* (London: HarperCollins, 1997), 347; and Bychkov, *Tainy liubvi*, who says that this story "allows us to concretize that which remained 'behind the scenes'" in the correspondence between Mizinova and Chekhov (135).

72. Rayfield goes so far as to say that Chekhov "for once [. . .] appears in his own story" (*Chekhov: A Life*, 347); see also Bychkov, *Tainy liubvi*, 132.

73. Savely Senderovich, *Chekhov—s glazu na glaz: istoriia odnoi oderzhimosti A. P. Chekhova. Opyt fenomenologii tvorchestva* (St. Petersburg: Dmitrii Bulanin, 1994), 234. See my discussion in the previous chapter.

74. This interpretation of the significance of the rare emergence of a first-person narrator in Chekhov's late period is supported by A. P. Chudakov's finding that, in first-person narratives of Chekhov's last period (1895–1904), there is "no attempt to incorporate alien or oral

speech; they are very close in style to third-person stories of this period" (*Chekhov's Poetics*, 68). In other words, the use of the first person does not introduce a distinct "other" speaking subject and perspective into the narrative; if the results are stylistically indistinguishable from third-person narratives, the introduction of an I-narrator in this period therefore fulfills other functions.

75. On Zola's influence on Max Nordau and the theory of degeneration, see Hans-Peter Söder, "Disease and Health as Contexts of Fin-de-Siècle Modernity" (Ph.D. diss., Cornell University, 1991), 171–86; also helpful is the section "A Short History of Degeneration Theory's Scientific Background," 253–60. On the theme of heredity in Zola, and the novel *Dr. Pascal* in particular, see Pick, *Faces of Degeneration*, 74–87.

76. Émile Zola, *Doctor Pascal*, trans. Vladimir Kean (London: Elek Books, 1957), 7.

77. Savely Senderovich, "*The Cherry Orchard:* Čechov's Last Testament," *Russian Literature* 35 (1994): 233–34 and passim. This does not contradict the association between Gaev's *shkaf* and the Chekhov family heirloom, with which any visitor to the Chekhov home and museum in Yalta will be familiar. As with the black monk of Chekhov's dream, the fact of a concrete referential association in Chekhov's life and surroundings by no means limits or contradicts the broad range of potential intra-, extra-, and intertextual associations.

78. See my concluding chapter.

79. Rayfield, *Chekhov: A Life*, 296.

80. Zola, *Doctor Pascal*, 231.

81. Pick, *Faces of Degeneration*, 79, 82.

82. Zola, *Doctor Pascal*, 257. See the discussion of this "impossible performative" in Pick, *Faces of Degeneration*, 87.

83. For a discussion of these and Chekhov's very last words, see Maia Sheikina, "'Davno ia ne pil shampanskogo,'" in *Tselebnoe tvorchestvo A. P. Chekhova (Razmyshliaiut mediki i filologi)*, ed. M. E. Burno and B. A. Voskresenskii (Moscow: Rossiiskoe obshchestvo medikov-literaterov, 1996), 42–45.

84. Chekhov's evaluation of Zola is reported in Aleksandr Kuprin, "Pamiati Chekhova," in Gitovich, *A. P. Chekhov v vospominaniiakh sovremennikov*, 533. See also Rayfield, *Chekhov: A Life*, 181–82.

85. Édouard Toulouse, *Enquête médico-psychologique sur les rapports de la supériorité intellectuelle avec la névropatie. Introduction générale: Émile Zola* (Paris: Société d'éditions scientifiques, 1896), vi. See the discussion in Pick, *Faces of Degeneration*, 76–78, and Frederick Brown, *Zola: A Life* (New York: Farrar Straus Giroux, 1995), 711–12.

86. See Winner, *Chekhov and His Prose*, 90; the discussion of Zola and Claude Bernard in Aleksandr Roskin, "Zametki o realizme Chekhova," in his *A. P. Chekhov. Stat'i i ocherki*, ed. N. A. Roskina (Moscow: Khudozhestvennaia literatura, 1959), esp. 196–206; and Dolzhenkov, *Chekhov i pozitivizm*.

87. Hugh Shelley, intro. to Zola, *Doctor Pascal*, 5–6; Brown, *Zola*, 751.

88. Senderovich, "*The Cherry Orchard.*"

4. Erotic and Mythic Visions

1. Chekhov's notes for the unfinished *History of Medicine in Russia* (*Vrachebnoe delo v Rossii*, S 16:277–356) contain many (though not disproportionately so) citations regarding dreams,

troubling visions, and, for that matter, eye problems. That Chekhov's writings take dreams and dreaming as a central concern is an argument of Karl D. Kramer, *The Chameleon and the Dream: The Image of Reality in Čexov's Stories* (The Hague: Mouton, 1970), esp. 76–92.

2. For a discussion of Chekhov's reading of Grigorovich's story, and what it reveals about Chekhov's poetics and a story in which Chekhov explores the terrain of dreams and delusions, "Sleepy" ("Spat' khochetsia," 1888), see Gleb Struve, "On Chekhov's Craftsmanship: The Anatomy of a Story," *Slavic Review* 20 (October 1961): 465–76.

3. Patricia Cox Miller, *Dreams in Late Antiquity: Studies in the Imagination of a Culture* (Princeton: Princeton University Press, 1994), 80–81 and passim. Artemidorus was the author of *Oneirocritica* (Interpretation of dreams).

4. See Jean Laplanche and J. B. Pontalis, *The Language of Psycho-Analysis*, trans. Donald Nicholson-Smith (New York: Norton, 1973), 96–97; Sigmund Freud, *The Interpretation of Dreams*, trans. James Strachey (New York: Avon Books, 1965), 196–221.

5. Mikhail P. Chekhov, *Vokrug Chekhova: vstrechi i vpechatleniia* (Moscow: Moskovskii rabochii, 1960), 249–51.

6. Savely Senderovich, *Chekhov—s glazu na glaz: istoriia odnoi oderzhimosti A. P. Chekhova. Opyt fenomenologii tvorchestva* (St. Petersburg: Dmitrii Bulanin, 1994); Julie de Sherbinin, *Chekhov and Russian Religious Culture: The Poetics of the Marian Paradigm* (Evanston, Ill.: Northwestern University Press, 1997). Both proceed on the assumption, shared here, that, "as in poetry" (and in dreams as *oneiros*), "few of Chekhov's words are random," and they advance interpretations that "depend in large part on attention to the cumulative meanings of unobtrusive details" (de Sherbinin, *Chekhov and Russian Religious Culture,* 144). An early and condensed version of Senderovich's study may be found in English in his "Anton Chekhov and St. George the Dragonslayer (An Introduction to the Theme)," in *Anton Chekhov Rediscovered: A Collection of New Studies with a Comprehensive Bibliography,* ed. Savely Senderovich and Munir Sendich (East Lansing, Mich.: Russian Language Journal, 1987), 167–87.

7. Salman Akhtar, "Object Constancy and Adult Psychopathology," *International Journal of Psycho-Analysis* 75 (1994): 446. See also Robert D. Stolorow and Frank M. Lachmann, *Psychoanalysis of Developmental Arrests: Theory and Treatment* (New York: International Universities Press, 1980), esp. 88–98.

8. On this, see Savely Senderovich, "O chekhovskoi glubine, ili iudofobskii rasskaz Chekhova v svete iudaisticheskoi ekzegezy," in *Avtor i tekst: Sbornik statei,* ed. V. M. Markovich and Volf Shmid [Wolf Schmid] (St. Petersburg: Izdatel'stvo S.-Peterburgskogo universiteta, 1996), 330–31.

9. This episode was reflected in the second part of Chekhov's 1888 story "Beauties" ("Krasavitsy").

10. Donald Rayfield, *Anton Chekhov: A Life* (London: HarperCollins, 1997). Some of Rayfield's inferences have been contested by Russian scholars with mastery of the primary materials. See V. B. Kataev's review of the book in *Chekhovskii vestnik,* no. 2 (1997): 6–12.

11. Janet Malcolm, *Reading Chekhov: A Critical Journey* (New York: Random House, 2001), 35–36.

12. M. P. Chekhov, "Anton Chekhov na kanikulakh," in *Chekhov v vospominaniiakh sovremennikov,* ed. N. I. Gitovich and I. V. Fedorov (Moscow: Gosudarstvennoe izdatel'stvo khudozhestvennoi literatury, 1960), 83; also in Chekhov, *Vokrug Chekhova,* 67–68. According to Rayfield, this took place at the Kravtsov estate, when Chekhov was left on his own in Taganrog (*Chekhov: A Life,* 51).

13. Though somewhat disputed by Ivan Bunin; see his *O Chekhove (Nezakonchennaia rukopis')* (New York: Izdatel'stvo imeni Chekhova, 1955), 58.

14. I have relied on the translation of this story in Anton Chekhov, *Stories,* trans. Richard Pevear and Larissa Volokhonsky (New York: Bantam Books, 2000), 375. Further references to this translation are cited in the text.

15. See the commentary in *S* 10:421–22.

16. See her letter from January 1900 in *Perepiska A. P. Chekhova i O. L. Knipper,* 2 vols., ed. and commentary A. B. Derman (Moscow: MIR, 1934), 1:123. Iurii Sobolev sees the ending of the story "as the personal confession of Chekhov: it is like a chapter from the biography of his emotions (*Chekhov. Stat'i. Materialy. Bibliografiia* [Moscow: Federatsiia, 1930], 262).

17. For treatments of this relationship and its reflections in Chekhov's art, see Leonid Grossman, "Roman Niny Zarechnoi," *Prometei* 2 (1967): 218–89; Iurii Bychkov, *Tainy liubvi, ili "kukuruza dushi moei". Perepiska A. P. Chekhova s sovremennitsami* (Moscow: Druzhba narodov, 2001); Zinovii Papernii, *Taina siia . . . Liubov' u Chekhova* (Moscow: B. S. G.-Press, 2002), 69–100; Carolina De Maegd-Soëp, Chekhov and Women: Women in the Life and Work of Chekhov (Columbus: Slavica, 1987), 117–30.

18. *Perepiska A. P. Chekhova v trekh tomakh,* ed. M. P. Gromov, vol. 2, ed. and commentary A. M. Dolotova (Moscow: Nasledie, 1996), 279.

19. Ibid., 2:277.

20. Ibid., 2:306 (November 1892).

21. Her letter of 4 October 1897 is cited from Ronald Hingley, *A Life of Anton Chekhov* (Oxford: Oxford University Press, 1989), 233.

22. This trope coordinating arousal, vision, and distance appears elsewhere in Chekhov, for instance, in this notebook entry: "Having had a look at a plump, appetizing woman: that's not a woman, but a full moon!" (*S* 17:60).

23. See Chekhov's letter to Aleksei Suvorin of 8 October 1898, and his letter to Lidiia Mizinova of 21 September 1898.

24. Letter to Knipper, 27 September 1900.

25. See Ol'ga Knipper, "Neskol'ko slov ob A. P. Chekhove (1898–1904), in *Perepiska A. P. Chekhova i O. L. Knipper,* 1:40–41.

26. See the discussion of this in chapter 1.

27. Of these, 433 items were sent by Chekhov to Knipper, and over 400 from Knipper to Chekhov; see *Perepiska A. P. Chekhova v trekh tomakh,* vol. 3, ed. and commentary V. B. Kataev (Moscow: Nasledie, 1996), 139.

28. Ibid., 1:107; see also Harvey Pitcher, *Chekhov's Leading Lady: A Portrait of the Actress Olga Knipper* (New York: Franklin Watts, 1980), 60.

29. *Perepiska A. P. Chekhova i O. L. Knipper,* 1:138.

30. Ibid., 1:180 (4 September 1900).

31. Senderovich, "O chekhovskoi glubine," 331.

32. *Perepiska A. P. Chekhova i O. L. Knipper,* 1:80, 88.

33. Ibid., 1:252 (28 December 1900).

34. For helpful summaries of key features of these theories and their departures from Freud, see Michael St. Clair, *Object Relations and Self Psychology: An Introduction* (Monterey, Calif.: Brooks/Cole Publishing Co., 1986); Stephen A. Mitchell and Margaret J. Black, *Freud and Beyond: A History of Modern Psychoanalytic Thought* (New York: BasicBooks, 1995), esp. 112–80. For a rare positive take on the transformation of the self in connection with love, see the

following notebook entry (the context of which, however, remains obscure—is this Chekhov speaking or one of his characters?): "That which we experience when we're in love is perhaps in fact a normal condition. Being in love shows a person how he ought to be" (*S* 17:14).

35. Elena Tolstaia, *Poetika razdrazheniia: Chekhov v kontse 1880-kh nachale 1890-kh godov* (Moscow: Radiks, 1994), 54.

36. See Senderovich, "O chekhovskoi glubine," and Tolstaia, *Poetika razdrazheniia*, 15–55.

37. Rayfield, *Chekhov: A Life*, 83, 178–79.

38. See *Letopis' zhizni i tvorchestva A. P. Chekhova*, vol. 1 (1860–1888), ed. L. D. Gromova-Opul'skaia and N. I. Gitovich (Moscow: Nasledie, 2000), 51.

39. So too in 1889 Chekhov signed a letter to Elena Lintvareva "A. Panov" "to make fun of the rumors that he was to marry Glafira Panova," an actress; see Rayfield, *Chekhov: A Life*, 212.

40. See Sander Gilman, *The Jew's Body* (New York: Routledge, 1991), and *The Case of Sigmund Freud: Medicine and Identity at the Fin de Siècle* (Baltimore: Johns Hopkins University Press, 1993); Daniel Rancour-Laferriere, *Signs of the Flesh: An Essay on the Evolution of Hominid Sexuality* (Bloomington: Indiana University Press, 1985), 331–40. Freud interpreted circumcision as a symbolic substitute for castration in *Totem and Taboo* (*The Standard Edition of the Psychological Works of Sigmund Freud*, vol. 13, trans. James Strachey [London: Hogarth, 1955], 153).

41. For a different interpretation of this lace, see Tolstaia, *Poetika razdrazheniia*, 41. Interestingly, one of Chekhov's earliest and most embarrassing episodes from his medical practice involved circumcision. Soon after graduation from the medical faculty in 1884, Chekhov took a temporary position at a small hospital near Voskresensk, where his brother Ivan was teaching. Mikhail Chekhov recounts, not without amusement, the first surgical intervention Chekhov was called upon to carry out: a boy presented with paraphimosis (an inflamed and constricting foreskin); he was already showing signs of gangrene "and would lose his sex" if not operated upon. Chekhov began but became flustered and unable to proceed with the very minor procedure called for in such instances—circumcision—and had to summon a doctor from elsewhere to operate (*Vokrug Chekhova*, 133–34).

42. *Letopis' zhizni i tvorchestva A. P. Chekhova*, 1:369.

43. See editor's commentary in *Perepiska A. P. Chekhova i O. L. Knipper*, 1:157.

44. See the commentary in *S* 5:634–35. Vladimir Nabokov exploited the metapoetic potential of the theme of voyeurism in "Romance with a Contrabass" in his own *The Eye* (1965; first published in Russian in Paris as *Sogliadatai*, 1930). There the narrator, a White Russian émigré who is earning his keep as a tutor, is interrupted while reading Chekhov's story to his charges and severely beaten by the jealous husband of his mistress. This shaming leads to a suicide attempt and a splitting of the narrator's "I" into the eye from which the narrative emanates and a character, Smurov, whom the narrator's spying eye follows, and who, we learn only at the short novel's end, is in fact the narrator. D. Barton Johnson identifies *Sogliadatai* as "the first of Nabokov's 'double' novels," the first to explore the technical and thematic implications of the fractious mirroring, splitting, or disembodiment of the observing and speaking narrator ("The Books Reflected in Nabokov's *Eye*," *Slavic and East European Journal* 29, no. 4 [winter 1985]: 394). And this innovation, which would become a hallmark of Nabokov's work, issues from a reading of Chekhov; in addition to the overt allusion to "Romance with a Contrabass," the novel is suffused with characters and plot situations taken from Chekhov, the most prominent of which are "The House with the Mezzanine ("Dom s mezaninom," 1896) and "Story of an Anonymous Man" ("Rasskaz neizvestnogo cheloveka," 1893).

45. The other two stories were "A Fragment" ("Otryvok"), also under the signature of "Man without a Spleen," and "The History of One Commercial Enterprise" ("Istoriia odnogo torgovogo predpriiatiia"), published under the signature "The Rook" ("Grach").

46. I borrow the phrase "land diving" from Robert Morgan, *Land Diving: New Poems* (Baton Rouge: Louisiana State University Press, 1976).

47. George Kennan, *Siberia and the Exile System,* vol. 2 (New York: Century Company, 1891), 189.

48. It also suggests that at some level Chekhov *sought* or *staged* the epistemological crisis that, Cathy Popkin has convincingly argued, he experienced during his visit to Sakhalin and in his efforts to write about it; see her "Chekhov as Ethnographer: Epistemological Crisis on Sakhalin Island," *Slavic Review* 51, no. 1 (1992): 36–51. Mircea Eliade's remarks on the "eschatological implications of colonization" are very interesting in this respect; see *The Quest: History and Meaning in Religion* (Chicago: University of Chicago Press, 1969), 89–111. See also Mikhail Bakhtin's discussion of connection between the descent in Rabelais and the exploration of the New World in *Rabelais and His World,* trans. Helene Iswolsky (Bloomington: Indiana University Press, 1984), 397–400.

49. Given the parallel these connections establish, the ending of *Sakhalin Island* becomes particularly significant. Dr. Chekhov devotes this highly marked structural position to a description of the appalling conditions at the infirmary at Aleksandrovsk: it is a kind of last circle of hell. Many features of the infirmary at Aleksandrovsk are repeated in the description of the hospital in "Ward 6" (see editors' commentary, *S* 7:449), which certainly belongs among Chekhov's hellish visions. For additional parallels between *Sakhalin Island* and Dante's *Inferno,* see Kenneth John Atchity, "Chekhov's Infernal Island," *Research Studies: A Quarterly Publication of Washington State University* 36, no. 4 (December 1968): 335–40. Popkin notes that, in a significant contradistinction to the principle of *contrapasso* in Dante's hell, Chekhov finds no connection between the crime and the punishment on Sakhalin ("Chekhov as Ethnographer," 44).

50. Thus, Laurence Senelick has observed that whenever Chekhov makes a classical allusion, it is just as likely to point to an Offenbachian perversion of Virgil or Homer as to the original; see his "Offenbach and Chekhov; or, La Belle Elena," in *Reading Chekhov's Text,* ed. Robert Louis Jackson (Evanston, Ill.: Northwestern University Press, 1993), 201–13. For a concise typology of the descent motif, see John G. Bishop, "The Hero's Descent to the Underworld," in *The Journey to the Other World,* ed. H. R. Davidson (Cambridge: Rowman & Littlefield for Folklore Society, 1975), 109–29.

51. This has become a contentious point in Chekhov studies. One thing is certain: whether believer or skeptic, Chekhov had profound mastery of Russian religious culture, and he employed it as one of the most widely significant cultural codes creating meaning in his texts. See Julie de Sherbinin, "Chekhov and Christianity: The Critical Evolution," in *Chekhov Then and Now: The Reception of Chekhov in World Culture,* ed. J. Douglas Clayton (New York: Peter Lang, 1997), 285–99; and A. S. Sobennikov, *"Mezhdu 'est'' Bog' i 'net Boga' . . ."* (o religiozno-filosofskikh traditsiiakh v tvorchestve A. P. Chekhova) (Irkutsk: Izdatel'stvo Irkutskogo universiteta, 1997).

52. See Linda Ivanits, *Russian Folk Belief* (Armonk, N.Y.: M. E. Sharpe, 1989), 64–70.

53. On this somewhat obscure process, see Donald Rayfield, *Uncle Vanya and the Wood Demon* (London: Bristol Classical Press, 1995).

54. L. Michael O'Toole, *Structure, Style, and Interpretation in the Russian Short Story* (New Haven: Yale University Press, 1982), 209. David Bethea reads the scene in "Peasants" depicting a black horse spooked by the fire and running wild as an apocalyptic motif signifying "a popular world falling apart in an orgy of drunkenness and ignorance" (*The Shape of the Apocalypse in Modern Russian Fiction* [Princeton: Princeton University Press, 1989], 57).

55. See Bishop, "The Hero's Descent," 116–17.

56. Fire breaks out similarly at a critical point in *Three Sisters*. For a treatment of hellish symbolism in that play, see Petr Dolzhenkov, *Chekhov i pozitivizm* (Moscow: Dialog-MGU, 1998), 172–85.

57. The sinner recalls Guido da Montefeltro of Dante's *Inferno* (canto 27): a warrior turned repentant monk, he is promised absolution by the pope for help in waging war; past sins are absolved in exchange for committing further, perhaps greater sins in the service of the church.

58. She is alluding to the character of Lermontov's narrative poem "Demon" (1839).

59. There the woman's kingdom, a pagan underworld, is located on the lower floor of the rich but lonely heroine's manor, while the diabolic lawyer Lyseich reigns above; see Robert Louis Jackson, "Chekhov's 'A Woman's Kingdom': A Drama of Character and Fate," in *Critical Essays on Anton Chekhov*, ed. Thomas A. Eekman (Boston: G. K. Hall & Co., 1989), 101–2.

60. For an alternative interpretation of this story as a hellish vision, see Robert L. Jackson, "Dantesque and Dostoevskian Motifs in Čechov's 'In Exile,'" *Russian Literature* 35, no. 2 (February 1994): 181–94.

61. See Fitzroy Richard Somerset, Baron Raglan, *The Hero: A Study in Tradition, Myth, and Drama* (London: Methuen & Co., 1936); Joseph Campbell, *The Hero with a Thousand Faces*, Bollingen series 17 (New York: Pantheon Books, 1949); Northrop Frye, *The Secular Scripture: A Study of the Structure of Romance* (Cambridge: Harvard University Press, 1976), 102 and passim. See also Ol'ga Freidenberg, who demonstrates the centrality of the descent episode in Homer's *Odyssey* in "The Plot Semantics of the Odyssey," *Soviet Studies in Literature* 27, no. 1 (winter 1990–91): 22–32; the treatment of the heroes of ancient Greek religion in Erwin Rohde, *Psyche: The Cult of Souls and Belief in Immortality among the Greeks*, trans. from 8th ed. by W. B. Hillis (New York: Harcourt, Brace & Co., 1925), 115–55 and passim; and René Girard, *Deceit, Desire, and the Novel: Self and Other in Literary Structure*, trans. Yvonne Freccero (Baltimore: Johns Hopkins University Press, 1965), 253.

62. The paradigmatic opposition is between Prometheus and Orpheus. See Walter A. Strauss, *Descent and Return: The Orphic Theme in Modern Literature* (Cambridge: Harvard University Press, 1971), 10–12; and Herbert Marcuse, *Eros and Civilization: A Philosophical Inquiry into Freud* (Boston: Beacon Press, 1966), 161–71.

63. See Chekhov's letter to Suvorin of 9 March 1890.

64. The taxing and dangerous journey has often been understood as the act of a socially committed physician risking his life and bucking the regime. See Simon Karlinsky's criticism of this commonly held view in *Anton Chekhov's Life and Thought: Selected Letters and Commentary*, trans. Michael H. Heim and Simon Karlinsky, ed., intro., and commentary by Simon Karlinsky (Berkeley: University of California Press, 1975), 152–54. See also Chekhov's letter of 9 March 1890, in which he tells Suvorin that his chief reason for going to Sakhalin is to do medical research.

65. Raglan, *The Hero*, 171.

66. On Kundasova, see Chekhov's letter to his family of 23 April 1890; on the girl in Ceylon, see his letter to Suvorin of 9 December 1890, in Heim and Karlinsky, *Anton Chekhov's Life and Thought*, 174, as the relevant lines are censored out of *Pis'ma*. For a collection of such censored material, see A. P. Chudakov, "'Neprilichnye slova' i oblik klassika (O kupiurakh v izdaniiakh pisem Chekhova)," *Literaturnoe obozrenie* 11 (1991): 54–56. It should be pointed out that Chekhov also visited brothels along the way, "out of curiosity"; see an uncenscored version of his letter to Suvorin of 27 June 1890.

67. Senderovich, *Chekhov—s glazu na glaz.*

68. See Chekhov's letter to I. L. Leont'ev-Shcheglov, 10 December 1890.

69. To Suvorin, 15 April 1890.

70. G. I. Rossolimo, "Vospominaniia o Chekhove," in *A. P. Chekhov v vospominaniiakh sovremennikov*, ed. N. I. Gitovich (Moscow: Khudozhestvennaia literatura, 1986), 436.

71. The Russian title of this tremendously influential article was "Gamlet i Don-Kikhot." Turgenev's conceptualization of the Hamlet theme goes back to the 1840s; see the commentary in I. S. Turgenev, *Polnoe sobranie sochinenii i pisem v dvadtsati vos'mi tomakh*, vol. 8, ed. N.V. Izmailov et al. (Moscow: Nauka, 1964), 553.

72. *Bogatyrs* are the heroes of Russian folk epics (*byliny*).

73. Mircea Eliade, *Birth and Rebirth: The Religious Meaning of Initiation in Human Culture*, trans. Willard R. Trask (New York: Harper & Brothers, 1958), 128. One might rather say that the *story* of every life is made up of a series of ordeals, etc., and that the katabatic masterplot is a supremely attractive and powerful tool for narrativizing, and so making sense of, one's own life.

74. See Bishop, "The Hero's Descent," 117–18.

75. Some salient examples of such stories, all of which can be demonstrated to employ descent motifs, are "The Steppe" ("Step'," 1888), "An Attack of Nerves" ("Pripadok," 1889), and "Ward 6" ("Palata No. 6," 1892). On Chekhov and existentialism, see Marena Senderovich, "Chekhov's Existential Trilogy," in Senderovich and Sendich, *Anton Chekhov Rediscovered*, 77–91, and "Chekhov i Kirkegor," in *Anton P. Čechov, philosophische und religiöse Dimensionen im Leben und im Werk: Vorträge des Zweiten Internationalen Čechov-Symposiums, Badenweiler, 20.–24. Oktober 1994*, ed. Vladimir B. Kataev, Rolf-Dieter Kluge, and Regine Nohejl (Munich: Otto Sagner, 1997), 29–44.

76. On the meaning of this epigraph, see Jean Starobinski, "Acheronta Movebo," trans. Françoise Meltzer, *Critical Inquiry* 13, no. 2 (winter 1987): 394–407. For a few subsequent uses of the trope, see James Hillman, *The Dream and the Underworld* (New York: Harper & Row, 1979); Joseph L. Henderson and Maud Oaks, *The Wisdom of the Serpent: The Myths of Death, Rebirth, and Resurrection* (New York: George Braziller, 1963); and C. G. Jung, "The Psychological Aspects of the Kore," in C. G. Jung and C. Kerényi, *Essays on a Science of Mythology*, Bollingen series 22 (New York: Pantheon Books, 1949), 215–45.

77. Two monograph-length studies of the temporality of Chekhov's poetic world should be mentioned: C. J. G. Turner, *Time and Temporal Structure in Chekhov* (Birmingham: Dept. of Russian Language and Literature, University of Birmingham, 1994); and Daria A. Kirjanov, *Chekhov and the Poetics of Memory* (New York: Peter Lang, 2000).

78. Herbert Spencer, a cultural icon for the notion of progress, began his career as a railway engineer, and may be alluded to in the figure of Anan'ev. On the existential symbolism of space in "Lights," see Dolzhenkov, *Chekhov i pozitivizm*, 16–21. For a sharp discussion of

time in "Lights," see V. B. Kataev, *If Only We Could Know! An Interpretation of Chekhov,* trans. and ed. Harvey Pitcher (Chicago: Ivan R. Dee, 2002), 33–37.

79. On the autobiographical implications of this episode for Chekhov, see M. S. Voloshina, "Zagadka 'Nikolaia i Mashi,'" in *Chekhovskie chteniia v Ialte: Chekhov i xx vek,* ed. V. A. Bogdanov (Moscow: Nasledie, 1997), 267.

80. This "agnostic" position is understood as the "final authorial position in this work" (but not in Chekhov's life or oeuvre) in Dolzhenkov, *Chekhov i pozitivizm,* 21.

81. See Robert Louis Jackson, "'If I forget Thee, O Jerusalem': An Essay on Chekhov's 'Rothschild's Fiddle,'" in Senderovich and Sendich, *Anton Chekhov Rediscovered,* 35–49.

82. On Chekhov's own fragmentary King Solomon monologue and the ecclesiastical in Chekhov, see Peggy A. Burge, "Čechov's Use of Ecclesiastes in 'Step','" in Kataev, Kluge, and Nohejl, *Čechov, philosophische und religiöse Dimensionen im Leben und im Werk,* 399–404; Radislav Lapushin, *Ne postigaemoe bytie. Opyt prochteniia A. P. Chekhova* (Minsk: Propilei, 1998), 10–16; Sobennikov, *"Mezhdu 'est'' Bog' i 'net Boga' . . .",* 36–50; Peter Rossbacher, "Čexov's Fragment 'Solomon,'" *Slavic and East European Journal* 12 (1968): 27–34.

83. Frye writes: "The notion of a world of pure memory, where everything forever continues to be as it has been, is the core of the religious conception of hell" (*Secular Scripture,* 175).

84. Freud, *Interpretation of Dreams,* 617. Writes Frye: "Hence many descent themes, from the Harrowing of Hell to the psychological quests of Freud and his successors, center on the theme of the release, revival, or reemergence of parental figures buried in a world of amnesia or suppressed memory" (*Secular Scripture,* 121–22).

85. See Marena Senderovich, "Chekhov's 'Kashtanka': Metamorphoses of Memory in the Labyrinth of Time (A Structural-Phenomenological Essay)," in Senderovich and Sendich, *Anton Chekhov Rediscovered,* 63–75.

86. K. S. Stanislavskii, "A. P. Chekhov v Khudozhestvennom Teatre. (Vospominaniia)," in Gitovich, *A. P. Chekhov v vospominaniiakh sovremennikov,* 413.

87. O. L. Knipper-Chekhov, "O A. P. Chekhove," ibid., 631.

88. R. L. Jackson, "Chekhov's *Seagull:* The Empty Well, the Dry Lake, and the Cold Cave," in *Chekhov: A Collection of Critical Essays,* ed. R. L. Jackson (Englewood Cliffs, N.J.: Prentice-Hall, 1967), 100. See also the very relevant remarks in this brilliant essay on *Seagull* regarding Treplev's Oedipal fixations and psychological infantilism, and the motifs of water and the journey.

Conclusion

1. See the splendid collection in Peter Urban, *Anton Čechov. Sein Leben in Bildern* (Zurich: Diogenes, 1987).

2. The term is a pun on Chekhov's name (Anton) and a type of tart winter apple known as the *antonovka.*

3. On Chekhov's Yalta home, see M. P. Chekhova, *Dom-muzei A. P. Chekhova v Ialte* (Moscow: Gosudarstvennoe izdatel'stvo izobrazitel'nogo iskusstva, 1958); G. S. Perepelitsa, A. V. Khanilo, and V. F. Permiakova, *Dom-muzei A. P. Chekhova v Ialte: putevoditel'* (Simferopol': Krym, 1971); L. N. Shapovalov, "Kak byl postroen dom Chekhova v Ialte," in *A. P. Chekhov v vospom-*

inaniiakh sovremennikov, ed. N. I. Gitovich and I. V. Fedorova (Moscow: Khudozhestvennaia literatura, 1960), 468–72. I do not mention the Chekhov home in Taganrog because I have not seen it firsthand; moreover, as the house in which Chekhov was born, rather than one of the homes he made, it is of least interest in the present context.

4. The translation is taken from *Anton Chekhov's Life and Thought: Selected Letters and Commentary,* trans. Michael H. Heim and Simon Karlinsky, ed., intro., and commentary by Simon Karlinsky (Berkeley: University of California Press, 1975), 144. Chekhov made this remark in the context of a small polemic regarding the French novelist Paul Bourget's *The Disciple;* see the discussion in Katherine Tiernan O'Connor, "Čechov the Materialist versus Suvorin the Anti-materialist or the Unboring Story of Čhekhov, Suvorin, and Paul Bourget," in *Anton P. Čechov, philosophische und religiöse Dimensionen im Leben und im Werk: Vorträge des Zweiten Internationalen Čechov-Symposiums, Badenweiler, 20.–24. Oktober 1994,* ed. Vladimir B. Kataev, Rolf-Dieter Kluge, and Regine Nohejl (Munich: Otto Sagner, 1997), 379–83.

5. Thus in his vigorous criticism of a story by Elena Shavrova (discussed in chapter 2), Chekhov ridicules her depiction of "love for a corpse." "You have never seen a corpse," he accuses (letter of 16 September 1891).

6. Mihaly Csikszentmihalyi and Eugene Rochberg-Halton, *The Meaning of Things: Domestic Symbols and the Self* (Cambridge: Cambridge University Press, 1981), 138.

7. John Cheever, "The Melancholy of Distance," in *Chekhov and Our Age: Responses to Chekhov by American Writers and Scholars,* ed. James McConkey (Ithaca: Cornell University Center for International Studies, 1984), 126.

8. Janet Malcolm, *Reading Chekhov: A Critical Journey* (New York: Random House, 2001). Both Malcolm and Cheever, lovers of Chekhov, tend to portray the curators and guides working at Chekhov's home-museums as somehow un-Chekhovian, alien, and distorting the heritage of Chekhov; the writer-visitor, by contrast—perhaps because of his or her own credentials as an author who can truly understand Chekhov—is properly at home in Chekhov's house. This is a very typical response, though in a large sense we are all *antonovki,* violating Chekhov's privacy.

9. Chekhova, *Dom-muzei A. P. Chekhova v Ialte,* 5.

10. A quite different interpretation of these colored panes is suggested by Aleksandr Chekhov's 1891 denunciation of Chekhov and Suvorin as looking at the world "from afar" through the colored glass windows of their offices (see *P* 4:259, 492); coming after Chekhov's trip to Sakhalin, such criticism seems preposterous.

11. Personal communication. Here, too, a visitor to the house is sure to learn that Chekhov sat at this window while chatting with Maksim Gorkii.

12. Mariia P. Chekhova, *Iz dalekogo proshlogo* (Moscow: Khudozhestvennaia literatura, 1960), 48; Ronald Hingley, *A Life of Anton Chekhov* (Oxford: Oxford University Press, 1989), 71–72.

13. Mikhail P. Chekhov, "Anton Chekhov na kanikulakh," in Gitovich and Fedorova, *A. P. Chekhov v vospominaniiakh soveremennikov* (1960), 97.

14. N. S. Butova, cited from V. A. Freider, *A. P. Chekhov: Literaturnyi byt i tvorchestvo po memuarnym materialam* (Leningrad: Academia, 1928), 356–57.

15. I. A. Bunin, *O Chekhove (Nezakonchennaia rukopis')* (New York: Izdatel'stvo imeni Chekhova, 1955), 207.

16. Aleksandr Chekhov, "Iz detskikh let A. P. Chekhova," in *Chekhov v vospominaniiakh*

sovremennikov, 2d ed., ed. N. L. Brodskii et al. (Moscow: Gosudarstvennoe izdatel'stvo khudozhestvennaia literatura, 1954), 29.

17. The tradition of emphasizing the importance of the personal relations and the reciprocal artistic emphasis between Chekhov and Levitan goes back to the very first years of the museums in Moscow and Yalta. See Iurii Sobolev, *A. P. Chekhov. Literaturnye ekskursii: Muzei Chekhova v Moskve. Chekhovskie ugolki pod Moskvoi. Ialta. Komnata Chekhov v Taganroge* (Moscow: V.V. Dumnov, 1924), 5.

18. I have seen only three published photographs of Chekhov in his study. One of the other two also shows him beside the fireplace, in front of his father's walking sticks (though the photograph has been published backwards, which makes it look as if he were on the other side of the fireplace); in the third, he is in the alcove behind his desk and under the photograph of his mother (see Urban, *Anton Čechov. Sein Leben in Bildern,* 234, 295).

19. E. J. Simmons, *Chekhov: A Biography* (Boston: Little, Brown and Company, 1962), 360.

20. Anna Khanilo, *Lichnaia biblioteka A. P. Chekhova v Ialte* (Frankfurt: Peter Lang, 1993). On Chekhov's library from the earliest days, see E. A. Dinershtein, *A. P. Chekhov i ego izdateli* (Moscow: Kniga, 1990), 7–31.

21. I. M. Geizer cites a letter from Mariia Chekhova about this point, and Chekhov's professional identity as a physician, in *Chekhov i meditsina* (Moscow: MEDGIZ, 1954), 45.

22. Evgenii D. Ashurkov, *Slovo o Doktore Chekhove* (Moscow: MEDGIZ, 1960), 7.

23. For instance, to Stanislavskii, regarding Hauptmann: "He's a real dramatist. I'm not a dramatist. Listen, I'm a doctor" (cited from Simmons, *Chekhov,* 304).

24. Mikhail Gromov, *Chekhov* (Moscow: Molodaia gvardiia, 1993), 156. See also Evgenii B. Meve, *Meditsina v tvorchestve i zhizni A.P. Chekhova* (Kiev: Gosudarstvennoe meditsinskoe izdatel'stvo SSSR, 1961), 132.

25. Likhachev was speaking with the artist Pavel Smotritskii; see Dmitry S. Likhachev, *Reflections on the Russian Soul: A Memoir,* trans. Bernard Adams (Budapest: Central European University Press, 2000), 147.

26. I. A. Bunin, "Chekhov," in *A. P. Chekhov v vospominaniiakh sovremennikov,* ed. N. I. Gitovich (Moscow: Khudozhestvennaia literatura, 1986), 496.

27. Chekhova, *Dom-muzei A. P. Chekhova,* 28. See chapter 3 for another interpretation of the *shkaf* in *Cherry Orchard.*

28. Salman Akhtar and Steven Samuel, "The Concept of Identity: Developmental Origins, Phenomenology, Clinical Relevance, and Measurement," *Harvard Review of Psychiatry* 3, no. 5 (January–February 1996): 261.

29. It is utterly characteristic of Chekhov that these two calendars were functionally different and marked the passage of two different types of time. One was a tear-off calendar, which showed only the current date, and which marked, therefore, the progress of linear, chronological time; the other was a monthly calendar showing church holidays, that is, time in its cyclical and recurring aspect. The juxtaposition of these two temporalities is a central feature of Chekhov's poetic world.

30. I. A. Bunin, "Chekhov," in Gitovich, *A. P. Chekhov v vospominaniiakh sovremennikov* (1986), 497.

31. From the painter Korovin; see K. S. Stanislavskii, "A. P. Chekhov v khudozhestvennom teatre. (Vospominaniia)," ibid., 412.

32. I. N. Al'tshuller, "O Chekhove (Iz vospominanii)," ibid., 553.

33. Csikszentmihalyi and Rochberg-Halton, *The Meaning of Things,* 96.

34. See the portrayal of Chekhov's catch and release policy in I. A. Bunin, "Chekhov," in Gitovich, *A. P. Chekhov v vospominaniiakh sovremennikov* (1986), 496.

35. A similar configuration may be seen in a posed 1902 photograph of Chekhov with his mother, sister, and wife. All of the women look directly into the camera's lens, while Chekhov distinguishes himself by a gaze down and to his right; the photo may be found in Gitovich and Fedorova, *A. P. Chekhov v vospominaniiakh sovremennikov,* (1960), 608–9.

36. See M. Dolinskii and S. Chertok, "Poslednii put' Chekhova," *Russkaia literatura,* no. 2 (1962): 194. Among Western biographers in particular, there is considerable confusion regarding the details of Chekhov's last journey, and accounts vary wildly. For a creative reading of Chekhov's death, see Katherine Tiernan O'Connor, "Chekhov's Death: His Textual Past Recaptured," in *Studies in Poetics: Commemorative Volume: Krystyna Pomorska (1928–1986),* ed. Elena Semeka-Pankratov (Columbus, Ohio: Slavica, 1995), 39–50.

37. S. M. Chekhov, "Iz vospominanii Marii Pavlovny Chekhovoi," in *Khoziaika chekhovskogo doma: vospominaniia, pis'ma,* ed. S. G. Bragin (Simferopol': Krym, 1969), 19.

38. M. P. Chekhov, *Vokrug Chekhova: vstrechi i vpechatleniia* (Moscow: Moskovskii rabochii, 1960), 252.

39. See Simmons, *Chekhov,* esp. 306–10.

40. See also discussion in Simmons, *Chekhov,* 88–91.

41. Aleksandr's letter is cited in the commentary to *P* 5:500.

42. The formulation is Cathy Popkin's; see her "*Historia Morbi* and the 'Holy of Holies'—Scientific and Religious Discourse and Čechov's Epistemology," in Kataev, Kluge, and Nohejl, *Anton P. Čechov—Philosophische und Religiöse Dimensionen im Leben und im Werk,* 366.

43. See the discussion of these points in Boris M. Shubin, "Doktor A. P. Chekhov," in *Dopolnenie k portretam: Skorbnyi list, ili Istoriia bolezni Aleksandra Pushkina. Doktor A. P. Chekhov,* rev. ed. (Moscow: Znanie, 1998), 176–79. On the illness of the narrator of "Boring Story," see Jefferson Gatrall, "The Paradox of Melancholy Insight: Reading the Medical Subtext in Chekhov's 'A Boring Story,'" *Slavic Review* 62, no. 2 (summer 2003): 258–77.

44. N. I. Gitovich, *Letopis' zhizni i tvorchestva A. P. Chekhova* (Moscow: Gosudarstvennoe izdatel'stvo khudozhestvennoi literatury, 1955), 298; see also Simmons, *Chekhov,* 254.

45. As Freud famously wrote, "The ego is first and foremost a bodily ego" (*The Ego and the Id,* trans. Joan Riviere, ed. James Strachey [New York: Norton, 1960], 16); see also the remarks on body image in Akhtar and Samuel, "The Concept of Identity," 259.

46. "Dnevnik Alekseia Sergeevicha Suvorina," manuscript deciphered by N. A. Roskina, ed. Donald Rayfield and O. E. Makarova (Moscow: Izdatel'stvo Nezavisimaia Gazeta, 1999), 286.

47. M. M. Kovalevskii, "Ob A. P. Chekhove," *Birzhevye vedemosti,* 2 November 1915, cited in Zinovii Papernyi, *Taina siia . . . : Liubov' u Chekhova* (Moscow: B.S.G.-Press, 2002), 239.

48. See Chekhov's letters to his brother Ivan and to Suvorin of 26 and 27 October 1898, as well as the commentary to them in *P* 7:312–13, 648–49.

49. Gitovich, *Letopis',* 495.

50. Julie de Sherbinin, "American Iconography of Chekhov," paper read at "Chekhov the Immigrant: Translating a Cultural Icon," a symposium sponsored by the National Endowment for the Humanities at Colby College, Waterville, Maine, October 2004. The remark about sniffing horseradish was made in a letter of 23 March 1898.

51. Claudine Herzlich and Janine Pierret, *Illness and Self in Society,* trans. Elborg Forster (Baltimore: Johns Hopkins University Press, 1987), 32–33. An error-ridden chapter on Chekhov in a more recent history of tuberculosis defines Chekhov's mature dramaturgy as "unique insider studies of the tuberculous destiny without once mentioning the illness"; see Thomas Dormandy, *The White Death: A History of Tuberculosis* (New York: New York University Press, 1999), 189.

52. Sander Gilman, *Franz Kafka, the Jewish Patient* (New York: Routledge, 1995), 185.

53. In his 1830 lyric "SILENTIUM!"

Index